PSYCHEDELICS AND INTERNAL FAMILY SYSTEMS

A partnership in relational healing

by Curt Kearney

Cover painting, "Dawn," by Cecilia Kearney. Used by permission.
Cover design by Keelin Kennedy (http://barefootdesign.com) and Majid Khan.

"RIPPLE, " Words by ROBERT HUNTER Music by JERRY GARCIA
© 1971 (Renewed) ICE NINE PUBLISHING CO., INC.
All Rights Administered by WC MUSIC CORP.
All Rights Reserved
Used by Permission of ALFRED MUSIC

Library of Congress Control Number 2025904671
ISBN 979-8-218-30537-6

First edition, 2025

"... making your friends family, and your family friends."
— Kate Ruhl

Acknowledgements:

This book has grown and developed one conversation at a time, one friendship at a time (I hope). I'm not going to try to list them all, that would be a ridiculous errand. I will just say my thanks. If you think you might be in any way one of those conversations, one of those hopeful friendships, I can assure you that you are. Thank you.

I would like to particularly acknowledge and thank my patients. We've been on the frontiers together, often figuring it out as we go. We have learned so much together. I hope you can be proud and gratified that your contributions will hopefully help other people.

Maybe we're all always on the frontiers together.

TABLE OF CONTENTS

CHAPTER 4
STARTING TO BRING PSYCHEDELICS AND IFS TOGETHER
91

INTRODUCTION TO PART II   105

CHAPTER 5
PREPARATION WORK   107

CHAPTER 6

MEDICINE SESSIONS   *183*

CHAPTER 7
INTEGRATION WORK 248

CHAPTER ONE

INTRODUCTION AND OVERVIEW

The die is cast. Psychedelics are rapidly entering the mainstream of Western mental healthcare. In this nascent stage, those of us in this field need to get ready, and we need to do it fast and well, both for our patients now and for generations to come.

Use of psychedelics, just about any use, seems to be beneficial.[1] [2] [3] Still, gunpowder with expert fuselage becomes a rocket that can go places that an explosion never will. And part of good rocket travel is doing it safely, and that once we've gotten somewhere, being able to get off the rocket, get our feet on the ground, and live a life there. The point can't be to ride rockets non-stop.

An axiom of this book is that without adequate containers, without adequate cultures of psychedelia, the power of psychedelics can dissipate quickly or fuel limited, strange, or even dangerous journeys. Those of us in Western mental healthcare need to find or create pairings that are worthy of the work – and the ease – at hand with psychedelics. Enter the psychotherapy part of psychedelic assisted psychotherapy (PAP). And very notably, enter Internal Family Systems therapy (IFS). Astoundingly, Internal Family Systems is an already existing form of psychotherapy that partners extremely well with psychedelics.

Exploring and delineating some of the epic contributions that IFS can make to truly adequate Western PAP practice is the topic of this book.

---

[1] Peter S Hendricks et al., "Classic Psychedelic Use Is Associated with Reduced Psychological Distress and Suicidality in the United States Adult Population," *Journal of Psychopharmacology* 29, no. 3 (March 2015): 280–88.

[2] Grant Jones et al., "Associations between Classic Psychedelics and Opioid Use Disorder in a Nationally-Representative U.S. Adult Sample," *Scientific Reports* 12, no. 1 (April 7, 2022): 4099.

[3] Peter S Hendricks et al., "The Relationships of Classic Psychedelic Use with Criminal Behavior in the United States Adult Population," *Journal of Psychopharmacology* 32, no. 1 (January 2018): 37–48.

Psychedelics and IFS have radical overlap in that they each invite soul or mind to show up in direct, powerful, and thoroughly relational healing. That is, they are each psychedelic and psychotherapeutic in the etymological sense of the words; psychedelic for "soul or mind manifesting" and psychotherapeutic for "soul or mind attending."

We will explore how IFS can help make powerful and fairly unique contributions to PAP in each of the three general types of psychedelic work:

- In preparatory work, IFS therapy can facilitate radically respectful dialogues with our patient's whole diverse psyche about a potential upcoming medicine session. This can lead to rich and real consent and collaboration from all "parts" of our patients, deepening the journey to come as well as making it more humane and safer. ("Parts" is an IFS term for the diverse aspects of our psyches. This will be discussed much more in the next chapter, An Overview of IFS.)
- In medicine sessions, IFS can expertly guide both overt therapy in the medicine session, as well as help guide crucial, relational, non-verbal companioning of our patients, again greatly deepening medicine sessions and making them safer.
- In integration work, we don't want psychedelic healing to be just a flash of health, no matter how beautiful. Flashes by their nature fade. However, relationships can remain vital and endure if they are engaged in directly and actively. In IFS integration, we can help our patients integrate the healing of psychedelic medicine sessions within a living ecosystem: the relationships with and within their multifaceted psyche, and with and within their world and their daily lives. Here, integration *is* relationship.

We will explore clinical theory in trying to elaborate a wide and flexible palette in working with the novel clinical situations that can and do arise in psychedelic assisted psychotherapy. As part of this, we will explore how both IFS and psychedelics are radically relational healing modalities and as such can naturally partner together so well.

We will explore paradigm questions, questioning what our field is now in light of psychedelics, a truly profound innovation (or shocking rediscovery) in Western mental healthcare. Thomas Kuhn, who coined the term paradigm transition, wrote in his seminal book *The Structure of Scientific Revolutions*, "When the transition is complete, the profession will have changed its view of the field, its methods, and its goals."[4] When this paradigm transition is complete, we will view our field differently; we will have different methods; and our goals will be different. Whatever all that might be, that is where we are going as a field.

We will explore how IFS as a broad and relational systems model can make great contributions to paradigm considerations. An assumption here is that good Western PAP is going to take a village, that no one paradigm will be adequate to psychedelics. That is, instead of a sole victor, "last one standing" battle of paradigms, how we might co-create, by the participation of each of us, an interrelating, diverse ecosystem of paradigms for psychedelic Western mental healthcare. By such a co-created ecosystem of paradigms, we could finally help our field realize its long held vision of an integrated biopsychosocial model — so integrated that we don't even write it with a space in between each. And for some of our patients, optionally, an even further enriched, complexified, and integrated biopsychosocialspiritual model.

When we look cross culturally and across time, we can see psychedelics paired with practices and traditions of healing relationships. Such practices and traditions have often been

---

[4] Kuhn, Thomas S. 1962. The Structure of Scientific Revolutions. University of Chicago Press.

completely integrated with whole cultures. We can see this in Indigenous cultures, in the East, and possibly even at the roots of Western culture.

The Indigenous examples of cultures of psychedelia, past and present, are too numerous, too varied, and too unknown to the West to list. And they would be very difficult for a Westerner such as myself to describe in anything but at best a ham handed way. But it must be said that some of these traditions and peoples have been foundational to the current psychedelic West. I'll return to this crucial topic at the end of this chapter.

In the East, examples of psychedelic cultures include the foundational, ancient Vedic culture with their Soma, likely a psychedelic drink, especially prominent in the *Rig Veda* and the *Upanishads*.[5] Mike Crowley also makes a case that there is a tradition of psychedelics in Tibetan Buddhism.[6]

In the West, prominent examples of entire cultures integrated with psychedelics are, by the best evidence available, the Ancient and Classical Greek and Roman worlds and the proto-Western and early Western cultures that were foundations for these.[7] [8] If evidence continues to bear out the West as one of the great psychedelic cultures of the world, this would, of course, have profound implications for Western identity.

I realize these are big statements about possible psychedelic roots of the West. Chapter 3, An Overview of Western Psychedelic Assisted Psychotherapy, has a short history of psychedelics in the West and we will briefly review some of the evidence there.

Shockingly enough, IFS can be seen as a contemporary Western culture of psychedelia. And it is a small and portable one. It can fit

---

[5] Hu, Jane C. "India, Hinduism, and Psychedelics: 5 Questions for Scholar Swayam Bagaria." India, Hinduism, and psychedelics: 5 Questions for scholar Swayam Bagaria, December 16, 2024. https://themicrodose.substack.com/p/india-hinduism-and-psychedelics-5.

[6] Mike Crowley and Ann Shulgin, *Secret Drugs of Buddhism: Psychedelic Sacraments and the Origins of the Vajrayana*, Second edition (Santa Fe: Synergetic Press, 2019).

[7] Brian C. Muraresku and Graham Hancock, *The Immortality Key: The Secret History of the Religion with No Name* (New York: St. Martin's Press, 2020).

[8] E. Guerra-Doce et al., "Direct Evidence of the Use of Multiple Drugs in Bronze Age Menorca (Western Mediterranean) from Human Hair Analysis," *Scientific Reports* 13, no. 1 (April 6, 2023): 4782.

in a clinical hour, giving IFS a great strength as a highly applicable culture of psychedelia in Western mental healthcare.

This brings us back to some of the great shared strengths and overlaps of IFS and psychedelics.

IFS, like psychedelics themselves, can traverse seamlessly and gracefully from general practice focuses, such as depression, anxiety, relationship concerns, and complex or developmental trauma, through to psychospiritual focuses, such as focuses on meaning, divinity, ontology, and ethics. By this, IFS can companion psychedelics in just about their full scope. Most other Western psychotherapies would need secondary spiritual models added on, perhaps awkwardly, to adequately extend to what might be called spiritual focuses. And from the other direction, most spiritual traditions require a clinical add-on to address general clinical concerns, again maybe introducing awkwardness.

Both IFS and psychedelics could also be classified as humanistic, that being a movement in psychology that is focused on human beings as just that, as beings, not as simply mechanisms, however complex.

Much of Western mental healthcare can see our minds and mental health, wittingly or not, as roughly just issues of hardware or software, of mechanistic neurobiological hardware or as cognitive software information processing. That is, minds and people as roughly computers to be fixed, debugged, rewired, or reprogrammed. This obviates our patients and ourselves as full beings, as "Selves." ("Self" is a technical IFS term that we might think of as each of us as a being; Self will also be discussed in the overview of IFS in the next chapter.) As Barry Magid, a psychiatrist, relational psychoanalyst, and Zen teacher writes, "Minds belong to people, not brains.... The mind is no more inside the brain than a dance is inside the muscles."[9] IFS cannot be a mechanistic psychology without ceasing to be IFS.

---

[9] Magid, Barry. (2020, February 14). "'Why I'm NOT a Neuroscientist' Thompson offers an incisive deeply informed critique of Buddhist modernism's mutual love affair with neuroscience." https://www.facebook.com/profile/804313867/search/?q=dance%20muscles%20brain

I should underline that this is not an argument against reductionistic science in the study of psychedelics. Psychedelics are mind-breakingly interdisciplinary and supradisciplinary. But this is an argument against simplistic or overly ambitious extrapolations from reductionistic science.

Psychedelics have been massive in restoring soul, true beings, to a central place at the table in Western mental healthcare. This pushes open new paradigmatic options in Western mental healthcare and dusts off old ones. Again, IFS, with its bedrock focus on Selves, is an excellent companion here.

IFS and psychedelics are also both radically somatic. There is the literal physicality of the psychedelic "substances" themselves entering and becoming one with the "substance" of our bodies. In psychedelic sessions, much of the psyche manifests in the body. Some examples are shaking, relaxing, urges to move, movements themselves, postures, temperatures, vomiting, urinating on oneself. Yes, it apparently happens. A research participant in a psilocybin study unknowingly urinated on himself during a medicine session. At first, he experienced a warm, oceanic bliss. Then, realizing what had happened, shame. He was helped to the bathroom and given clean clothes by a female therapist. Soon after, he broke through to "finally," in his word, grieving his deceased mother.[10] Soma and psyche, sides of one coin.

IFS is also highly somatic in its focus. Some of Richard Schwartz's earliest collaborators as he was creating IFS were Hakomi therapists, including Kay Gardner, Susan McConnell, and even Ron Kurtz, the founder of Hakomi therapy. They collaboratively built a somatic focus right into the foundations of IFS, into every IFS session. Like many therapists using IFS, I have found that relationships with parts of the psyche are far more powerful if there is a somatic focus. This is easy to do in IFS by the patient finding the part in or on their body as one way that it is manifesting.

---

[10] Anderson, Brian. "CIIS Class." Class lecture, 2021.

Most contemporary psychotherapies require an add-on to integrate the somatic while most somatic psychotherapies require an add-on to work with the more conventional manifestations of the psyche. The elegance of IFS across a great range of psyche and soma is exceptional.

I would like to underline again that IFS and psychedelics share a sense of somatic work in mental health as entirely part of humanism. IFS and psychedelics seem to share a sense of the body as inseparable from us as beings, including body as meaning, not just body as mechanism or information.

Another natural pairing of psychedelics and IFS is that they share a focus on both inner and outer relationships, of both the intrapsychic and community. Western psychology has often struggled to truly integrate these, variously foregrounding the individual or the community. At one extreme, this can result in something of a solipsistic sense of the "real me" as my inner, private experience and the world as a sort of theater scene for this "main character" self. At the other extreme, there can be a view of the self as nothing much more than something to be shaped by psychology on a Procrustean bed to fit "the real world."

I will go ahead and assert that psychedelics themselves don't seem to fall into these false dichotomies. With psychedelics, people often seem to heal and grow both as citizens and as psyches.

IFS is a good match, a good partner in this. Richard Schwartz, with his steadfast background in systems thinking, has made IFS much less prone to imbalances of foregrounding either self or community. Schwartz has consistently emphasized IFS as relevant to a wide range of meaningful systems at different scales, including individual intrapsychic psychology, couples, families, groups, organizations, and cultures. Self can be present, in relationship, and leading equally in our so-called inner worlds and outer worlds.

But the most important ground that I think IFS and PAP share is almost embarrassingly simple: they both provide options for healing, growth, and health through relationships of mutual respect. By this, in healing, our patients do not become "fixed." They get in better, richer, more harmonious relationships, inner and outer.

We will see this in action in the clinical chapters to follow: the rich relationships of mutual respect with all parts of our patient's psyche that are necessary for good preparation work for a psychedelic medicine session. The rich, healing relationships that often come to the fore in medicine sessions, intrapsychically and "in the room." And what is in the room in psychedelic sessions can get, shall we say, "trippy!" And in integration work, we will see that this simple and rich relationality is what makes true integration possible.

FRAMES, LIMITS, AND WARNINGS ON THIS BOOK

The major frame of this book is psychotherapy and psychology. But psychedelic work and interest includes people of goodwill from many paths and many angles. I want this book to be widely welcoming.

Using the language of psychology will, I hope, give a consistency here that can be useful. But it is a fairly everyday language. We all have psyches and we all have relationships, the stuff of psychology. So feel free to make this book your own, whether you come with professional expertise in some or all of the areas focused on here, you are a trainee, you are reading this to help with your own healing, or you are reading this out of curiosity or general interest.

Some parts of the clinical chapters do get into quite technical discussions of IFS technique. I want this book to help clinicians in their work. The good news is that all of the IFS in this book is covered in any level 1 IFS training. The bad news is that without that clinical background, some of the technique discussions here might seem quite opaque!

Another limitation on this book and this work is that I think it is only ethical and safe to work with others in IFS and PAP to the extent of one's expertise and training. I would urge patience, humility, and ongoing training in applying this work with others. I think it's very notable that many traditional ways of working with psychedelics to help others involve apprenticeships of maybe ten years or so.

I think we can have confidence in doing this work with others if we have done a level 1 IFS training, a good general PAP training program, had our own experience as a patient in IFS PAP, and are in ongoing IFS PAP consultation.

Without those, this work can be dangerous and can hurt people. I would particularly urge respect of "exiles" (an IFS term for the most vulnerable parts of ourselves) by not trying to help them very much in IFS PAP until we have the above training and support in place.

The spirit of this work is respect, of ourselves and of our communities. By honoring our limits honestly, even as they grow, we are doing this work: we are serving others, our community, and ourselves.

I also want to underline that this book is not meant to be a total take on psychedelics or on psychedelic assisted psychotherapy. The topic here is more narrow, on some of the great contributions that IFS can make to psychedelic assisted psychotherapies.

Lastly, this is not a treatment manual or a "how to" book. This work is far more fluid and varied than those can hold. As we will see, this work has to come primarily from relationships, not from techniques or steps.

A BIT ABOUT WHO I AM AND WHERE I'M COMING FROM

I want to give some information on myself and my background. I hope this will help make it easier to triangulate on what I am presenting here and make it easier to understand and evaluate.

I'm a psychotherapist in private practice in Evanston, Illinois, just north of Chicago. My practice is mostly "standard" IFS, that is, IFS therapy without psychedelic medicines. With many of my patients, ketamine sessions have organically become part of our work together. I do other psychedelic work, such as some teaching on IFS and PAP, some work in psychedelic research studies, and some consulting in psychedelic practice.

I'm married and have three kids. The opening quote of the book is actually from my wife.

I've been working with psychedelics myself since I was sixteen, in the mid-1980's, driven by my deep need for relief from depression and PTSD. I was trying the available treatments, including working with an excellent therapist. But things were very bad and steadily getting worse.

My therapist mentioned once, seemingly offhandedly as I was walking out the door of a session, that some people who had taken LSD had found it helped their mental health quite a bit. I was shocked. Did my therapist just recommend I take LSD? I respected him greatly, and I also knew the topic was too hot to follow up on.

I was a reader, so I got a hold of all the books on psychedelics I could find. Eventually I wound up at the Northwestern University library during public access hours. There I found, in literally dusty, untouched bound volumes on a library shelf, the crucial information that I needed, the research from the first wave of the Western psychedelic renaissance, from the 1950's and 60's. (Thank you, Northwestern library system.)

I was astounded by what I read. Most of the studies were on LSD. The reports of the great therapeutic efficacy and especially of the excellent medical safety of psychedelics were not at all what the culture was telling me at the time. This was during Reagan's second term, an intense reboot of the "war on drugs."

I was something of a straight edge kid, and I also dearly did not want to fry my brain like an egg. But based on the research that was available and my desperation, I decided that Nancy Reagan was probably wrong and that the risk of not trying psychedelics was likely far greater than the risk of trying them.

I studied all I could about working with psychedelics safely and effectively. After months of careful and, in retrospect, shockingly good preparation with a friend, we gave it a heartfelt go. All went very well, and I turned a corner.

Things definitely didn't get "all better," but the trajectory was no longer downward. And although I knew I had a long, varied, and in many ways hard road ahead of me, I knew I could walk it. I am, of course, deeply grateful.

I can attest as an "*n* of 1" that psychedelics are usually not an automatic cure. But they can be a key part of a path.

It quickly became apparent to me that my friends and I could not reliably create adequate containers for working with psychedelics, a *temenos*, the necessary cauldron of alchemy that Jung rightly saw as usually essential for rich transformational processes. (Jung's work was the main model I had available at the time.) It seemed to me that without finding or building adequate containers I was wasting the power of psychedelics and thereby not respecting them. I just couldn't do that. So I worked with psychedelics rarely, only when there seemed to be a truly adequate, respectful setting.

I also quickly realized that psychedelics were not a standalone practice. I finally took up Zen practice, now seeing that there were no shortcuts. I also went to a lot of Grateful Dead shows. These both influence this book greatly...

I eventually knew that I wanted to be a therapist, but I very sadly realized that with psychedelics being illegal I could not use them to help other people. So in my work I tried to find the most psychedelic and legal ways of helping people. I trained and worked in long backcountry expeditions, including Outward Bound. I thought I would become a Jungian analyst. I sought out the most psychedelic schools I could find. I had the honor of doing my undergrad at the great Hutchins School at Sonoma State University. I chose Pacifica Graduate Institute for graduate school.

I worked in a residential group home and a school in inner city Chicago. I later worked as a therapist in a local hospital system for ten years and slowly grew my current full-time private practice.

In midlife, I was called to re-engage with psychedelic practice again within — finally — an adequate *temenos*.

But I again quickly realized that psychedelics were not a standalone practice. Psychedelics led me to IFS (pretty literally). Finally, a worthy psychological companion to psychedelics.

I asked around and was referred to an IFS therapist who was interested in psychedelics. Through a comical misunderstanding, my therapist was *interested* in psychedelics, but she didn't actually work with psychedelics herself! But we hit it off. We've since learned much together over the years, and it's been a joy and of profound help to me. The fact that much of my IFS PAP has been with an IFS therapist naïve to psychedelics has powerfully highlighted to me again and again the natural pairing of IFS and psychedelics.

In a very real way, I have been a patient in a long term IFS psychedelic therapy. I often think that one of the best ways to learn about a treatment is to go through it as a patient. The root of the word "patient" is the Greek word *pathos*, for "feeling or suffering." I highly recommend that clinicians interested in working with IFS PAP in their practices do their own IFS PAP truly as a patient, as one who presents their feelings and suffering, not just as an academic exercise. There is much that most of us simply cannot learn otherwise. This is, again, something of an apprenticeship model.

Eventually, the current Western "psychedelic renaissance" took off, shocking the hell out of me. I never saw that coming! To put it mildly, thank you Rick Doblin and many others for keeping going on working to make PAP a legal and widely available treatment, a goal that I and so many others "knew" was impossible. I am very glad to have been wrong on this.

With the current psychedelic renaissance, I could then shift my work more explicitly towards psychedelics, including, as I mentioned, bringing ketamine assisted psychotherapy (KAP) into my practice, teaching, doing some work in research studies, and doing some consulting.

As part of finding my way in this new professional terrain, I badly wanted to read a book on IFS and psychedelics. But sadly, one didn't exist. So I grudgingly went ahead and researched and wrote this book.

It's been a real trip. Long, at times grueling, at times joyous, and ultimately richly transformative and satisfying. Part of this has been classes and generous conversations with some of the masters of IFS and PAP, including Richard Schwartz, Michael Mithoefer, Robert Grant, Robert Falconer, as well as general training in PAP through the Usona Institute, MAPS (Multidisciplinary Association for Psychedelic Studies), the California Institute for Integral Studies (CIIS), and Healing Realms.

As I said in the acknowledgements, this book has grown and developed one conversation at a time, one – I hope – friendship at a time. Again, my thanks.

A NOTE ON TERMS

I will use the words "West" and "Western" here a good bit. I do that to be clear on what form of PAP I am talking about in this book. Psychedelic practices are very diverse, going far beyond Western culture and Western mental healthcare. So I think it's important and respectful to be clear about what kind of psychedelic practice is the topic here.

Having said that, I should define how I am using the terms West and Western. I'll borrow from David Graber in his book *There Never was a West*, of what "...one might call... the Great Books theory of civilization."[11] This is a sense of a culture or a civilization not as so much the culture of a particular geography at a particular

---

[11] David Graeber, "There Never Was a West," 2007, https://theanarchistlibrary.org/library/david-graeber-there-never-was-a-west.

time, but a culture as a long, diverse, curated tradition. By this, the "list" of the Great Books of the West has always been in flux and has always been dialogically and relationally co-created. I see the current Western psychedelic renaissance as part of this dynamic tradition.

Psychedelics as becoming, once again, part of the "official" Western Great Books? This could get funky.

In this sense of co-created cultures, we are shaped by the cultures, large and small, that we live in. And, we shape those cultures. Then we live in those cultures more and are shaped by them again. And on and on and on. By this, what those of us in this Western psychedelic renaissance do and say now is part of the ongoing dialogue and co-creation of our field and "the West."

STRUCTURE OF WHAT'S TO FOLLOW

This book is in three parts. Part I of this book is roughly overviews. We'll start that in the next chapter with an overview of IFS therapy. Chapter 3 is a brief overview and history of psychedelics in the West. Chapter 4 starts trying to bring PAP and IFS together on some neutral terrain by looking at Peter Webster's salience hypothesis of psychedelics and Martin Buber's work on I-Thou and I-it relationships.

Part II is the clinical heart of the book. There are three chapters on clinical technique, theory, and case material. Chapter 5 is on IFS in psychedelic preparation work. Chapter 6 is on IFS in psychedelic medicine sessions. And chapter 7 is on IFS in psychedelic integration work. These are fairly long chapters, with a lot of clinical material and discussion of many topics.

Part III closes the book. Chapter 8 is a conclusion that attempts to explore larger paradigm considerations. And then there is an Epilogue, with some of my personal reflections on where this has all been and where it might be going.

A PERSONAL NOTE

I've been in relationship with these psychedelic terrains for 39 years now, for my whole adult life plus change. But I am young here. I think we're all young here. Of course, this book is nothing like "final answers." Like I said, I mostly wrote it because I needed to read something like it.

Robin Wall Kimmerer, a member of the Potawatomi Nation, botany professor, and writer, wrote beautifully of our youth in her gift of a book *Braiding Sweetgrass: Indigenous Wisdom, Scientific Knowledge and the Teachings of Plants*. Here is Kimmerer:

> In the Western tradition there is a recognized hierarchy of beings, with, of course, the human being on top—the pinnacle of evolution, the darling of Creation—and the plants at the bottom. But in Native ways of knowing, human people are often referred to as "the younger brothers of Creation." We say that humans have the least experience with how to live and thus the most to learn—we must look to our teachers among the other species for guidance.... They've been on the earth far longer than we have been, and have had time to figure things out.... Plants know how to make food and medicine from light and water, and then they give it away.[12]

Again, we're all young here. We're all learning this PAP stuff on the fly. My sense is that we will never get *there* with psychedelics. That is maybe part of the "point." As the Talmud says, "We plan, God laughs." We could say, "We try to understand psychedelics, God laughs." We're all young here, and hopefully growing, and doing it together. That might be about all we get.

It can be pretty damn good.

---

[12] Robin Wall Kimmerer, Braiding Sweetgrass: Indigenous Wisdom, Scientific Knowledge and the Teachings of Plants (New York: Milkweed Editions, 2013).

We need each other, like members of an ecosystem need each other. We need dialogue. We need questions at least as much as we need answers. We need disagreements. And optimally, we need our disagreements to be mutually respectful, even of some friendship, and to be forward moving.

THE PSYCHEDELIC WEST BEING IN HONORABLE RECIPROCITY WITH THE NATIVE PEOPLES AND TRADITIONS IT HAS BENEFITED FROM SO MUCH

It may seem off topic here to discuss the relationships between the psychedelic West and Native psychedelic traditions, but I think these relationships are so foundational to the psychedelic West and there are so many current and pressing problems in these relationships that this cannot rightfully be ignored in any discussion of the psychedelic West.

Without the West's relationships with Native psychedelic traditions, there might not be any or much of a current psychedelic West. Native traditions brought many of the literal psychedelic medicines to the awareness of the West, and provided the West with rich cultural, medical, psychological, and religious frameworks on psychedelics.

Psychedelic medicines occur naturally worldwide, but in the West for much of Western history until quite recently, when someone accidentally ate a psychedelic plant or fungi, the "trip" was mostly classified as a painful or weird effect of a poison, like a fever dream. Nothing of much meaning or helpfulness. It seems that without a framework, without a "set" or "mindset" on psychedelics, there is no rich psychedelia.[13][14] So in a very real way, Native peoples provided both the medicines and the necessary "sets" for modern Western psychedelia to exist. Arguably, no Native psychedelic traditions, no contemporary psychedelic West.

But there are great breaks, imbalances, and harms in the relationships between the psychedelic West and some of these

---

[13] Leary T, Litwin G, Metzner R (1963) Reactions to psilocybin administered in a supportive environment. J Nerv Ment Dis 137: 561–73.

[14] Hartogsohn I. Constructing drug effects: A history of set and setting. Drug Science, Policy and Law. 2017;3.

Indigenous peoples and traditions. Some breaks are subtle, and some are not at all subtle.

One major example of a break in these relationships is that the West got access to psilocybin through Gordan Wasson going to the Sierra Madre mountains in present day Mexico hoping to get the mushrooms that were rumored to cause religious experiences.

Wasson set up expeditions and traveled to Indigenous villages in Oaxaca State. He was eventually introduced to Maria Sabina, a Mazatec woman skilled with the mushrooms in ceremony.

Sabina told Wasson that he could attend the ceremonies, but that outsiders were highly forbidden from eating the mushrooms. Wasson knew that in her tradition the mushrooms and the ceremonies were not for simple curiosity, but for healing and for finding lost people or belongings. So Wasson told her a lie that he didn't know where his son was and that he was worried about his wellbeing. Sabina was also told by a higher-up in her town to allow Wasson into the ceremony and to give him mushrooms to eat. Based in Wasson's lie, her compassion, and maybe pressure as a relatively poor woman, Sabina decided to go against her tradition and let an outsider eat the mushrooms in ceremony. But she first negotiated a promise from Wasson that he would only share the story with his intimates who he trusted and who sincerely needed to know, and that Wasson would not share her name or the name of her town.[15]

Wasson ate the mushrooms, deceitfully pocketed some for later identification, and had an astounding experience. He returned to New York, and promptly violated his agreement with Sabina by publishing a story in *Life Magazine* and writing a book naming Sabina and her town.[16] [17] [18]

---

[15] Andy Letcher, Shroom: A Cultural History of the Magic Mushroom, 1st Harper Perennial ed (New York: HarperCollins, 2008).

[16] Seeking the Magic Mushroom. Life 13 May 1959 42(19) 100-102, 104-110, 112, 114, 117-118, 120. R. Gordon Wasson

[17] Wasson, Valentina Pavlovna, R. Gordon Wasson, Stephan Francis De Borhegyi, D. Jacomet, Stamperia Valdonega, and Fratelli Alinari. 1957. Mushrooms, Russia, and History. New York: Pantheon Books.

[18] Stephan V. Beyer, Singing to the Plants: A Guide to Mestizo Shamanism in the Upper Amazon (Albuquerque: UNM press, 2009).

The West got knowledge of psilocybin mushrooms and a "set" of working with them in ceremonies.

Wasson became a psychedelic celebrity. He held mushroom "ceremonies" in his Manhattan apartment for friends and influential people. Already a vice president of a New York bank, he became even richer through his books and articles on psychedelics and eventually was made a director of a chemical company that hoped to profit off psilocybin mushrooms.[19]

But Sabina and her culture were trampled badly by the West. By the curious, by the desperate, by Mexican police looking to shut down these Indigenous "drug dealers."[20]

In the fallout of this, Sabina wound up living an extremely difficult life. Her son was murdered before her eyes. Her house and beloved store were burnt down. She was never sure if these were from her breaking tradition and letting an outsider eat the mushrooms. She wound up very alone and impoverished in her old age and ultimately died of malnutrition.[21]

Respect goes a long way.

Wasson later made a deeply flawed apology, but an apology nonetheless, lamenting what had happened to the Mazatec people and Sabina, while disavowing his repeated dishonesty to Sabina and his direct responsibility for what happened to her and her people.[22] By his disavowal, I imagine that what he had done gnawed at his soul badly.

Now, in purest tragic irony, we have Western corporations valued in the hundreds of millions of dollars based on their business plans of fighting tooth and nail for the exclusive "rights" to psilocybin.[23] The Conquest is continuing.

---

[19] Andy Letcher, Shroom: A Cultural History of the Magic Mushroom, 1st Harper Perennial ed (New York: HarperCollins, 2008).

[20] The Tragedy of Maria Sabina | Singing to the Plants. (2008, February 17). https://singingtotheplants.com/2008/02/tragedy-of-maria-sabina/

[21] Chloe Aridjis, "On María Sabina, One of Mexico's Greatest Poets," March 30, 2015, https://www.britishcouncil.org/voices-magazine/maria-sabina-one-of-mexicos-greatest-poets.

[22] R. Gordon Wasson, "Drugs: The Sacred Mushroom," September 26, 1970, https://timesmachine.nytimes.com/timesmachine/1970/09/26/90615979.html?pageNumber=21.

[23] Dave Hodes, "Pending Patents: Can Any Company Own Psilocybin?," January 13, 2022, https://www.greenmarketreport.com/pending-patents-can-any-company-own-psilocybin/.

Like with most things regarding psychedelics, these current issues are complex. There are open source patent methods that could be the most workable and honorable patent method for integrating already existing psychedelics into Western mental healthcare. The Usona Institute is spearheading such an approach. But the drug development costs of novel psychedelics may be so great that time limited, for-profit patents may be necessary and appropriate. But certainly, dishonorable "patent trolling" should have no place and should not be tolerated by ethical professionals in our field.[24] [25]

The current psychedelic West owes many Native peoples massive debts of honorable reciprocity. I would urge the psychedelic West to make honorable reciprocity with these Native peoples foundational to our field, in financial and political support and in relationships of respect. Many of these peoples are in a time of great need, even genocidal need, precisely from injuries from the West: from global warming, from habitat destruction from agribusiness, oil extraction, mining, and from often very grave racism.[26] Those of us in the psychedelic West are generally in positions to help materially and politically.

Some ways for the psychedelic West to begin being in honorable reciprocity with these Native peoples could include joining and donating to organizations such as Chacruna's Indigenous Reciprocity Initiative (especially for businesses), Survival International, Amazon Aid, Amazon Watch, or other similar Indigenous advocacy organizations. And for those of us from the West to humbly and honestly try to be in truly respectful relationship with these peoples and cultures. This can include knowing where we as Westerners stand and to be in respectful relationship and dialogue from there. That might mean decentering

---

[24] Christian Angermayer, "An Open Letter to Tim Ferriss about the Value of Patents in the Psychedelic World," March 9, 2021, https://www.linkedin.com/pulse/open-letter-tim-ferriss-value-patents-psychedelic-angermayer/.

[25] Steve Paulson, "Psilocybin, the 'God Molecule,' and the Quest to Revolutionize Mental Health Care" (Wisconsin Public Radio, August 6, 2022).

[26] Flavia Milhorance, "Jump in Child Deaths Reveals Impact of Industrialisation on Amazon's Indigenous Peoples" (The Guardian, June 5, 2023).

from ourselves and listening more. After all, the main theme of this book, and I think of this work, is rightful relationships.

CHAPTER TWO

AN OVERVIEW AND REVIEW OF IFS

"The primary healing relationship in internal family systems therapy is between the client's Self and her young, injured parts."

— Richard Schwartz, Ch 1, *IFS: New Dimensions*[27]

IFS is a psychotherapy that does an excellent job of taking our psychological lives very seriously and very directly. By that, I mean that IFS isn't *about* our psyches. It's not a removed, bird's eye view or an interpretive stance on our psyches. IFS does have excellent maps of the psyche, but it is ultimately entirely experiential and relational. That is, it is about helping our patients get directly into better relationships with and within their own psyches, and ultimately with and within their world. IFS is entirely about lived relationships.

IFS tends to be deeply satisfying for patients, and for therapists, even if it is quite challenging at times. When I work with new patients with IFS, they are often nearly mute with gratitude at relating to themselves via IFS therapy. Over time, and not a lot of time, they are very often pleased that their lives, inner and outer, seem to be richly if subtly improving via the therapy.

And of course, IFS can deeply and fruitfully partner with psychedelics. But the overview of IFS in this chapter will not be about an adaptation of IFS to partner with psychedelics. One of the most shocking things is that we don't need to modify IFS much, if at all, to partner with psychedelics.

[27] Martha Sweezy, ed., Internal Family Systems Therapy: New Dimensions (New York: Routledge, 2013).

This is all the more shocking because Richard Schwartz developed IFS in the 1980's when psychedelics just weren't on his radar. As Schwartz stated in an interview with Tim Ferris, when the current wave of the Western psychedelic renaissance started, his stance was that with standard IFS we could do everything that psychedelic assisted psychotherapy does, and in some ways do it more safely and simply. And he was right. But eventually he decided to get empirical about it and did some IFS PAP himself with Robert Grant, a physician very skilled in IFS and ketamine assisted psychotherapy. Soon after that – very soon after that! – Schwartz changed his stance on the benefits of psychedelics. Since then, he has been a great proponent, practitioner, and teacher of IFS and psychedelics.[28]

I want to reiterate something from the Introduction chapter: IFS *is* psychedelic. IFS therapy skillfully and lovingly helps manifest our psyches, our minds, our souls. Patients and therapists doing IFS therapy are doing psychedelia all the time.

I have a personal list of criteria of what, for me, makes an excellent psychotherapy. IFS meets this list very well. IFS is or can be:

- Non-dogmatic. No one needs to become a true believer to get relief.
- Ecological. Nothing is attempted to be thrown out of or destroyed in the psyche. This is both a pragmatic and a moral commitment.
- Democratic. No authoritarian stance by the clinician. Empowers the patient. The therapist and patient are equals in the relationship even if they occupy usefully differentiated roles.
- Of depth and richness. All in the deep and complex psyche can be met directly. It doesn't traffic in simplistic or overly limited understandings.

---

[28] Tim Ferris and Schwartz, "Richard Schwartz — IFS, Psychedelic Experiences without Drugs, and Finding Inner Peace for Our Many Parts (#492)," January 14, 2021.

- Effective. It can actually help people with their often deep needs. It isn't something that works only "in theory" or in rare, special cases.
- Accessible to everyday people. That is, most people can tolerate it and it can be logistically implemented. It isn't especially expensive or time consuming. No one needs to become a monk or a fanatic or go on extended foreign odysseys to get some relief or healing.
- It can be a real companion to the depth and richness of psychedelics.
- Interdisciplinary. It can be in rich, useful conversation with fields from materialist science to the humanities, to religions, to cross cultural dialogues, and beyond.
- It has values. Amorality in a difficult world, especially a world unduly difficult for some, is immoral.
- Scalable. It can be taught to therapists easily enough and widely enough to actually become available in the world. An excellent treatment modality that is very difficult, very expensive, or very time consuming to learn is not going to have enough real world impact.
- Relational. That is, it uses the dynamics of the relationship between therapist and patient as a healing force, both in the positive aspects of the relationship and in the difficult aspects of that relationship.

Let's get into some specifics.

A BRIEF OVERVIEW OF IFS THEORY, TECHNIQUE, AND SPIRIT OF HEALING

For the rest of this chapter, we will get to know the main players of the IFS therapy model, Self, parts, and burdens. We will discuss the main "spirit" of healing in IFS: Self to part relationship. And we will look at one of the most crucial techniques in IFS, unblending.

After discussing these, we will ground this all in a demonstration session of IFS that Richard Schwartz did at a recent online conference. Fortunately, there is a video of this session freely available, making it an extremely helpful resource. We will review a transcript of this session and we will discuss a section of it, fleshing it out "play by play."

The main topics that we will look at here – again, Self, parts, burdens, unblending, and healing – are so deeply interrelated that to understand one we must understand the others. They form a sort of circle. Because of that, we've got to start somewhere, so we'll start with parts. We will naturally cycle through each of these topics many times throughout this chapter and this book. That way, as we go along we will wind up elaborating on them from different angles and in different contexts, hopefully coming to a four dimensional, living, and relational sense of them, because that's what they are.

Parts

IFS is often called a "parts model" of psychotherapy in that it recognizes the multiplicity of the psyche. That is, that our psyches are "peopled" by multiple agents.

This can sound whacky, and we will get into objections to IFS later. But multiplicity of mind is an observation that has come up over and over in the history of psychology (and seemingly has been forgotten over and over as well). As a quick sampling, we see a recognition of the multiplicity of mind in Freud's structural model of id, ego, and superego. In his later "internal object relations" model. In Jung's "complexes" ("Complexes are in truth the living units of the unconscious psyche"[29]). In Kohut's "splits" in the psyche. In Schema Therapy Modes. And in contemporary psychoanalysis, in Philip Bromberg's "multiple self-states." There are also many other models that recognize the multiplicity of mind.

I personally often just think of parts as inner children, as the members of our internal families.

---

[29] C. G. Jung, The Collected Works of C.G. Jung, ed. Herbert Read, Michael Fordham, and Gerhard Adler, trans. R. F. C. Hull (New Jersey: Princeton University Press, 2024).

Schwartz has said that he started using the term "parts" because it was just the word that his patients would use as they got to know their psyches better in therapy. As Schwartz was stumbling into what would become IFS, he was often working with people with eating disorders, so they might say something like, "A part of me doesn't want to restrict, but another part of me gets absolutely terrified about stopping."

In IFS therapy, multiple "parts" are seen as just a natural, very important way that we are.

Of the multiplicity of mind psychologies, IFS might have the richest sense of the relationships between parts. This might be because Schwartz was originally trained as a family systems therapist, so he was primed to notice and explore relationship dynamics. He soon noticed that the relational dynamics that families go through when there is trauma or deprivation were about the same relational dynamics that parts of his patients' psyches went through when there was trauma or deprivation.

Hence the name, Internal Family Systems therapy.[30]

This relational sense of parts can bring some real clarity to how the roles and relationships of parts of the psyche, of the inner family, can be changed profoundly by experiences of trauma or deprivation. Once the roles and relationships of our inner parts are changed by trauma or deprivation, our inner world is likely not inhabited by a happy family. Instead, it's probably a family trying its best to survive, even if other members of the family have to be fought or suppressed to try to make it through.

This leads us to discussing "burdens."

Burdens and trauma and deprivation

"Burdens" are what parts of us often take on and carry after experiences of trauma or deprivation. The word "suffering" etymologically means to "carry a burden." Parts of us wind up carrying the sequela of trauma or deprivation. These could be the

---

[30] Tim Ferris and Schwartz, "Richard Schwartz — IFS, Psychedelic Experiences without Drugs, and Finding Inner Peace for Our Many Parts (#492)," January 14, 2021.

feelings, the beliefs, the relational configurations, and the sense of self from trauma or deprivation. These could also be the crisis management protective moves following trauma or deprivation.

Parts carrying burdens, if not helped, if not healed, can go on carrying those heavy burdens for a lifetime.

Parts of us seem to especially take on burdens when we were too alone in and after a trauma or deprivation. Experiences of trauma or deprivation within a larger context of good enough relational connection don't seem to lead to parts taking on burdens so much. Perhaps in circumstances of good enough relationships, parts aren't stuck carrying the burdens alone. They can then heal, they can unburden, in the healthy relationships.

So relational isolation — too much aloneness — is central to trauma or deprivation becoming what we often think of as trauma or deprivation. By that, real relational togetherness is then of profound importance to healing.

A relational sense of both burdening and of healing will be a core theme all through this book.

Exiles

From an experience of trauma or deprivation, one part of ourselves, often one of the most sensitive parts of ourselves, might wind up carrying the burdens of the actual experiences of the trauma or deprivation. These burdens are often the emotions we experienced in the trauma or deprivation; the physical feelings and physical reactions; the memories (in some form or another); and meanings or messages that were implied or inferred by the trauma or deprivation. For example, from trauma or deprivation, a part might wind up carrying emotions of hurt, sadness, confusion, or shame. That part might also wind up carrying the physical feelings or physical reactions, maybe of shaking, physical weakness, recoiling, or shrinking. The part might also carry the memories of the experience of trauma or deprivation, maybe not as a sort of a video replay, but as flashes or atmospheres of one kind or another, perhaps of being powerless, of being alone. And the part might wind up carrying beliefs such as, "I'm awful," "I'm broken," "People are dangerous and unreliable," "I'm fundamentally alone," or "This is my lot, this kind of thing is what happens to someone like me."

Ouch.

From there, in crisis management, other parts of us then can try to push this part out of us in one way or another. That is because the burdens the sensitive and vulnerable part carries are terribly painful and can seem truly overwhelming and even extremely dangerous. When one part tries its best to get rid of or silence or ignore another part, that is called "exiling." The part that is being exiled, often the part carrying the direct experiences of the trauma or deprivation, is then often called an "exile."

Protectors

The part or parts trying to do the exiling are then called "protectors," because they are trying to protect both from the noxious, horrible burdens that the exile has been stuck carrying, and the protectors might be trying to protect from further, similar traumatization in the world or external relationships.

So the burdens of protectors are the heavy, difficult loads of constantly trying to exile a vulnerable, sensitive part and of constantly trying to protect the patient and their parts from further dangerous situations.

There can also be multiple different protectors trying to do the same basic protective and exiling goals with the same exile, but with different and possibly conflicting strategies. So in addition to working nearly constantly and very diligently to try to keep the exile and all of its burdens out, protectors can also be in tense and conflictual relationships with other protectors.

From all this, protectors can often be at or near their wits end and leading very tense lives.

It's important to note that burdened protectors aren't "the bad guys" in IFS. They aren't the problem, and getting rid of them (a simplistic "being less defensive") isn't the goal. Parts who have taken up protective burdens are inner children who are doing their damndest to help, and they are often suffering badly. Like all parts of ourselves, they need and deserve their own loving, respectful relationship and ultimately their own healing. And that is going to be necessary if the inner family is going to be harmonious and if our patient is going to have some real peace and freedom.

Parts carrying protective burdens will only truly heal, will only lay down their external burdens and return to their primary natures, to themselves, when the exile or exiles they protect and protect from are healed and are safe enough.

Managers and firefighters

There are roughly two kinds of protector roles based on different types of strategies of protecting. The main difference is about timeframe, of long term or short term.

Some burdened protective parts try to set up long term or permanent systems or strategies of inner exiling and outer world safety. These parts are then often called "managers" or "manager protectors." The term comes from the image of managers of an organization, like a business, who try to create procedures, routines, and policies that will ensure the organization is safe basically forever.

Other protector parts might take on very short term strategies for blocking out exiles and protecting from the outside world. These parts are then often called "firefighters" or "firefighter protectors," from the image of real world firefighters who might dump thousands of gallons of water on a burning building to put out the fire without worrying about water damage. They just try to get rid of the present danger as soon as possible.

Again, the main difference between manager protectors and firefighter protectors is just about the time frame of their strategy.

But there can be some common stylistic differences between them that can help us at least start guessing about their job in the inner world.

Manager protectors might have strategies of trying to "keep everything together." Of succeeding in school or work or family. Of being nice. Of being powerful. Of being attractive. Of being intimidating. Of being smart. Of being dependent. Of being disciplined. Of restricting eating. Of being "super spiritual." Strategies like these are hoped by the manager protector parts to be permanent strategies of avoiding crisis and trouble, inner and outer.

Firefighter protectors might have protective strategies of zoning out on the internet. Avoiding a daunting responsibility. Substance abuse. Impulsive sex. Bursts of rage. Binging and purging. Suicidal thoughts. Flights into otherworldly experience. Exiling and protective strategies like these *tend* to be more immediate term emergency measures.

From all this we can start to see more clearly that if someone has been through a lot of trauma or deprivation in too much relational isolation, then their inner relationships, the "politics of experience" of their inner family, as R.D. Laing might put it, can become quite rough.[31] Manager protectors and firefighter protectors can come to really hate each other, and hate the exile who keeps evading them and popping up with their burdens of suffering no matter what they try to do. A firefighter part might see a manager protector as a failure whose procedures are bossy and incompetent. A manager protector might see a firefighter protector as childish, undisciplined, not sticking to the system, and just making things worse, water damage and all. And the exiles might be not only carrying the burdens of the trauma or deprivation, but living deeply alone, shunned and manhandled in the main relationships they have, with the managers and firefighters.

---

[31] R. D. Laing, The Politics of Experience (New York: Pantheon Books, 1967).

Again, ouch. It's a horrible thing that those who go through trauma and deprivation not only have to experience the trauma or deprivation itself but, without adequate support and healing, carry all these burdens from the trauma or deprivation, day by day, for the long term.

This is a lot of what we are dealing with in psychotherapy. No wonder we need all the help we can get in helping heal our patients, and how wonderful that we have the option of the partnership of psychedelics.

It's important to underline that burdened parts, whether exiles or protectors, are not their burdens. They are inner children. But because the burdens can be so intense, parts can very much come to identify with the burdens they carry and other parts can simply see them as their burdens. By the intensity of the burdens, parts can totally forget who they are originally and who all these other parts of the psyche are. Again, in truth, they are all wonderful inner children. But they can appear to each other and to themselves as the most horrid monsters or as heartless enforcers.

Similarly and crucially, due to the intensity of the burdens, parts also become stuck in time. This isn't because of some whacky physics. This is from psychology: the intensity of the burdens can so dominate parts' attention, their whole field of perception, that *everything* effectively bends towards the burdens, even time. Just about all they see are the burdens. They do not see time pass.

A pop science analogy to this could be black holes in astrophysics, where light, time, and all dimensions bend towards the heart of the black hole.

Because burdened parts are stuck in time, they then see the themes, dangers, and atmospheres of the original traumatic or depriving situations as what is happening *now,* to some extent or another, sometimes more than others.

As Freud crucially observed, "In the unconscious there is no time."[32]

So just time doesn't heal these wounds.

(I am deeply grateful to my IFS colleague Madeleine Warren for helping me understand the crucial mechanism of how burdened parts get stuck in time: nose to the grindstone.)

The intensity of the burdens also forces the parts who carry them into what is called in IFS "extreme roles;" extreme roles of suffering or of protective strategies. If you want to find a burdened part, look for extreme roles.

And from all this, again, parts can really seem like they are their burdens, to ourselves, to the people in our lives, and even to our therapists. But when healed, when freed of their burdens, we then get to find out who they really are. And almost as a rule, we are surprised.

Discussing the intensity of burdens leads us to discuss "blending."

Blending

"Blending" is when a burdened part kind of takes us over. That is, "blends" with us. When a part blends with us, it becomes our psychology. We then see the world, other people, ourselves, and other parts through its eyes to a large extent. We think with its mind. We feel the emotions of that part, often its fears. We feel its physical reactions in our bodies. Given all this, when blended with a part we will also then act, or feel strong urges to act, in the extreme ways of the burdens of that part.

If it's a protector part who has blended with us, we then feel the fears and resolve of that protector, and we very much want to do its protective strategies.

If it's an exile who has blended with us, we feel at least tastes or atmospheres of what they felt in the trauma or deprivation.

---

[32] Sigmund Freud and James Strachey, The Interpretation of Dreams (New York: Basic Books A Member of the Perseus Books Group, 2010).

We feel their fears and panics, their vulnerability. We may also feel their desperate need for help.

Sometimes our various burdened parts blend with us one at a time rapidly in a chaotic inner scrum. Then various and often contradictory thoughts and feelings and motivations can be taking us over, one after another depending on who is "up" in the scrum at a given moment. This itself can be painfully confusing, in addition to the burdens of each part.

Blending is the experience of, "Why the fuck can't I stop doing that?" Or when the people in our lives say to us, "Why can't you stop doing that?" Blending helps describe what has often been called our "patterns," "tapes," or our "programming."

We'll discuss Self in IFS next. This follows naturally from our discussion of blending, because a crucial thing in IFS therapy is helping our patients, and ourselves as therapists, unblend to Self.

Self

Self is a big deal term in IFS. It's what makes IFS IFS. Again, there are many, many traditions in psychology and beyond that recognize parts, by whatever terms and with whatever differing nuances. But as we will see, in IFS therapy Self is entirely necessary for some of the deepest, fullest, and most real healing.

The great news is that Self in IFS is not only extremely important, but it is also extremely common. This is because Self is simply each of us, patients and therapists, when we are not blended with one of our parts. As common as dirt.

Because Self is just each of us, it can't be lost. It can't be damaged. No traumas or deprivations can hurt Self or weaken it. Self doesn't need adequate childhood environmental or relational conditions to exist or grow or to be made. It doesn't need to grow at all.

One way of thinking about Self might be as our ontology, that it is us as beings.

Because Self is just each of us, it's not something we have to find or get from outside ourselves. It's not something we need to try to "game," to hope to luck into, to float into, or muscle into.

We can't — and we don't have to — make water wetter.

Here, perhaps, is how Pablo Picasso put it: "I don't develop, I am."[33]

These are big statements. I can't cite studies that have found Self in some region of the brain or in some quantum process in microtubules in neurons. If we want experiments about the validity of what is called Self in IFS, I think the best way to do that is clinically. Experience is a form of experiment. And as pragmatism might put it, that which works is real. With probably just a small handful of sessions of IFS work in our own psychotherapy, we can experientially test the validity of Self and its healing power. And with adequate training and support, we can try IFS in our work as therapists. In doing that, we will naturally explore with our patients the validity of Self and the healing power of Self to part relationships.

I personally think that one of the greatest contributions that IFS has made to psychotherapy is that it can help us work pragmatically with Self, not just talk about it or theorize about it or hope to luck into it here or there. Which leads us to our next topic, unblending, or more fully stated, unblending to Self.

Unblending

Many schools of therapy and other healing traditions seem to have a real sense of something like what we might call the power of Self to part relationships. But unfortunately, they often haven't offered much pragmatically to help us actually get there. There is plenty of good, wise advice available: "You've got to love yourself." "Self-acceptance is the way forward." "Be compassionate with yourself." "Be present with all that is." "It's all about balance." "It's all about relationships."

---

[33] Quoted in, James Hillman, The Soul's Code: In Search of Character and Calling, Ballantine Books trade paperback edition (New York: Ballantine Books, 2017).

All true. But to a hurting person, just saying these things can be like telling them that healing is available in the seventh dimension. Great, it's nice to know it's there, but without offering any path to that health and healing, that advice is likely of no real help.

But in IFS, we have the technique of unblending. By helping our patients unblend, we can help them get into real-time relationships of Self with their hurting, burdened parts, and then real healing can happen.

And unblending can happen in just about any therapy session.

Again, by the intensity of their burdens, burdened parts are often struggling for dominance of our psyches. They blend with us. Exiles try to take us over to get out, to vent, to be seen and heard, and maybe, "this time," to be helped. Protectors try to take us over to keep pushing out the exiles with their seemingly impossible burdens and to try to avoid the dangers of the world, to keep us from getting traumatized again. Burdened parts can be battling fairly non-stop for who gets to blend with Self. There can be little room or time for our patient as Self.

So unblending is terribly important.

The technique of unblending is incredibly simple and it is fully relational: it's pretty much just acknowledging the part or parts who have blended with us, and then asking them to unblend from us. Maybe we briefly explain to them why we are asking them to unblend from us. And then they unblend from us or they don't. They are free agents, and we need to respect that.

As we'll see in the demo session at the end of this chapter, we as therapists can very much help our patients unblend. In fact, this is one of our main jobs as therapists in IFS therapy: to help our patients unblend to Self. Then, in Self to part relationship, they can help and heal their own parts. Often, our most important role is to be midwives to that.

There is technique to unblending, but again, the spirit of unblending is relational. Unblending is asking a question, a true question, of a part. Unblending is not an attempt to exile anything out of the psyche.

Unblending is, to borrow a term from structural family therapy, getting into rightful roles within the relationships of our psyche. Inner children deserve to be able to be in the role of child, not to have to try to run the show as a little "Self."

Our own unblending to Self as therapists is also key to IFS therapy. We as therapists are very important in the healing relationships of therapy. We are ingredients in the cauldron of healing with our patients. Our being there as Self is very important.

Because unblending is so important, we will return to it in detail in the clinical chapters in Part II. We will focus there on both helping our patients unblend to Self and in doing our own unblending to Self as therapists.

We've now discussed the view in IFS of how our patients come to suffer psychologically. And we've discussed Self and unblending to Self. Having done that, we can now more fully discuss healing in IFS therapy.

The spirit of healing in IFS

The opening quote of this chapter beautifully and simply describes healing in IFS. It will be a refrain all through this book, so I want to re-quote it: "The primary healing relationship in internal family systems therapy is between the client's Self and her young, injured parts."[34]

Again, relational aloneness made trauma and deprivation so much worse. So the relational togetherness of Self and part can be decisive for healing.

IFS has great technique that can help make these healing relationships happen, and we will discuss that and see it in action

---

[34] Martha Sweezy, ed., Internal Family Systems Therapy: New Dimensions (New York: Routledge, 2013).

in the example session later in this chapter and throughout this book. But before that, I would like to share a story of healing.

A STORY OF A PROTECTOR'S HEALING

This is a non-clinical story of healing which, in some ways, makes it more powerful to me. It is a story of Hiroo Onoda, a Japanese soldier during World War II. When I first learned about Onoda's story, I was struck by it as a beautiful parallel to healing in IFS.

Onoda was the most famous of the Japanese "remaining soldiers" (*zanryū nipponhei*) of World War II. These were Japanese soldiers who kept fighting the war well after it was over. Onoda didn't surrender until 1974, twenty-nine years after the war ended.

He was an intelligence officer, and he and a group of fellow Japanese soldiers didn't trust the leaflets repeatedly dropped by American planes on their island in the Philippines announcing the end of the war and telling them to come into a town and surrender. Onoda and his colleagues figured they might do something like that to trick Americans into a trap. So they decided to ignore those messages and keep fighting the war.

Over time, most of these soldiers did in fact surrender, but not Onoda. Tellingly, Onoda only surrendered after a very friendly young Japanese man, Norio Suzuki, made it his mission to leave Japan, travel to the island, find Onoda, and become friends with him.

Suzuki did come to Onoda's island and reached out to Onoda persistently, leaving notes at Onoda's camps and suggesting times to meet. I imagine the notes involved some jokes. And maybe mentions of Japanese food.

Onoda eventually agreed to meet with Suzuki, and over several meetings and fires together at night in the woods, they became friends. From a friend, from Suzuki, Onoda was able to accept that the war was over.

But Onoda stated that he could only surrender on orders from his commanding officer. The Japanese government found his old commanding officer, who had been running a bookstore in Tokyo for nearly thirty years, and flew him to the island. He ordered Onoda to surrender, which he did.

Onoda had developed an interest in cows during the years hiding in the countryside of the island. He eventually chose to move to Brazil with his wife and brother to work in the booming cattle industry. He also wrote a book of his story and became famous in Japan.

If we play with this story, we might say we can see a part getting into an extreme role: protect Japan, fight the war. Parts that become burdened with protective roles often take what amount to very strong vows to do their jobs. They will not back down because of reasoning, cajoling, or pleading. They will only shift their roles when healing and good enough safety are in place, and in some relationship of Self to part.

We might see blending: Onoda nearly completely functioning from that one burdened, protective part.

We can also see healing in relationship. Here, the young man Suzuki is perhaps a sort of external Self, reaching out to Onoda, meeting him more than halfway, and befriending him. Once in relationship, once not pathologically alone, Onoda could start to heal. When Onoda was unblended enough and the protector part unburdened, Onoda could then choose a new role for himself that fit his interests and talents far more: cattle farming.

We can see in Onoda's story integration of this healing as well. He acted on this new, truer vision of himself and his life. And crucially, he didn't have to do it alone. He could be in partnership with his wife and his brother.

IFS can seem very weird, like an "out there" psychotherapy. Maybe it is as simple as friendship.

Let's now look at a demo session of IFS.

A DEMO SESSION OF IFS THERAPY

How many words is a video worth? A lot. We are very fortunate that there are videos of demonstration sessions of IFS available, including the one we are going to look at now and discuss.

We will look at an edited transcript of the session and then we will discuss a portion of the session. That discussion will center on "the 6 F's". In IFS, the 6 F's are a mnemonic device for remembering some steps for helping our patient find and get into relationship with a part.

The video is from a presentation Richard Schwartz did for the Wisdom 2.0 Conference in 2019. The conference organizer, Soren Gordhamer, was interviewing Schwartz in his presentation, and wound up invited into a demonstration session! This piece of work centers very poignantly on Gordhamer getting to know and helping a protector part and an exiled part of himself who were burdened by his parents' sudden divorce when he was a child.

My great thanks to Gordhamer for helping present this work so richly.

I would highly recommend, if possible, watching the video as well as reading the transcript. The video is freely available on YouTube. Here is the link for the video: https://tinyurl.com/IFSdemosesh The demo begins at about 7:20.

Here is the transcript.

Transcript of example session

Participant: Let's start with the part that felt kind of burned. Yeah. And, and doesn't want to be burned again. So in order to not get burned again, that requires, you know, this certain strategy.

Therapist: Got it. So go ahead and find that one in your body or around your body. That feeling or that, that belief system or that emotion, just see where you find it.

Participant: Okay. Yeah, I can see it in, in my body.

Therapist: Where, whereabouts?

Participant: It's like right below my belly. Like right below kind of my belly button, I guess that would be like my *hara* [a rich Japanese term for that part of our bodies]. Like right below my belly button.

Therapist: And as you see it there, how do you feel toward it?

Participant: I don't actually have a strong desire either way with it. It feels like – It's interesting, I don't have like a strong interest in it. It just feels like it's more kind of a hollowness. It's, it's more like a hollowness, I guess is the best way to put it. I don't know if that's a feeling that makes sense, but yeah.

Therapist: But are you open to getting to know it?

Participant: Absolutely.

Therapist: Okay. So just focus on it again and ask it what it wants you to know about itself and don't think of the answer. Just wait and see what comes to you.

Participant: What just came without even thinking was, "I'm here to keep you safe."

Therapist: Okay. And how do you feel toward it as you hear that?

Participant: I feel, I feel positive towards that. I feel like I want people around me to help me feel safe.

Therapist: So let it know you appreciate that. And ask what it's doing inside of you to keep you safe these days.

Participant: Wow. Okay. It says, "I'm careful." "We're careful who we open our heart to."

Therapist: Yeah.

Participant: "I'm helping you be careful who you open your heart to."

Therapist: Okay. And that sounds valuable, right?

Participant: Yeah, yeah.

Therapist: Yeah. So again, just show it a lot of appreciation for that. [Pause] And ask it what it's afraid would happen if it didn't do that.

Participant: It's actually — it's an interesting part. It says, "I just want you to choose wisely. If you don't choose wisely, you could get hurt."

Therapist: Okay. And ask if it protects parts of you that have been hurt in the past.

Participant: Yes.

Therapist: And maybe ask if it'd give us permission to go to one of those parts and see what we could do to heal it.

Participant: It says sure.

Therapist: Okay, good. So Soren, go ahead and focus on one of those parts, the hurt. Find it in your body.

Participant: And this is a different part than the previous part? Okay, yeah. Okay.

Therapist: Where do you find this one?

Participant: This is more heart based, heart centered.

Therapist: And how do you feel toward it?

Participant: I feel very sweet towards it. Very, very curious and loving towards it.

Therapist: So let it know that and see how it reacts.

Participant: It reacts favorably.

Therapist: Good. And see if it wants you to know anything about that hurt that it carries.

Participant: It's, yeah, it wants me to know that, it wants me to know to look out for myself. Uh huh. Like, "I want you to look out for yourself."

Therapist: Okay.

Participant: And I, I agree with it. I want to look out for myself.

Therapist: Yeah. Okay. Yeah, stay with it for a second. [Pause] Okay. And just see if there's anything it wants you to know about when it got hurt in the past.

Participant: When it got hurt in the past. Um, it didn't see the signs. It's like, "I wasn't aware of the signs." I wasn't aware of – I didn't see it. It came as an alarm, as a shock. And as I was unprepared, it's like getting a punch and you're not prepared for the punch.

Therapist: Yeah. So it felt kind of blindsided.

Participant: Blindsided, yeah.

Therapist: Yeah. Does that make sense, Soren?

Participant: Yeah, very much.

Therapist: So let it know you get that and that that was really hard and bad for it. And see if, ask if it feels like you get how bad that was for it, or if it wants you to feel or see or sense more about that.

Participant: It feels like I get it. It feels like I get it, that it was actually the shock and the, um, blindsidedness that really impacted. Yeah.

Therapist: And ask if it's still stuck back in that time. Do we need to get it out of there?

Participant: Is, is it okay if the part says there's a percentage? It says it's 5% still there. But that it, it doesn't feel like that's where it lives right now.

Therapist: Okay. That's great. But would it like us to get that 5% out of there?

Participant: Yes.

Therapist: All right. So, so why don't you go to, to that younger you in that scene, in that time period and be with him again in the way he needed somebody. Just tell me when you're in there with him.

Participant: Okay. I'm with him.

Therapist: How are you being with him?

Participant: I'm just kind of holding him, and he's crying. Just comforting him.

Therapist: How old is he?

Participant: He's about 12.

Therapist: Okay. So we're just going to hang with him that way. And while you do that, you can see if he wants you to do anything for him back there, or if he just wants you to hold him.

Participant: Rubbing. Yeah. Just rubbing his hair. Like petting him.

Therapist: How's he reacting?

Participant: He likes that. He likes to be held and petted and just, like, comforted.

Therapist: Good. And ask if he's ready to leave that time and place or if there is anything else he wants to happen back there first.

Participant: He says he doesn't want to be blindsided. And I told him I get that. Yeah. That's his only thing. Otherwise he's ready to leave.

Therapist: Okay. All right. So let's take him wherever you want. He can join the other part, the 95% with you in the present, if that's what he wants to do, or he can go somewhere else, wherever he feels safe.

Participant: He wants to go into the forest.

Therapist: Great. Yeah, so take him there.

Participant: Okay. I see him in the forest.

Therapist: How's he seem?

Participant: He seems very relaxed and at ease. He's very small. But he seems very relaxed and at ease.

Therapist: Okay. And he wants to just stay there? Or does he want you to stay with him? Does he want other people with him?

Participant: What does he want? He wants to spend some time in the forest and he wants to go with me wherever I go.

Therapist: Okay. How's that sound?

Participant: Sounds great.

Therapist: So tell him that's what you're going to arrange. He never has to go back to that scene.

Participant: Okay.

Therapist: And you are going to take care of him now. And ask, given all that, if he's ready to unload the feelings and beliefs he got back there.

Participant: He is, definitely.

Therapist: And ask where he carries all that, in his body or on his body?

Participant: I can say his chest. He says his chest.

Therapist: Okay. And ask what he'd like to give it all up to. Light, water, fire, wind, earth, anything else?

Participant: Water, for sure.

Therapist: Yeah. So set that up for him and tell him to just let all that out of his chest.

Participant: Into the water, into the water. He can do that.

Therapist: Good. And how does he seem now without that?

Participant: He kind of becomes ephemeral. Like he's kind of misty. He seems very good. He kind of just becomes this misty energy form.

Therapist: Okay, great. And tell him he can invite into his body qualities he might want to have now, even though his body is misty now. But whatever he'd like to have come back, tell him he can open to that.

Participant: Okay.

Therapist: So how does he seem now?

Participant: He seems really good.

Therapist: Good. So let's go back to that original protector and have him come in and see he doesn't have to protect this 12-year-old anymore and just see how he reacts.

Participant: He's fine. He was tired of that job. He's very happy to not do that job.

Therapist: Yeah. So ask him what he'd like to do now instead.

Participant: He said he'd just like to relax.

Therapist: Yeah, he can just relax for a while anyway. Maybe figure out a new role when he's ready.

Participant: Maybe he'd like to be "Head of relaxation."

Therapist: Sounds good. So tell him that's his new role.

Participant: Okay.

Therapist: And does that feel complete for now, Soren?

Participant: It does. It does. Thank you.

Therapist: Yeah.

Participant: Thank you.

Therapist: Thank your protector for letting us do all that.

Participant: This is good. Thank you, Dick. You always take me somewhere.

Therapist: Thanks for being such a good sport.

Participant: I trust me. I trust you. I trust what wants to emerge.

The "6 F's," starting a relationship with a part

"The 6 F's" are a list of steps in IFS work that are very helpful for starting to establish Self to part relationship with a part. And again, as we saw in the demo session, once there is Self to part relationship, crucial healing can start to happen.

In this discussion will look at the 6 F's just in the beginning part of the demo session. Throughout the book we will revisit the sort of healing that happened later in the session.

I'll list and discuss each "F" in the order that they usually come up in a session and we'll discuss how that "F" seemed to play out in the demo session.

- **Find the part**. Ask our patient to find the part they want to work with. This will be the "target part," the main part focused on for the time being. Our patient might readily find the part as they check their emotions, body, mind, imagination, or the room. Or they might need to invite the part to be there with them.
    - In the demo, Schwartz asks Gordhamer if he wants to work with the part that they were already talking about. This is very typical of a session. Often patients start a session essentially talking about or from a part. If a patient begins a session saying they got very angry a couple of days ago, we might ask, "So one way of looking at this is that a part of you got very angry. Would you like to work with that part of yourself?" In the demo, Gordhamer readily found the part he wanted to work with.
- **Focus on the part**. Ask our patient to notice the part and to let it be there.
    - Schwartz just asks Gordhamer to find the part, and Gordhamer does, mostly in his body.
- **Flesh it out**. Notice how the part is there, how it is manifesting. Perhaps it's in their body, in their emotions, maybe they see the part in their imagination. Maybe it's somewhere in the room. Maybe there's just an inchoate sense, but they know it's there. Whatever, however.
    - Schwartz asks Gordhamer where it is in his body, and Gordhamer finds the part in greater detail in his belly, in his *hara*. As part of "fleshing out," I think it's good to help our patients find the part in both their body and emotions. Somehow, the Self to part relationship can be more powerful from there. The important thing is that our patient is noticing the part, in whatever ways it's there.

- **Feel toward — unblending**. Here we get into some technique for checking on blending, and if need be, unblending to Self. Again, being Self, well enough, is crucial to healing in IFS.
  - Schwartz asks the classic IFS checking question: "As you see it there, how do you feel toward it?" This checking question can give a good sense of some very important things: If our patient is in a Self to part relationship with the target part; if our patient is blended with another part as they relate to the target part; or if our patient is blended with the target part itself. If our patient replies with things that are different than "qualities of Self" — roughly, different than being in a respectful relationship with the part at the moment — then we can guess that another part has blended with our patient, or our patient is blended with the part. In this demo, Gordhamer responded that he was feeling a "hollowness" towards the part, and not a strong desire in one form or another. Schwartz asked to clarify, "Are you open to getting to know it?" Gordhamer responded, "Oh yes, absolutely." Schwartz seemed to take that as a good indication that Gordhamer was in Self to part relationship with the part.
- **Be[F]riend**. Once our patient is there as Self with the part, the healing has actually begun. At this point, it can be important to trust the patient as Self, to trust the patient's part, and to let them co-lead much of the actual healing path from here. Again, much of our work as therapists in IFS is to help "midwife," to help structure, some Self to part relationship. Then, to at least some extent, we need to get out of the way.

- Schwartz says to Gordhamer, "So just focus on it again and ask it what it wants you to know about itself and don't think of the answer, just wait until it comes to you." And later, because the target part seems to be a protector part, "Ask it what it's doing these days to try to keep you safe."
- **Fear.** This step is for when our patient is spending time with a protector part, which is the case at this point in the demo. Our patient can ask the protector about their fears, specifically about what they are afraid would happen if they didn't do their job. This can deepen the work.
  - Schwartz says, "Ask it what it's afraid would happen if it didn't do that?"

There is much more to this demo session, but because of brevity we'll need to end our discussion of the session here.

We will return to all these themes — Self, parts, burdens, unblending, healing — many times over the course of the book, and in different contexts, to elaborate them.

Cautions about inadequately trained IFS work

It's not talked about enough, but harm can be done in psychotherapy. I already stated a warning in the Introduction about doing inadequately trained IFS work in PAP. That same basic warning holds for standard IFS too.

As I think we've seen, IFS is pretty easy to understand conceptually. It can then seem easy to "jump in" and start healing. But sometimes we can best respect the inner family by compassionately doing less. As our skills grow, we will be meeting and working with more parts. My hunch is that they will have more respect and trust in us because we had the respect to not rush in and try to help parts when that could have hurt them.

Again, the big warning here is to not work with exiled parts much without having done a level 1 IFS training.

Protectors can be easier to work with. They tend to be more burly. And protectors truly appreciate the Self to part relationship. They are inner children who have been working alone and often non-stop for maybe many years. They appreciate the friendship and understanding of Self to part relationship.

Possible objections to IFS

As mentioned earlier, IFS can seem "out there," even ridiculous. Is that a bug or a feature? Maybe sometimes we need to get out of the ordinary for healing to happen. That can be another thing that psychedelics and IFS share!

Most people who come into psychotherapy have been through the ordinary attempts at helping. They've likely had good advice. They've maybe had heart-to-heart conversations. They've tried to "look at things from another perspective" and "to get their shit together." And those have maybe helped quite a bit. But they still show up in our practices, they need something more.

I get it that there are real epistemological challenges to the whole sense of "parts" having real autonomy, and why would everyone have this quality of unhurt healing wisdom and goodness regardless of how traumatic or depriving their development was?

One possible tack here is simply empirical and pragmatic: to just do IFS therapy and see how it goes. Do some IFS as a patient in therapy, in a workshop, or in a training. At its base, IFS is an entirely experiential, entirely relational therapy, so really, that's the only way we get to know it anyway.

Maybe we see some real benefits in the IFS work, even great benefits. But maybe we still can't buy "all that" about parts or Self. In that case, we could go ahead with IFS in clinical work simply acting "as if" parts and Self and burdens were real, but mostly just taking them as matters of good clinical technique. That somehow, they "work." That will probably go quite well clinically. We maybe just say to ourselves, and maybe to our patients, "I don't know" about the reality of parts and Self, but that it sure seems to help a lot.

Or we could frame for ourselves IFS technique as an excellent, very customized form of hypnosis. Or as an excellent, experiential way to get at neurological "memory reconsolidation." Or as an excellent form of a mentalization based therapy. A meta cognitive therapy. A somatic based therapy.

Psychoanalytically, we could frame IFS as an excellent "internal subject relations" therapy, in Thomas Ogden's great phrase.[35] One that crucially adds the healing power of Self to part relationships. Or as "something more than interpretation," in Glen Gabbard's term.[36]

Such "as if" approaches could be parallel to what is apparently going on in contemporary biology and philosophy of science in big discussions about "agents," "motivation," and "learning" in single celled organisms and plants. It can seem very daunting and weird, but such terms seem to fit the data very well. One school of thought in contemporary biology is that even if we can't prove or even hypothesize mechanisms that would "make sense" of single celled organisms and plants being real agents, that because that seems to fit the data, we can best go ahead "as if" that agency were true so that the field can move forward with further science.[37] [38] [39] [40]

Another criticism of IFS that I have heard is that IFS is inadequately relational in terms of the therapy relationship. That is, there can be a sense that in IFS therapy the therapist is a sort of detached

[35] Thomas H. Ogden, The Matrix of the Mind: Object Relations and the Psychoanalytic Dialogue (Lanham (Md.): J. Aronson, 2004).

[36] Gabbard, Glen O., and Drew Westen. 2003. "Rethinking Therapeutic Action." The International Journal of Psychoanalysis 84 (4): 823–41.

[37] Okasha, S. The Concept of Agent in Biology: Motivations and Meanings. Biol Theory 19, 6–10 (2024).

[38] Gershman SJ, Balbi PE, Gallistel CR, Gunawardena J. Reconsidering the evidence for learning in single cells. Elife. 2021 Jan 4;10:e61907.

[39] Kevin Jiang, "Unexpected Depths" (Harvard Medical School, December 5, 2019), https://hms.harvard.edu/news/unexpected-depths.

[40] "Aristotle's Biology" (Stanford Encyclopedia of Philosophy, February 15, 2006), https://plato.stanford.edu/entries/aristotle-biology/.

consultant simply helping facilitate the patient's own Self to part relationships; that the therapist is not a direct, real "ingredient" in their patient's healing process. Fortunately, this is very much not the case. As we've already seen and will continue to see over and over in this book, IFS is entirely, fundamentally a relational model, including in the therapist and patient relationship.

One of the best sources on the topic of relationality in IFS is a 2013 chapter from Richard Schwartz, "The Therapist-Client Relationships."[41] The opening quote of this chapter is from Schwartz's chapter. In that chapter, Schwartz skillfully explores and discusses IFS as a fully relational therapy, transference, countertransference, and all. I obviously highly recommend this excellent chapter. It is a bedrock of this book. As we will see and discuss extensively in the clinical chapters to come, the therapeutic relationship figures very prominently in good PAP work.

There can also be concerns that IFS is something of a cult. Well, there can be *a lot* of excitement about IFS from therapists and patients. And protector parts can take on IFS in an extreme way, as their new protective burden. This seems to be a pretty common move with just about any school of psychotherapy (or hell, brand of phone or music genre for that matter).

But ultimately, IFS is fundamentally incompatible with cultiness. Cults are primarily about attempts to hollow out the Self of the cult members. All the good stuff is purported to be outside the cult members and in the cult leader. Then, the only way cult members can get at any of that good stuff, any Self, is to be in relationship with the cult leader. So in cults, the only person perceived to have something like Self is the cult leader. This is a fundamental pathology of cults.

However, an IFS view is basically the opposite of that. In an IFS view, everyone has or is Self. Without that, there is no IFS. And being a Self means – well – being oneself, with all the wisdoms,

---

[41] Martha Sweezy, ed., Internal Family Systems Therapy: New Dimensions (New York: Routledge, 2013).

powers, objections, questions, and disagreements that that entails, and being an agent and in relationship with what is from there. Again, this is fundamentally different and incompatible with a cult view.

I'd also like to note that some patients (and some therapists) can struggle with the terminology of IFS. I personally think we can be natural and flexible with the language we use in IFS therapy. It's important to find words, images, metaphors, and analogies that we and our patient can connect on and that work well enough for both of us. These could vary from patient to patient.

I personally rarely use the term Self with my patients, unless they are an IFS therapist. The capital "S" of Self can sometimes cause problems. It can give an unhelpful sense of Self as some special, outside thing. I don't have a better term, so I just take Self as a technical term with a particular meaning and move on. In my clinical work, I tend to mostly just help my patients unblend and then talk about "you."

CHAPTER THREE

AN OVERVIEW OF WESTERN PSYCHEDELIC ASSISTED PSYCHOTHERAPY

> The future may teach us to exercise a direct influence,
> by means of particular chemical substances, on the
> amounts of energy and their distribution in the
> mental apparatus. It may be that there are other
> still undreamt-of possibilities of therapy. But for the
> moment we have nothing better at our disposal...
>
> — Sigmund Freud, *An Outline of Psychoanalysis,* 1940[42]

We need better ways to help people. Some people just clearly need more or different than standard psychotherapy and psychiatry can readily offer. Psychedelic assisted help, taking the term very broadly, is both an ancient and varied healing modality and a shockingly novel and highly promising introduction to modern Western mental healthcare. It is already helping many people who have not responded to standard treatments. It is even shaking current paradigms on what mental health is and what healing is. It looks like it could be one of the most efficacious and profound innovations in the history of Western mental healthcare.

We could say that there have been two main forces in modern Western mental healthcare: psychology implemented within a clinical relationship, that is, psychotherapy; and medications for mental health. Psychedelics are radically novel in ways that we do not understand now, and we may never understand, but one way of thinking about them is as a shocking combination of those two forces. As psychological medicines. Medicines that help partially via psychology.

---

[42] Quoted by Hanscarl Leuner in Passie T. (1997). Psycholytic and psychedelic therapy research 1931 - 1995 a complete international bibliography. Laurentius Publ.

This is not normal. This is no longer "normal science," in Thomas Kuhn's phrase. Kuhn noted that when a field passes beyond its "normal science," it has entered a paradigm transition.[43]

Adding to the shock, psychedelic assisted psychotherapy outcome studies show some of the best results ever seen in Western mental healthcare. Again, very notably, many people with previously treatment resistant conditions have gotten quite significant relief through PAP.

Even the governmental and legal categories of the old paradigm are shifting and creaking in the face of psychedelic medicines. The recent decision by the US FDA to not yet approve MDMA as a prescribable medicine, based in MAPS/Lycos' application, was partially because MAPS/Lycos rightly paired psychedelics and psychotherapy. The FDA — the Food and *Drug* Administration — had never regulated a psychotherapy before, and they were apparently quite uncomfortable, understandably, with what would have been a massive shift in their role. Clearly, psychedelic medicines are like no drugs the FDA has ever regulated.

To clarify some terms, psychedelic assisted psychotherapy, as the name says, is psychotherapy *assisted* by psychedelics. Psychedelics are not going to and should not replace psychotherapy. Properly respected and with best efficacy, psychedelic assisted help is not about psychedelics as simply standalone medicines. Psychedelics will be considered here as in a relational partnership with psychotherapy.

I will use the term "psychedelics" here very broadly, as any medicine that helps manifest the psyche. The term psychedelics here will not be restricted to 5-HT_{2A} agonists as in the "classic psychedelics" of LSD, mescaline, DMT, and psilocybin. Because this is a book of clinical psychotherapy, the psychological effects of medicines will be the consideration of what is psychedelic. Ketamine and MDMA will be fully included here as psychedelics

---

[43] Kuhn, T. S. (1962). The Structure of Scientific Revolutions. University of Chicago Press.

because psychologically, experientially, they can be as psychedelic as any 5-HT$_{2A}$ agonist.

As part of this psychotherapeutic and inclusive definition of psychedelics, I will not focus much on differences between psychedelic medicines. There do appear to be unique and important strengths and differences in psychedelic medicines, but that might be best addressed in general PAP training.

Psychedelic medicines here will be considered by a commonality they share: the healing power of more richly manifesting the psyche and then getting into better inner and outer relationships.

This broad take on psychedelics will also have the advantage of keeping the discussions here simpler and more organized.

I should note that ketamine looms large in this book because it is the medicine I have been using in my clinical practice. That is not only because ketamine is arguably the only psychedelic that is currently legally prescribable in the US, but also because it is an excellent healing psychedelic. Its direct healing effects can be shorter lived than those of the classic psychedelics, but often balancing that, ketamine is easier for many people to tolerate and is logistically easier to use, so ketamine can be more easily worked with frequently.

For the rest of this chapter, we will discuss several important topics:

- A broad history of psychedelics in the West
- The first wave of Western psychedelic research, of the 1950's to 1970's
- The current generation of psychedelic research
- Current structures or models of psychedelics in the West
- A difficult discussion of abuses by psychedelic "helpers"
- And we will end with a discussion of current policy considerations for PAP

SOME HISTORY OF PSYCHEDELICS IN THE WEST

Practices that we might call psychedelic assisted help seem to go back far if not wide in human history. As mentioned in the Introduction, we can see this in Native cultures, in the East, and in the West. Because Western mental healthcare is the frame of this book, we will focus here on a historical overview of psychedelics in the West.

Psychedelics seem to be embedded in the history of the West, possibly even in a foundational way. A quick and crucial example: if, as Alfred North Whitehead wrote, "The safest general characterization of the European philosophical tradition is that it consists of a series of footnotes to Plato,"[44] then what were Plato's sources? Largely, of course, Socrates. And what were Socrates' sources? Well, central to Socrates' life and work were the Eleusinian Mysteries, of which he was an active participant and a full initiate. The Eleusinian Mysteries were very likely psychedelic rituals. So by this historical line, is all (or a lot) of Western philosophy footnotes on psychedelics?

As mentioned earlier, this assertion of prominent or even foundational Western psychedelic roots is a big statement. The topic has been sharply controversial, mostly by the whole topic and its evidence being systematically belittled or ignored. But there is ample archeological, anthropological, archaeobotanical, and historical evidence that makes a very good case for important and widespread historical Western psychedelic use.

The story of the early West takes place largely in the basin of the Mediterranean Sea, the waters that connect the lands where the West matured. We might call the Mediterranean the "information superhighway" of the time.

There is recent evidence of early, intentional, repeated, and likely ritual use of psychedelics on the Mediterranean island of Menorca (present day Spain), from about 1000 BCE (Bronze Age).

---

[44] Alfred North Whitehead and David Ray Griffin, Process and Reality: An Essay in Cosmology, Corr. ed, The Gifford Lectures 1927/28 (New York: Free Press, 1985).

At a likely ritual site in a cave there, researchers found human hairs of many individuals that appeared to have been ritually stored. The researchers tested the hairs and found the presence of strong psychedelic alkaloids. These people seemed to have ingested these alkaloids several times over a year, the timeframe available for study by the length of the hairs. The setting and other archeological evidence suggests possible regular funerary rites, of rituals honoring the dead. The alkaloids found were atropine and scopolamine, apparently very strong and challenging psychedelics. Local plant sources could have been jimsonweed, henbane, and mandrake. The very challenging nature of these psychedelics suggests that these people were very sophisticated in the herbalism and the psychospiritual use of the plants. Clumsy or accidental use of these psychedelics would likely not have been repeated![45]

One could make an argument that one group of people on one island using psychedelics for intentional purposes does not make for even a significant subculture of Western or proto-Western psychedelia. But from about 300 BCE and just across the Balearic Sea, on the mainland of present day Spain, there is again very solid evidence of intentional, ritual use of psychedelics. This is from an ancient temple site in Mas Castellar de Pontós. There, herbalism tools, a chalice, and dental fragments from a man's skeleton all show the presence of ergot alkaloids. These are potent psychedelics akin to LSD-25 and the Meso-American *ololiuhqui*. They are widely available for preparation by expert herbalists as mold on grain products and grain plants.[46]

Deepening the argument for widespread Mediterranean, Western psychedelic use, Brian Muraresku points out in his book, *The Immortality Key*, that the temple site at Mas Castellar is a temple of Demeter and Persephone, and so is the temple of the just cited Eleusinian Mysteries. Possibly further linking the

---

[45] Guerra-Doce, E., Rihuete-Herrada, C., Micó, R. et al. Direct evidence of the use of multiple drugs in Bronze Age Menorca (Western Mediterranean) from human hair analysis. Sci Rep 13, 4782 (2023).

[46] Juan-Stresserras, J., & Matamala, J. C. (2005). Estudio de residuos microscópicos y compuestos orgánicos en utillaje de molido y de contenido de las vasijas [A study of the microscopic residue and organic compounds in grinding tools and jar contents]. In P. Bueno, R. Balbín, & R. Barroso (cur.), El dolmen de Toledo (pp. 235–241). Alcalá de Henares, Spain: Universidad de Alcalá.

temples at Mas Castellar and Eleusis is Peter Webster's very plausible circumstantial argument that the *kykeon*, the sacred drink of the Eleusinian Mysteries, was an expertly prepared ergot beverage from grain plants local to Eleusis.[47]

We should talk more about the Eleusinian Mysteries. The Eleusinian Mysteries were official and esteemed rituals conducted just outside Athens on a yearly calendar for about 2,000 years. In addition to Socrates, other deeply grateful initiates and participants were Sophocles, Marcus Aurelius, Aeschylus, Herodotus, Aristophanes, Plutarch, and Cicero.[48] Plato was not an initiate, but he wrote admiringly of the Eleusinian Mysteries.[49]

As part of their prep work, we might say, participants in these grand group rituals made a vow of secrecy — and they stuck to it! Because of that, very much is unknown about what actually happened in these rituals that are clearly so central to some of the foundations of Western culture.

However, there are hints. An Athenian tablet from the Classical period states that the Mysteries taught or showed that "the greatest good among people is acquaintance with one another and trustworthiness."[50]

Cicero, a Roman, had this to say of the Eleusinian Mysteries:

> For among the many excellent and indeed divine institutions which your Athens has brought forth and contributed to human life, none, in my opinion, is better than those mysteries. For by their means we have been brought out of our barbarous and savage mode of life and educated and refined to a state of civilization; and as the rites are called "initiations," so in very truth we have learned from

[47] Carl Ruck and Peter Webster, "The Mythology and Chemistry of the Eleusinian Mysteries," https://www.youtube.com/watch?v=uwfkJkvbR-I.

[48] "Eleusinian Mysteries," 2025, https://en.wikipedia.org/wiki/Eleusinian_Mysteries.

[49] Plato. 2017. Euthyphro ; Apology ; Crito ; Phaedo. Edited by C. J. Emlyn-Jones and William Preddy. Loeb Classical Library /. Cambridge, Massachusetts: Harvard University Press.

[50] Quoted in, Individuals in the Eleusinian Mysteries: choices and actions, in M. Fuchs, A. Linkenbach, M. Mulsow, B.-C. Otto, R.B. Parson, J. Rüpke (ed.), Religious individualisation. Historical dimensions and comparative perspectives, Berlin 2019

them the beginnings of life, and have gained the power not only to live happily, but also to die with a better hope.[51]

The Eleusinian Mysteries and other similar, likely psychedelic rituals were thriving during the peak of the Roman Empire and the time of the creation of Christianity. Muraresku even makes a plausible suggestion that Christianity could have started as a psychedelic religion or soon had important psychedelic sects. There clearly were early Christian illegal, regular funerary rites, some maybe psychedelic, reliving the Last Supper in the burial catacombs under Rome. These catacombs are now part of the Vatican.[52]

But in 380 CE, Theodosius I, one of the early Christian Roman emperors, made Christianity the official, sole religion of the Roman Empire. As the theologian Hans Kung wrote of this time, "What a revolution! .... the persecuted church had become a persecuting church."[53] As part of this persecution, in 392 CE Theodosius I outlawed the Eleusinian Mysteries and the other likely psychedelic Western rituals, like the Dionysian festivals, and possibly Christian psychedelic sects.

With this decree, psychedelics became deeply lost to the West, at least by all official sources. Lost even into a kind of historical amnesia.

We take this story up further in the Epilogue. But for this historical overview, we can note that having been thoroughly divorced from its likely psychedelic roots, the history of psychedelics in the West doesn't start up again until about 1,000 years later, until soon after Columbus' fateful journey to the present day Americas.

---

[51] Marcus Tullius Cicero, On the Commonwealth: And, On the Laws, ed. James E. G. Zetzel, Second edition, Cambridge Texts in the History of Political Thought (Cambridge: Cambridge University Press, 2017), https://doi.org/10.1017/9781316498934.

[52] Brian C. Muraresku and Graham Hancock, The Immortality Key: The Secret History of the Religion with No Name (New York: St. Martin's Press, 2020).

[53] Hans Küng, The Catholic Church: A Short History, trans. John Bowden, Modern Library ed (New York: Modern Library, 2001).

In the Americas, Westerners encountered ritual, regular psychedelic use among Indigenous cultures. As early as 1496, Friar Ramón Pane marveled at Indigenous psychedelic use by the Taina people on the island of Hispaniola (present day Haiti and the Dominican Republic). Pane reported the ritual use of *yopo* snuff, containing DMT and 5-MeO-DMT and other psychedelic alkaloids. The plants for *yopo* are not native to the island. It was likely imported, showing how valuable *yopo* was to the Taina people.[54]

As European colonization of the Americas intensified, so did the West's exposure to Indigenous psychedelic medicines and to the rituals of these cultures. *Peyote* was central to this. *Peyote* was and is prominent in some Indigenous religious, cultural, and healing practices. *Peyote* is native to what is now the Southwest of the United States and parts of Northern Mexico.

By 1897, Arthur Heffter, a Western scientist, had isolated single molecule mescaline from *peyote*, consumed it, and confirmed it to be psychedelic.[55] William James, one of the earliest American psychologists, experimented with *peyote* and mescaline himself. But nitrous oxide was far easier on his GI system, so he preferred it to explore psychedelia, including, famously, "varieties of religious experience."[56]

This brings us to the early twentieth century.

I would like to explore what we might loosely call an accidental case of psychedelic assisted psychotherapy. It is both historically important and clinically informative. This is of Bill Wilson's psychedelic treatment for alcoholism and his founding of Alcoholics Anonymous (AA) in 1934.

[54] Schultes, R. E. (1969). The Plant Kingdom and Hallucinogens: (Parts I-III). Available at https://www.unodc.org/unodc/en/data-and-analysis/bulletin/bulletin_1969-01-01_4_page004.html
[55] Wikipedia contributors, "Mescaline," Wikipedia, The Free Encyclopedia, https://en.wikipedia.org/w/index.php?title=Mescaline&oldid=1275508602
[56] Jane S. Moon, Catherine M. Kuza, Manisha S. Desai, William James, Nitrous Oxide, and the Anaesthetic Revelation, Journal of Anesthesia History, Volume 4, Issue 1, 2018, Pages 1-6

Wilson was a tormented alcoholic. He was a patient at the Towns Hospital in New York City four times. The Towns Hospital was an inpatient treatment program that drew on powerful psychedelic plants well known in European herbalism, specifically belladonna, henbane, and berries of the prickly ash tree. Interestingly enough, these are very similar to the psychedelics likely used on the island of Menorca, discussed earlier. But it is important to note that even though the Towns Hospital drew on powerful psychedelic plants, their official treatment protocol was actively anti-psychedelic, as we will soon see.

To begin the story at the end, perhaps in a failure of the Towns Hospital's anti-psychedelic protocols, during Wilson's fourth and last stay at Towns he had a profound psychedelic experience with the plants, and, we might say, founded AA with the 12th Step, by having a profound "spiritual awakening." This spiritual experience seemed to help power his sobriety for the rest of his life and inspired his founding of AA.

Very notably, Wilson's first three treatments at the Towns Hospital had produced no psychedelic experience and were of very short lived usefulness for his alcoholism. The botanical treatment offered there was considered solely a medical treatment to purge poisons associated with and perpetuating addiction. Any "hallucinations" were seen as an unwelcome side effect to be avoided. In 1909, Alexander Lambert, the founding physician of the Towns Hospital, described their treatment protocol in an article and advised physicians how to differentiate between the hallucinations of alcohol withdrawal and the hallucinations of the plants they used: "The various hallucinations of alcohol follow each other so quickly that a man is busily occupied in observing them one after another. The belladonna delirium is apt to be confined to one or two ideas on which the patient is very insistent. If these symptoms of belladonna intoxication occur, of course, the specific must be discontinued; then beginning again with the original smaller dose."[57]

But days before his fourth and fully psychedelic treatment at Towns, Wilson had been taken by a newly sober drinking buddy to a mission church for alcoholics run by the Christian Oxford Group.[58] The Oxford Group church made a big impression on Wilson. Perhaps the culture of the church provided him with an adequate set, something of an adequate culture of psychedelia, to bring into the treatment at Towns, helping the experience become meaningfully psychedelic and healing.

And who knows what happened with dosing during this fourth treatment? Perhaps the treatment team somehow didn't lower the dose of the psychedelics when things started to get weird.

But here's what happened, according to one of Wilson's official biographers:

> In his helplessness and desperation. Bill cried out, "I'll do anything, anything at all!" He had reached a point of total, utter deflation — a state of complete, absolute surrender. With neither their faith nor hope, he cried, "If there be a God, let Him show Himself!" What happened next was electric. "Suddenly, my room blazed with an indescribably white light. I was seized with an ecstasy beyond description. Every joy I had known was pale by comparison. The light, the ecstasy — I was conscious of nothing else for a time.
>
> Then, seen in the mind's eye, there was a mountain. I stood upon its summit, where a great wind blew. A wind, not of air, but of spirit. In great, clean

---

[57] Lambert, A. The Obliteration of the Craving for Narcotics. Journal of the A.M.A., 1909, LIII(13):985-989.

[58] Markel, Howard. "An Alcoholic's Savior: God, Belladonna or Both?" The New York Times, The New York Times, 19 Apr. 2010.

strength, it blew right through me. Then came the blazing thought 'You are a free man.'

I know not at all how long I remained in this state, but finally the light and the ecstasy subsided. I again saw the wall of my room. As I became more quiet, a great peace stole over me, and this was accompanied by a sensation difficult to describe. I became acutely conscious of a Presence which seemed like a veritable sea of living spirit. I lay on the shores of a new world..."[59]

Soon after this experience a friend brought Wilson a copy of William James' *The Varieties of Religious Experience*, which was, as mentioned earlier, itself partially psychedelically inspired. James' work seemed to serve as a further enriching culture of psychedelia for Wilson, as a sort of integration aid, and profoundly shaped Wilson's understanding of his psychedelic experience. Wilson soon began to formulate what would become AA. He credited James as one of the foundational influences of AA.[60]

Years later, Wilson underwent psychotherapy assisted by LSD, especially for his lingering depression, and became a great proponent of the healing power of LSD.[61] Eventually, he and the AA Board mutually decided to end their relationship so that Wilson's ongoing interests in PAP (and the occult) wouldn't confuse the mission and identity of AA.[62]

THE FIRST WAVE OF THE WESTERN PSYCHEDELIC RENAISSANCE

By the 1950's, the story of modern, Western psychedelic assisted psychotherapy really takes off, and it does so fast and wide.

---

[59] Alcoholics Anonymous. (1984). *Pass it on: the story of Bill Wilson and how the A.A. message reached the world*. Alcoholics Anonymous World Services.
[60] Amelia Hill, "LSD Could Help Alcoholics Stop Drinking, AA Founder Believed" (The Guardian, August 23, 2012).
[61] Ibid.
[62] ibid.

Luke Williams, a psychedelics researcher at Imperial College London, explains some of the timing of this Western psychedelic renaissance:

> The subsequent explosion of interest in LSD and psychedelics in general in the postwar period can be explained by several factors: Firstly, the discovery and manufacture of LSD only became possible after the emergence in the 20th century of large scale industrial chemistry, with all its techniques and equipment. Before this period, individual chemists did not have the resources to investigate and, importantly, produce chemicals of high purity. Second, the relatively new fields of psychiatry and psychoanalysis gave a range of possible applications for the new drug.[63]

We might expand on this to say that psychoanalysis and the fairly mainstream *zeitgeist* it created in the 1950's and 60's made available something of a "set" for psychedelic practice. Again, arguably, no set, no meaningful psychedelia. The set provided by the *zeitgeist* of psychoanalysis was largely a frame of an individual inward gaze, of making the unconscious conscious, and all this within a medicalized frame of "mental health."

And as discussed in the Introduction chapter about Maria Sabina and Gordan Wasson, during this same timeframe, from the fateful meeting of Indigenous cultures and Westerners in the Sierra Madre of Mexico, the medicine of psilocybin was brought into Western culture. And so was a further "set," a ceremonial one like Wasson had participated in with the Mazatec people.

With the explosion of available psychedelics made possible by industrialized chemistry, a psychoanalytic mindset, and the collision of the Western and Indigenous worlds, the first wave

---

[63] Luke Williams, "Human Psychedelic Research: A Historical and Sociological Analysis." Undergraduate Thesis, Cambridge University, 1999.

of the Western psychedelic renaissance had begun: the first widespread, "official," and even mainstream intentional use of psychedelics in Western culture since the repression of Western psychedelics 1,600 years prior.

The clinical research on psychedelics during this first wave of the Western psychedelic renaissance was large and highly positive. Torsten Passie researched a bibliography of this period and found 687 major papers published that specifically focused on therapy and psychedelics. These papers have a combined total of about 10,500 research participants.[64]

In this first wave of research, there was a large focus on alcoholism, depression, and neurosis. LSD was the medicine most often studied. None of these early studies were in the form of the currently favored blinded randomized control trials (RCT). Because psychedelics were unregulated and therefore legal at the time, many of these studies were of general practice clinical treatment programs open to the public.

The studies of this first generation found about 66% of participants benefited from these treatments.[65] It is important to note that the great majority of these research participants were considered to have had treatment resistant conditions. As we will discuss shortly, this efficacy rate of about 66% for previously treatment resistant conditions is strikingly similar to what meta-analyses of the current generation of PAP outcome research are showing.

Three retrospective safety analyses of approximately 9,000 participants in treatment and research programs of the time found no greater risk to participants than conventional psychotherapy

---

[64] Passie T. (1997). Psycholytic and psychedelic therapy research 1931 - 1995 a complete international bibliography. Laurentius Publ.

[65] Passie T, Guss J, Krähenmann R. Lower-dose psycholytic therapy - A neglected approach. Front Psychiatry. 2022 Dec 2;13:1020505. doi: 10.3389/fpsyt.2022.1020505. PMID: 36532196; PMCID: PMC9755513.

(considering suicides, suicide attempts, and prolonged difficult psychological reactions).[66][67][68]

Passie also discusses that in this first wave, the dominant model in Europe was of an intensive, residential, broadly psychoanalytic, and often partially group psychotherapy. In these treatments, several medicine sessions of a range of doses were interspersed within such programs over several months.

In the US and Canada, the dominant model was of a few high dose medicine sessions in short term, individual treatments.

The differences in these treatment protocols are particularly notable now because given the constraints of randomized control trials, pretty much all of the current, second generation PAP research is on short term models. The more complex, longer term, European style model would be just about impossible to implement in a randomized control trial, because the confounds and cost would be overwhelming. So Passie rightly urges that because we have almost no current research on longer term, more psychotherapeutically focused models of PAP, the literature of the first wave of the Western psychedelic renaissance deserves far more attention than it is currently getting.[69]

In the current generation of PAP research, we also have little research directly on complex or developmental trauma. The first wave of research did focus on such conditions, under different names, also making the earlier period of research valuable to study these days.

The US government funded much of the research of the first wave of the Western psychedelic renaissance. This was sometimes done overtly through research grants, and sometimes covertly via illegal, secret military research programs such as the infamous MK-Ultra.

---

[66] Cohen, S. (1960): Lysergic Acid Diethylamide: Side Effect and Complications. In: J of Nervous and Mental Disease 130; 30-40.

[67] Gasser, P. (1995): Die Psycholytische Psychotherapie in der Schweiz (1988-1993). Eine katamnestische Erhebung. In: Yearbook of Cross-Cultural Medicine and Psychotherapy 1995; 143-162.

[68] Malleson, N. (1971): Acute Adverse Reactions to LSD in Clinical and Experimental Use on the United Kingdom. In: British Journal of Psychiatry 118; 229-230.

[69] ibid.

In MK-Ultra and in similar programs under other governments, including in Nazi Germany, military and intelligence services were hoping to weaponize psychedelics for use in interrogations, torture, mind control, and assassinations.[70] Untold numbers of people were hurt and killed, including Jewish prisoners in the Dachau Nazi concentration camp and, after World War II, Soviet prisoners in secret US torture and military experimentation sites in Germany. A CIA officer prominent in these studies, Morse Allen, wrote of what he saw as a great feature of the German torture sites, "disposal of the body is not a problem."[71]

It's very notable that these military research programs were abandoned because they failed to reach their goals. The conclusion of these programs seems to have been that it did not appear to be possible to use psychedelics reliably as weapons. The CIA decided that torture and interrogation were more effective by psychological and behavioral means than by psychedelics. However, as we've seen, research into psychedelics for health has consistently gone very well. This can make for an argument against the idea that psychedelics are simply neutral tools.

Having said that, as we will see, an assumption throughout this book is that we are agents and that psychedelics do not simply program us, not even "programing" us for peace and health. With psychedelics, things are always complex. And unfortunately, psychedelics do appear to be usable to dark ends.[72]

By the late 1960's, a confluence of factors against psychedelics coalesced. Culturally, psychedelics had become a proxy battle in "the generation gap" between an often anti-war and anti-capitalist youth and the "establishment" older generation. Unfortunately, the hippie movement sometimes leaned into using psychedelics in provocative and extreme ways. For example, farcical or ridiculous

---

[70] McCoy, A.W. (2007), Science in Dachau's shadow: HEBB, Beecher, and the development of CIA psychological torture and modern medical ethics. J. Hist. Behav. Sci., 43: 401-417.

[71] ibid.

[72] Pace BA, Devenot N. Right-Wing Psychedelia: Case Studies in Cultural Plasticity and Political Pluripotency. Front Psychol. 2021 Dec 10.

calls to "dose the water supply" or "levitate the Pentagon" with the help of LSD. These may have been fun and provocative statements for the young people involved, but they also made psychedelics more of a target to attack such young people.

As well, a cottage industry of therapists or guides, often with questionable or fully dangerous methods, had spring up and charged large sums of money for psychedelic help from often desperate people. The medical and psychological establishments called for greater government regulation of psychedelic therapies.

There was also a general movement at the time towards greater regulation of all medical drugs, not just of psychedelics.

Taking advantage of these factors, particularly the mainstream backlash against psychedelics, "drugs," and hippies, the right wing Nixon administration saw an opportunity. In a stock move from the fascist playbook, the Nixon administration trumpeted issues of "law and order" as a pretext to kill, imprison, punish, harass, and quiet political enemies. Nixon declared a "war on drugs" and therefore "drug users."

Here is how Nixon's domestic policy advisor at the time, John Ehrlichman, put it in a 1994 interview with the journalist Dan Baum:

> The Nixon campaign in 1968, and the Nixon White House after that, had two enemies: the antiwar left and black people. You understand what I'm saying? We knew we couldn't make it illegal to be either against the war or black, but by getting the public to associate the hippies with marijuana and blacks with heroin, and then criminalizing both heavily, we could disrupt those communities. We could arrest their leaders, raid their homes, break up their meetings, and vilify them night after night

on the evening news. Did we know we were lying about the drugs? Of course we did.[73]

In 1971, against truly overwhelming scientific evidence, psychedelics were made profoundly illegal in the United States, and then quickly thereafter in the West generally. They were categorized into the newly created legal designation of "Schedule I," a category for substances with no hope for any possible good to humanity. Psychedelics were classified as essentially chemical evil. Governments would scarcely approve them to be synthesized even for basic chemical or animal research. The goal was that they should not exist on the face of the earth.

In the "war on drugs" to follow, including a massive reboot during the Reagan administration, Black and Latino communities were by far the most targeted. Many, many lives were lost and badly impeded. Families and communities were decimated.

As is common with prohibition laws, higher ups in organized crime grew rich and powerful in the new black market. The political right wing in the US was invigorated. And with some of the best mental health treatments being outlawed, the mental health of untold millions suffered gravely based in no scientific grounds.

This same basic story repeated with MDMA in the 1970's and 80's: MDMA was unregulated for a period of time. It showed great clinical promise as part of psychotherapy and helped many people. It became a cultural phenomenon, as Ecstasy in rave culture. And in 1985 it was outlawed by the US FDA, again against all available scientific evidence, exiled into the dark box of Schedule I.

Rick Doblin and his colleagues were central to fighting these unscientific laws against MDMA, but to no avail.

These were bleak, harsh years for psychedelics in the West. I remember them all too well. Somehow, during these dark years, against what seemed to me and many others literally impossible odds, Doblin and his colleagues continued their work for legal PAP.

---

[73] Dan Baum, "Legalize It All" (Harper's Magazine, April 2016).

The story of "official" psychedelic research picks up a bit again in the early 1990's with Rick Strassman's federally authorized research on basic medical responses to DMT in human subjects.[74]

In 2000, a MAPS study in Spain of MDMA assisted psychotherapy for PTSD was the first clinical trial of psychedelic assisted psychotherapy since the early 1970's. But it was shut down well before completion, apparently by political forces in the Spanish government who were hostile to the study.[75]

So it's not until 2006 that the first publication of clinical research on psychedelics reemerges into Western medical healthcare, with Francisco Moreno and colleagues' small pilot study of psilocybin for treatment resistant OCD. That study went very well in terms of safety and effectiveness, "with acute reductions in core OCD symptoms in several subjects."[76]

The second, current wave of the Western psychedelic renaissance had begun.

AN OVERVIEW AND DISCUSSION OF SOME OF THE CURRENT GENERATION OF RESEARCH ON PAP

The current generation of clinical research seems to again show PAP as being quite safe and generally effective for a number of conditions, including good outcome data so far on treatment resistant PTSD, unipolar depression, generalized anxiety, anxiety and depression associated with a life threatening illness, alcohol

---

[74] Strassman RJ, Qualls CR. Dose-Response Study of N,N-Dimethyltryptamine in Humans: I. Neuroendocrine, Autonomic, and Cardiovascular Effects. Arch Gen Psychiatry. 1994;51(2):85–97.

[75] The Brakes Put on Ecstasy Research, Alberto Gayo, Interviu, April 28, 2003 Translation from Spanish by Marcela O'talora

[76] F.A. Moreno, C.B. Wiegand, E.K. Taitano, P.L. Delgado Safety, tolerability, and efficacy of psilocybin in 9 patients with obsessive-compulsive disorder J. Clin. Psychiatr., 67 (2006), pp. 1735-1740

abuse, cigarette smoking, social anxiety among autistic adults, and chronic suicidal ideation. [77] [78] [79] [80]

Even though the total number of participants in the current psychedelic studies is small by typical drug research standards, we are fortunate that the field has matured enough that there can be meta-analyses done of the outcome research. Looking at these, we see moderate to large favorable outcomes. Again, these studies have usually been working with people suffering from very difficult, treatment resistant conditions.[81]

This second wave of psychedelic research is very much in the currently favored research model of blinded randomized control trials. The research designs are generally short term protocols of one to a few preparation sessions, a medicine session, and then one to a few integration sessions. Some studies do one block like this, some studies do two or three blocks, resulting in two or three medicine sessions within a psychedelic assisted psychotherapy.

Some study designs have built in more psychotherapy, some less.

Based in the very positive safety and clinical outcomes of these studies, PAP is quickly becoming mainstream in Western mental healthcare. Australia recently made PAP with psilocybin and MDMA prescribable treatments.[82] Switzerland has long standing compassionate use pathways for legal PAP.[83] Canada has recently been approving PAP treatments on a case by case basis, and Health Canada, the national health insurance, is willing to

---

[77] Luoma JB, Chwyl C, Bathje GJ, Davis AK, Lancelotta R. A Meta-Analysis of Placebo-Controlled Trials of Psychedelic-Assisted Therapy. J Psychoactive Drugs. 2020 Sep-Oct;52(4):289-299.

[78] Kwonmok Ko, Emma I. Kopra, Anthony J. Cleare, James J. Rucker, Psychedelic therapy for depressive symptoms: A systematic review and meta-analysis, Journal of Affective Disorders, Volume 322, 2023,Pages 194-204.

[79] Sipan Haikazian, David C.J. Chen-Li, Danica E. Johnson, Farhan Fancy, Anastasia Levinta, M. Ishrat Husain, Rodrigo B. Mansur, Roger S. McIntyre, Joshua D. Rosenblat, Psilocybin-assisted therapy for depression: A systematic review and meta-analysis, Psychiatry Research, Volume 329, 2023.

[80] Leger RF, Unterwald EM. Assessing the effects of methodological differences on outcomes in the use of psychedelics in the treatment of anxiety and depressive disorders: A systematic review and meta-analysis. J Psychopharmacol. 2022 Jan;36(1):20-30.

[81] Ibid.

[82] Zagorski, Nick. Australia Legalizes Psychedelics for Use in Depression, PTSD Therapy. Psychiatric News, PN, 58, no. 09 (September 2023).

[83] Claire-Marie Dikanska, "Is Psychedelic Therapy about to Go Mainstream?" (swissinfo.ch, July 8, 2024).

cover claims for the treatments.[84] The Netherlands seems poised to approve MDMA for treatment resistant PTSD.[85]

A giant exception to this is the US FDA's recent decision to not yet approve MDMA for treatment resistant PTSD. Rather than approving MDMA to become a prescribable medicine, the FDA asked Lycos/MAPS to do an additional phase 3 study. Best case scenario, that would take at least a couple of years, making 2027 or later the next possible date for approval of MDMA as a prescribable medicine in the US.

The US FDA's decision to not reschedule MDMA to be a prescribable medicine is controversial and deserves some discussion here.

At the time of this writing, clarity has not emerged, at least in the public record, about why the FDA did not approve the rescheduling of MDMA. So, most of us are left to speculate. There were hearsay claims made that MAPS staff cajoled research participants to inflate their positive outcome reports and to hide adverse reactions, including increased suicidal ideation. If these allegations are true, they would be tragedies and profound ethical, scientific, and clinical violations. But to date, these allegations have not been backed by any clear evidence.[86] [87]

Based in a case of abuse in a MAPS study in Canada (which we will address in a section later in this chapter), in 2022 Health Canada launched an investigation into the MAPS MDMA studies that took place in Canada.[88] As of this writing, about two and a half years later, Health Canada has not reported results of this investigation. But it is notable that Health Canada has been

---

[84] Kimberly Burns, "The State of Psychedelics in Canada in 2023" (lexpert.ca, May 24, 2023).

[85] Mari Eccles, "Dutch Panel Recommends MDMA for Post-Traumatic Stress Disorder" (politico.eu, June 6, 2024).

[86] Andrew Jacobs and Rachel Nuwer, "How a Leftist Activist Group Helped Torpedo a Psychedelic Therapy" (New York Times, February 4, 2025).

[87] Will Stone, "Transformation or Trouble? Research into MDMA Plagued with Allegations of Misconduct" (National Public Radio, May 13, 2024).

[88] Mattha Busby, "MDMA Trials under Review in Canada over Alleged Abuse of Study Participants" (The Guardian, June 20, 2022).

approving further MDMA studies and, as just mentioned, is approving MDMA assisted psychotherapy on a case by case basis.[89]

If the FDA made a crucial scientific and regulatory decision even partially based in hearsay, that would have been very poor science. If these hearsay allegations were factors in the FDA's decision, perhaps the FDA could have investigated the claims before making such an important decision.

Some members of an earlier FDA advisory board, which did not make the final decision, did cite concerns about functional unblinding, expectancy effects, and placebo effects in MAPS' data. This also deserves some discussion.

Expectancy and placebo responses are poorly understood but are probably psychosocial effects that can boost the effectiveness of even a non-active treatment.

Functional unblinding is when research participants and study staff can readily guess who got active treatment and who got placebo treatment. This is usually pretty easy to guess with psychedelics because it is very hard to find good active placebos for psychedelics. Once participants and staff know or guess who got active treatment versus placebo, that can consciously or unconsciously set off a wide range of different behaviors and expectations resulting in changes in reports on outcome measures.

But expectancy and placebo responses and functional unblinding are not at all unique to psychedelic research. They are part of long running issues and controversies for nearly all medical and psychological outcome research. These often come to a head in debates between "real world evidence" versus randomized control trials. These are well established issues that the FDA deals with to some extent with the vast majority of medical treatments they are called on to evaluate.[90]

---

[89] "Numinus Wellness Gets Health Canada Nod for MDMA Therapy Group Study" (patsnap.com, June 7, 2024).

[90] Eichler, H.-G., Pignatti, F., Schwarzer-Daum, B., Hidalgo-Simon, A., Eichler, I., Arlett, P., Humphreys, A., Vamvakas, S., Brun, N. and Rasi, G. (2021), Randomized Controlled Trials Versus Real World Evidence: Neither Magic Nor Myth. Clin. Pharmacol. Ther., 109: 1212-1218.

It does appear that functional unblinding, expectancy, and placebo responses are quite common and intense in psychedelic outcome research. Again, it's just very hard, and maybe impossible, to come up with research designs that can fully prevent these effects in psychedelic RCT's. Suresh Muthukumaraswamy and colleagues have done excellent work looking at these issues in the current PAP research and found massive effects skewing the results in psychedelic RCT's in favor of psychedelics.[91][92]

However, the FDA had signed off on the study designs and had even collaborated with MAPS on the design of these phase 3 studies, with their predictable limitations before the studies began. So it would at best be puzzling if in its final evaluation the FDA turned around and critiqued the study designs as flawed and their data as therefore unreliable.

Again, at the time of this writing the FDA's decision making process is still unclear. MAPS/Lycos apparently has a letter from the FDA stating their reasons for asking for another phase 3 study, but MAPS/Lycos has not made it public. It is important for the field that clarity emerges sooner rather than later. It's not good for the field scientifically or clinically to have the outcome of the first major US decision on the prescribability of psychedelics to be murky.

Besides MDMA, the FDA has designated psilocybin as a "breakthrough therapy," meaning that by the current research it appears to be so superior to existing treatments that the FDA is fast tracking its final evaluation to be a prescribable medicine. There should be adequate phase 3 data on psylocibin assisted psychotherapy available for review by the FDA in about 2027. So, possibly in 2027 both MDMA and psilocybin could become prescribable medicines in the US.

[91] Suresh D. Muthukumaraswamy, Anna Forsyth & Thomas Lumley (2021) Blinding and expectancy confounds in psychedelic randomized controlled trials, Expert Review of Clinical Pharmacology, 14:9, 1133-1152.
[92] Rich Harldy, "The Problem at the Heart of Modern Psychedelic Clinical Research" (New Atlas, June 13, 2021).

Other "established" psychedelic medicines, such as DMT, LSD, ibogaine/iboga, and 5-MeO-DMT are also showing very good outcome research and could follow in becoming prescribable medicines.

There are also novel psychedelics that are focuses of intense research and development efforts. Many of these research programs are seeking to create or find psychedelics that are easier to tolerate for patients, so that psychedelic based treatments can be more widely used. Some of these efforts are seeking "psychedelics" that have no experiential, psychological impact. I personally welcome any options for helping suffering people, but if there are no psychological or experiential aspects to a medicine, I don't think they could be called psychedelic anymore. Not that the terms would matter much to the people they can hopefully help.

Compared to the established psychedelics, these novel research programs are much earlier in drug development processes and their outcomes as viable medicines are far more uncertain.

As we wrap up this section on the current research, it's important to underline that this field is moving fast and it is very hard to keep up with new research and new thinking in PAP. One of my favorite ways to keep up with current research is to find a video of a recent grand rounds presentation on PAP. Natalie Gukasyan at Johns Hopkins has regularly done excellent grand rounds presentations that not only lay out the research, but also unpack it in terms of clinical utility and policy. She also brings a laudable critical eye to the literature. A "group think" field of uncritical positivity about psychedelics will not make for a healthy field over the long run. I highly recommend keeping up with her presentations. Videos of her grand rounds are readily available on the internet.

One area for future research that is very relevant to this book is researching outcomes of different psychotherapies in partnership with psychedelics. The field is still too young for that. Such research will likely have to wait until psychedelics are more widely prescribable. But there are likely very rich PAP research programs to come in the years ahead.

Structures of PAP; relational considerations

There are currently two major structures of what we might call PAP. One is a short term, time limited "bubble form" of PAP. The other form of PAP could be called a "long form" model.

The bubble form is very similar to the current RCT studies, and is often directly based on them. The bubble form generally consists of one to a handful of preparation sessions, a medicine session, and then one to a handful of integration sessions. Just like in the current randomized control trials on PAP, blocks like this might be strung together, forming a longer treatment that includes a few medicine sessions.

The bubble format might also be revisited in a sort of ever-so-often, as needed way by a patient and clinician, making for an *ad hoc* longer term therapy.

The long form model could be simply a regular psychotherapy relationship with PAP work interspersed as needed, including preparation work, medicine sessions, and integration work. At times there might be more intensive periods of PAP work, like in an intensive series of ketamine sessions.

Group PAP is another format that is looking very important and has some great advantages. Group PAP can be less expensive than individual PAP and draws on the general and time honored benefits of group therapies. Group PAP is currently mostly being done in a bubble format.[93]

Group PAP is often being done in a retreat format, with the preparation and integration sessions taking place remotely over video and the participants and staff gathering at a retreat location for the medicine sessions.

[93] Marseille E, Stauffer CS, Agrawal M, Thambi P, Roddy K, Mithoefer M, Bertozzi SM and Kahn JG (2023) Group psychedelic therapy: empirical estimates of cost-savings and improved access. Front. Psychiatry. 14:1293243.

There are also highly medicalized forms of psychedelic use for health, like the ketamine and Spravato clinics that frame the treatments as purely medical interventions for mental health.

I personally think it will be important for many of our patients that the PAP they receive is relational enough. Many of our patients need ongoing relationships and even ongoing community to help them come to health. A powerful weekend, week, or several weeks of PAP, even in a group format, that is otherwise isolated from their lives could have a hard time getting to truly adequate relationality. I think this is a major challenge for the current Western psychedelic world, and Western mental healthcare generally, and is an area in need of innovation and creativity.

Other "models" of current Western psychedelic assisted help

Besides psychedelics as traditionally prescribable medicines, the current Western psychedelic landscape is far more complex. Looking just at the US, there are very novel state level programs for clinical use of psychedelics, such as in Oregon and Colorado with psilocybin "service" centers.

There are also religious traditions and practices with psychedelics. Arguably, these are already legal in the US under the First Amendment freedom of religion clauses. The US Drug Enforcement Agency (DEA) has been forced by courts to respect some of these religions as legal.[94] [95] Although, in a seeming contradiction of separation of church and state, the DEA has been allowed to dictate some of the practices of these religions in terms of importing and storing their sacramentals and some of their other practices.

There are also widespread decriminalization movements afoot, which do not exactly make psychedelics legal. In decriminalization, laws against psychedelics stay on the books, but governments make explicit that in particular circumstances, such as personal use, those laws will not be enforced.

---

[94] Gonzales v. O Centro Espírita Beneficente União do Vegetal, 546 U.S. 418, 430–31 (2006).
[95] Church of Holy Light of Queen v. Mukasey, 615 F. Supp. 2d 1210 (D. Or. 2009).

The psychedelic terrain is complex and is rapidly changing in ways that are difficult or impossible to foresee now.

Brian Anderson at the University of California San Francisco has observed that as psychedelics continue to enter the mainstream in the West, some of the novel formats in place or to come might not look like treatment models at all. They might seem quite "out there" compared to a conventional Western mental healthcare model. Some examples could be psychedelics as a religious practice with a congregation; Westerners participating in Native or Mestizo psychedelic practices; psychedelic use at music concerts or festivals; psychedelics worked with amongst a group of friends; and sincere, intentional, solo work with psychedelics.

Even if mental health professionals have no interest in these seemingly non-clinical models, because their patients will likely be engaging in them more and more, mental health professionals might need to form some type of relationship or even partnership with such psychedelic work.

Anderson reflected that mental health professionals forming such relationships or loose partnerships with "outside" models could also allow more conventional professionals to essentially outsource the great "weirdness" of psychedelics.[96] I have talked with many wonderful, fairly conventional colleagues who say about PAP something like, "This is truly impressive safety and outcome research. I am very excited about this. And I want nothing to do with it." As Hunter S. Thompson put it, "When the going gets weird, the weird turn pro."

Some might balk at the idea of psychedelics at a music concert or festival as having any health relevance. But I have had some patients who have worked with psychedelics sincerely in such settings to great personal benefit.

None other than Joseph Campbell weighed in on Grateful Dead shows, one of the homelands of the Western psychedelic renaissance, after his experience at a Dead show in 1985. I believe

---

[96] Personal communication, December, 2021

he didn't take a literal psychedelic. He "just" went to the show, which was apparently fully psychedelic for him. Not long after that night, Campbell, Grateful Dead musicians Jerry Garcia and Mickey Hart, and the Jungian analyst and psychiatrist John Weir Perry participated in a day long symposium titled "Ritual and Rapture: From Dionysus to The Grateful Dead." It included a live performance of a long piece of music by Garcia, Hart, and other musicians. It is a sort of truly epic "space." This symposium's presentations and music seemed lost to time for many years, but gratefully there is now audio of the symposium available on YouTube.[97][98]

Campbell said of his experience at the Grateful Dead show:

> The first thing I thought of was the Dionysian festivals, of course.... This is more than music. It turns something on in here. And what it turns on is life energy. This is Dionysus talking through these kids. Now I've seen similar manifestations, but nothing as innocent as what I saw with this bunch. This was sheer innocence.... It reminded me of Russian Easter. Down in New York we have a big Russian Cathedral. You go there on Russian Easter, at midnight and you hear *Kristos anesti!* Christ is Risen! Christ is Risen! It's almost as good as a rock concert. It has the same kind of life feel.[99]

Part of the therapies I've had with people who work with psychedelics at festivals or concerts, for example, has been sometimes offering them the possibility of being in a more respectful relationship with the medicines. This can be like being

---

[97] Joseph Campbell et al., "Ritual and Rapture: From Dionysus to The Grateful Dead," November 1, 1986, https://www.youtube.com/watch?v=bPAH5JnPjAY

[98] Nicholas Meriwether, "Documenting The Dead: Joseph Campbell and the Grateful Dead," October 29, 2015, https://www.dead.net/features/blog/documenting-dead-joseph-campbell-and-grateful-dead

[99] Unknown, "Joseph Campbell and the Grateful Dead," Unknown, https://sirbacon.org/joseph_campbell.htm

a respectful friend to the medicines. It's not being a good friend that whenever one is bored or uncomfortable to say, "Hey, I'm bored, you have a cool house and you're interesting, I'm coming over." Instead, being in respectful relationship can mean being clear about why one might ask for a medicine's help, and if it's not a good reason, then maybe not bothering.

Robert Hunter, the main lyricist for the Grateful Dead, who knew a thing or two about psychedelics at concerts, cautioned in the song "Franklin's Tower" that we take care in what we ask for, that planting ice might lead to a very thin harvest.

ABUSE OF PATIENTS BY PSYCHEDELIC HELPERS

A very difficult but real topic is abuse of patients in psychedelic assisted psychotherapies and in broader psychedelic assisted help.

As mentioned earlier, this has even occurred in one of the recent psychedelic studies. In a MAPS phase 2 study, a study therapist violated the sexual boundaries of a research participant during a study medicine session. There is very disturbing video available of what this study therapist did during that medicine session.[100] The study therapist went on to have a long term sexual relationship with the research participant. Unsurprisingly, this wound up hurting her gravely.[101]

This is one clear and well documented case. There are of course others, including in "underground" therapies, psychedelic religious settings, and in Indigenous led psychedelic traditions. We know of these abuses and can therefore try to do better as a field largely because of the brave honesty of those who have been treated horribly by so called psychedelic helpers.[102] [103]

There is a rich literature on sexual boundary violations by therapists in standard, non-psychedelic psychotherapy. I think we

[100] Bethany Lindsay, "Footage of Therapists Spooning and Pinning down Patient in B.C. Trial for MDMA Therapy Prompts Review" (Canadian Broadcast Corporation, March 29, 2022).
[101] Bethany Lindsay, "B.C. Psychiatrist Resigns Licence after Patient Complains of Abuse during Psychedelic Therapy Study" (Canadian Broadcast Corporation, October 16, 2023).
[102] Will Hall, "Psychedelic Therapy Abuse: My Experience with Aharon Grossbard, Francoise Bourzat... and Their Lawyers" (Medium.com, September 18, 2021).
[103] Cover Story, "Cover Story: Power Trip" (Cover Story, November 10, 2021).

in the field of PAP can learn from that literature. Glen Gabbard, a psychoanalyst, has studied these situations throughout his career and has been a "go to" referral for therapists and psychoanalysts who have done sexual boundary violations with their patients.

From Gabbard's work, and again, from the courageous first person accounts of those abused by psychedelic helpers, I think we can start to understand some of these abuses.

Gabbard doesn't use IFS and he doesn't write about psychedelics, but I think we can extrapolate from his work to see that in PAP one class of sexual boundary violations can have their genesis when therapists (or others in psychedelic helping roles) seem to have gotten blended with burdened parts of themselves who want to help "too much" when a patient is in intense distress during a medicine session or a therapy. This can then lead to some small, well meaning violations of "the frame" to try to alleviate the patient's intense distress. For instance, in desperation, a therapist might try to help their patient get through a very difficult part of a medicine session by hugging the patient and expressing their love for them. Again, this could be very well meaning. And it might even seem to be somewhat helpful for the patient. Or it might clearly make things much worse for the patient, a new level of difficulty on top of what they're already dealing with in the medicine session. Regardless, such "well intentioned" boundary violations can escalate fairly quickly to greater and greater violations. For instance, to sexual touch as an attempt to "heal" or distract the patient from distress, or as an attempt to "save" them.

These "desperate to help" countertransference reactions from therapists have of course led to true disaster for patients, as well as for the therapists. And like most things, countertransference reactions from therapists and their parts can get particularly intense in PAP given the intensity of psychedelics.

Another class of abuses in PAP seems to be that some therapists have parts with straight up abusive, sociopathic burdens. This is probably a minority of cases, but they are of course important. This is when sexual predators become psychedelic helpers. With burdens like that, parts of a therapist can just fully want to "use" the patient as a sexual or sadistic object.

These parts of these psychedelic "helpers," as part of their burdens, seem desperate for the power of violating their patient. One way of starting to understand these burdens is by considering what Freud called "turning passive into active": that the therapist was profoundly violated and disempowered in their own life at some point, so protector parts took on roles of exiling the therapist's vulnerability and of getting into a position of abusing others — a position of power instead of the dreaded powerlessness that the therapist experienced maybe as an abused child. Again, passive into active.

These protector parts can then be desperate to get the therapist into positions where they are both an invulnerable figure and one who can abuse others. Having a career as a psychedelic helper is an extraordinarily great way to act on those goals. In this cultural moment, people often idolize psychedelic helpers, attributing all sorts of vague superhuman powers to them. This is very attractive to parts with burdens of needing to appear and feel beyond normal human vulnerability, to feel and appear superhuman.

At the same time, patients in psychedelic treatments can become extremely vulnerable during a medicine session. They may become confused, physically weakened, and unable to leave. So parts with "passive into active" burdens can see medicine sessions as an extraordinarily good opportunity to abuse others and thereby hope to douse the flames or smoldering of their own exiles, of the therapist's own painful vulnerability.

Again, in these cases, the boundary violations can start small, in a sort of grooming. The psychedelic helper might start with subtle ways of violating the boundaries of their vulnerable patient, even in the prep work. This would likely involve relatively small and subtle ways of trying to violate the patient as Self, as a free, respected, and co-equal agent; to subtly disempower them in the treatment relationship. This could be pressures that the patient "do" the psychedelic session according to the therapist's "flight instructions," or to come to understand the PAP from the therapist's point of view. Again, if these are *pushed* on the patient, subtly and even seemingly sweetly, these are relatively minor but real violations of the patient as Self, and of the autonomy, value, and consent of their parts.

Then during difficult times in a medicine session, these therapists might up the intensity of the boundary violations. To try to force their patient to "surrender" or "let go of control." To "guide" the medicine session, to make it about the psychedelic helper's sense of things, and again to disempower the patient. And maybe ultimately to try to get their patient to accept and "surrender" to sexual touch as a needed healing intervention.[104]

Particularly in the Medicine Session chapter, we will look at case material illustrating true surrender. True surrender cannot be cajoled or ordered by a therapist or other psychedelic helper. That would not lead to surrender, but to domination. Intended or not, that would be a violation of Self.[105]

In the Preparation Work chapter, we will discuss not making therapy a Procrustean bed, but instead honoring our patient as Self and honoring their parts; of not trying to force patients to chop parts of themselves off to fit the therapy, nor having to stretch parts of themselves to try to fit the therapy.

These cases of abuse by psychedelic helpers are extremely daunting problems and I won't pretend to have some fix. The countertransference issues going on are fairly well studied, but it's proven very difficult to actually prevent or change these dynamics. Gabbard recently wrote an article reflecting on his thirty years of work in the area of sexual boundary violations by

---

[104] Maira Evelyn Clancy, "Creating Greater Safety in Psychedelic-Assisted Therapy Spaces" (San Fransico State University, 2023).

[105] Perna, J., Trop, J., Palitsky, R. et al. Prolonged adverse effects from repeated psilocybin use in an underground psychedelic therapy training program: a case report. BMC Psychiatry 25, 184 (2025).

mental health professionals. He stated that his "previous optimism about the potential to prevent such transgressions has given way to a pessimistic view in light of the pervasive self-deception of analysts and therapists."[106]

Again, this is a very tough, very important problem. But I do think that IFS provides novel options for therapists working with their burdened parts, in their own consultation or therapy, to prevent such abusive therapeutic relationships. In the same chapter where Richard Schwartz explicitly and richly describes IFS as a fully relational therapy, he not surprisingly includes an excellent discussion of various countertransference phenomena.[107]

Again, PAP is fully, completely relational. And of course, that relationality includes the inner relationships of the therapist.

POLICY CONCERNS IN THE CURRENT FIELD OF PAP

We in this field stand at a historical, foundational stage not just in clinical considerations, but also in policy considerations. I'm no policy expert, but I have been dragged into policy considerations and positions by professional and ethical duties and commitments. I think we are all in that boat now.

Policy choices we make now could lead to psychedelics being available for the help of people now and for generations to come, or possibly to psychedelics becoming exiled again. A risk here is that in this current Western psychedelic renaissance we could in our own ways repeat some of the hasty and loose cannon excitement of the 1960's about psychedelics.

This is particularly plausible because there is little clear current structure around psychedelics in the West. With the MAPS/Lycos application of summer 2024, the FDA had an opportunity to create a clear US implementation for psychedelic assisted psychotherapy. But as we saw, they essentially chose to wait until about 2027 to possibly implement federal clarity.

---

[106] Gabbard, G. O. (2017). Sexual boundary violations in psychoanalysis: A 30-year retrospective. Psychoanalytic Psychology, 34(2), 151–156.

[107] Martha Sweezy, ed., Internal Family Systems Therapy: New Dimensions (New York: Routledge, 2013).

So in the meantime, in the US we have a confusing landscape. We have state and local laws popping up here and there with very novel and, I think it must be said, fairly chaotic clinical structures, like in Oregon and Colorado with psilocybin "services."

Beyond these state clinical implementations, as mentioned earlier, there is a varied landscape including psychedelic religious practices, some of which have been overtly affirmed as legal by US courts. But other psychedelic churches and religions are in a nasty double bind: Are their religious practices considered legal or not? Do they dare ask the DEA for clarification? It would obviously be very fraught for them to reach out to the DEA asking something like, "We just want to clarify whether or not you think we're repeatedly committing felonies. Please reach us at this address. Thank you." And many people, lacking clear implementations for psychedelic help, are simply doing their best in a DIY way (do it yourself).

We in the psychedelic West are currently in a chaotic landscape.

Let's look in more detail at the first state laws implemented, Oregon and Colorado's novel implementation of psilocybin "services."

Under Oregon and Colorado's laws, there isn't even clarity if they are healthcare programs. The overt wording of these laws is that they do not provide mental health treatment, psychotherapy, or medical care, but instead, the vaguely termed "psilocybin services." But of course, and predictably, the public are often seeking out these "services" for mental health concerns and treatment. (That's why I keep putting "services" in quotes; I don't know what words to use and I don't know what they mean.)

StatNews quotes Myles Katz, co-founder and director of business development at Synthesis Institute, one of the earliest and best funded businesses active under Oregon's implementation: "Oregon very much is going to allow for diagnosis and treatment. I'm not sure they're calling it those words, but they did craft the measure in such a way where depression, PTSD, addiction are things that will be supported here." This legally implemented unclarity can obviously lead to confusion for the public, and even for professionals.

In another radical departure from just about all pervious mental health implementations, under these laws the diagnosing and treating – done under whatever terms – can be done by someone with a high school diploma and less than 200 hours of training. These are the requirements to be a "psilocybin facilitator."

And established licensing boards, like for therapists and psychiatrists, seem unsure if they will allow their licensees to also be licensed in a federally illegal practice, such as with psilocybin. So actual mental health professionals may be blocked from providing diagnosis and treatment under these laws.

This is obviously all a mess.

Oregon and Colorado's laws, and similar laws proposed in other states, of course have some truly good intentions behind them, such as getting these crucial treatments to suffering people as soon as possible. And there have been arguments made that these laws provide a fairness by being an avenue for long experienced "underground guides" to be able to work legally without having to go to graduate school and getting licensed as mental health providers.

But I am concerned that, in worst case scenarios, such good intentions might be getting "played" and co-opted by powerful and very skilled business interests. Both Oregon and Colorado's state programs have been made law by ballot measures. Ballot measures were created to be a highly democratic method of law making, a form of direct democracy. Very unfortunately, in actual practice, ballot measures have often been able to be manipulated by business interests pushing their agendas via hiring high paid, professional marketers and lobbyists. This can then often completely overwhelm true, "grassroots" democracy.

In Oregon and Colorado, there are already instances playing into concerns about national, well funded lobby groups bypassing democratic processes. One documented case is the OPEN Project in Oregon. Mason Mark, an attorney who does some of the best coverage of these laws in his Substack, Psychedelic Week, writes about, "OPEN Project, a secretive plan to collect data from all participants in Oregon's psilocybin services program. Emails obtained through a public records request reveal behind-the-scenes collaboration between officials of the Oregon Health Authority, lobbyists from the Healing Advocacy Fund, and members of the Oregon Psilocybin Advisory Board."[108]

Similarly, in Colorado under ballot proposition 122, Mason writes that a "...multi-state lobbying group called the Healing Advocacy Fund, which has close ties to New Approach [a political action committee], interviewed potential board members for its list of preferred candidates.... When [Governor] Polis announced his board appointments on January 27, local activists saw few names they recognized. No one from the Nowak Society or Natural Medicine Colorado was appointed. Groups that had opposed Proposition 122, like SPORE and Decriminalize Nature Boulder, were also passed over."[109]

I have been unable to find full lists of who has financed the lobby groups behind these ballot measures. But they have clearly been major investments.

One possibility is that the radically new structures and chaos of Oregon and Colorado's laws are in part a Silicon Valley-style business strategy to "disrupt an industry," in this case, the "industry" of Western mental healthcare. To "move fast and break things" as part of an attempt to "Uber-ize" Western mental healthcare via psychedelics.

"Move fast and break things" is obviously a terrible model for healthcare.

---

[108] Mason Marks, "Oregon Psilocybin Emails Show Secret Data Collection Plans" (Psychedelic Week, November 20, 2022).

[109] Mason Marks, "The Disappearing Colorado Psychedelic Advisory Board" (Psychedelic Week, March 22, 2023).

If there are Silicon Valley-style business interests partially behind or hoping to exploit Colorado and Oregon's laws, then these business models would likely be based in a standard internet business model: companies rushing to be "first to market" in a newly possible technological service and thereby hoping to secure a monopoly or duopoly in that service. The goal is that a few relatively rich owners and investors can then profit immensely off a vast and captive customer base. The monopoly is further cemented by one (or two) corporations owning and controlling the relevant data, protocols, and servers for the service. As well, in standard internet business models most of the "labor" is done by computers, such as web servers.

This has been the basic business plan for many internet companies since the 1990's.

Uber innovated on this model by bringing the delivery of a service out of web servers and into the physical world, into taxis. The stated ultimate goal for Uber was and is robot, computerized taxis, like the computerized web servers. This would slash their labor costs to nearly zero.

Despite clear, early warnings about the potentials for dangerous internet monopolies, governments did little to rein in any of this.[110]

What we are seeing with these very novel state psychedelic laws could be a further iteration of such an internet-style business model: Disrupt an established industry, taxis or Western mental healthcare, to then create one huge corporate monopoly or duopoly of that industry. Like Uber or Lyft, a key part of such business models is to have a vast pool of poorly paid and poorly protected "gig workers." Hence maybe the interest in Oregon and Colorado in not having professional mental healthcare providers providing psychotherapy in PAP, but creating a new class of labor in inexpensive and poorly organized "facilitators." Ultimately, these gig workers could be replaced by so-called "artificial intelligence"

---

[110] John Perry Barlow, "Stopping the Information Railroad" (Electronic Frontier Foundation, January 17, 1994).

"agents." Again, labor costs would be close to zero and investors and owners would increase their profit margins greatly.

The end goal could be novel, self-driving "psychedelics" that are linked to a corporate app that tries reprogram people to "mental health," or whatever the corporations are selling as such.

In such a model, expensive relationality would be removed as much as possible. Suffering people would be "serviced" alone and relationally isolated.

These would also be essentially neo-feudal business models.[111] [112] As the old school feudal ladies and lords knew, being not just the economic power but also the governing power was good for the bottom line. So a further part of such business models would be trying to find ways to ignore, violate, work around, buyout, or replace existing government regulation and social structures, as huge internet companies and Uber have done. To disrupt the "industry" of Western mental healthcare, professional organizations like the American Medical Association (AMA), the American Psychological Association (APA), existing governmental professional licensing agencies, existing professional ethics boards, and established universities must optimally be bypassed, bought out, controlled, or broken.

Organizations such as the AMA, APA, state professional licensing boards, and universities are of course all flawed organizations, but they are at least quasi-democratic organizations. Corporations are not. Corporations have made themselves well insulated from democracy. By current US law (which can be changed), it is actually illegal for corporations to consider anything but financial return for their shareholders.

These are worst case scenario considerations. But I think professionals and citizens in this current psychedelic renaissance need to be prepared for big picture ethical issues.

---

[111] Kotkin, J. (2020). The Coming of Neo-Feudalism: A Warning to the Global Middle Class. United Kingdom: Encounter Books.
[112] Varoufakis, Y. (2023). Technofeudalism: What Killed Capitalism. United Kingdom: Penguin Random House.

In the revolutionary fervor of the psychedelic 1960's, Pete Townsend wrote of his observations and concerns in the song "Won't Get Fooled Again." I'm concerned that if we are not thoughtful and careful, in the psychedelic 2020's or '30's we could wind up with, "Meet the new corporate, feudal boss / Worse than the old boss."

The paradigm shift now afoot with psychedelics offers us a chance to make Western mental healthcare more humane, more communitarian, more relational and social, not more feudal and atomized. But this will only happen by the choices we make as agents, as Selves.

CHAPTER FOUR

STARTING TO BRING PSYCHEDELICS AND IFS TOGETHER:
PETER WEBSTER'S SALIENCE HYPOTHESIS OF PSYCHEDELICS AND
MARTIN BUBER'S I-THOU RELATIONSHIPS

This chapter will discuss Peter Webster's "salience hypothesis of psychedelics"[113] as a simple, powerful, and non-mechanistic take on some of what psychedelics "do." We will also look at and discuss Martin Buber's work on I-Thou relationships, a rich framework on relationality and being. These two perspectives can provide us with something of meta or theoretical views on our topics here, on PAP and IFS. They might help us reflect on these topics from a somewhat abstract or outside vantage point, and thereby open more perspectives for bringing psychedelics and IFS together.

PETER WEBSTER'S SALIENCE AMPLIFICATION HYPOTHESIS OF PSYCHEDELICS

Peter Webster is an independent scholar who has been doing creative work in the field of psychedelics since, like many people, the 1960's. Here we will discuss some of his work from his 2018 book, *KOSMOS: A Theory of Psychedelic Experience*.

In his salience amplification hypothesis, Webster argues that much of what psychedelics do is take what is already there, what has always been there for us, and make it more salient; that is, make it matter more to us. Like — ***Matter***. Sometimes I think about this increased salience as turning the volume up, like to 11. In this sense, psychedelics don't actually show us anything new.

This can sound counterintuitive, even a letdown — aren't psychedelics all about great discovery, great novelty?

---

[113] Available online, https://www.psychedelic-library.org/books/Kosmos+Cover.pdf

But I think the implications of Webster's salience hypothesis are even more revolutionary than that. For instance, in PAP we often see and feel parts of ourselves more acutely. Exiles, the most vulnerable parts of us, can come powerfully to the forefront. Protector parts and what they've been doing for maybe nearly our whole lives can become vividly clear, in your face clear. Self can be there in spades. Our minds or souls manifest. As does the world. By this hypothesis, psychedelics don't make us hallucinate, they don't make us "see things that aren't there" or create new worlds to inhabit for a while. Instead, by Webster's hypothesis, we see and feel what's already there, what's always been there. Maybe we then hear or notice some very important things.

If we follow this, it can have profound implications clinically and beyond.

For some of us, myself included, at some point we might need to hear important things at volume 11 to notice them.

But like with a guitar amp, there can also be distortions in listening to things at super high volume. Hence the psychedelic truism, "Don't make important decisions for a couple of weeks after a medicine session." Yes, a psychedelic session may make real, important things about a relationship quite salient, but that doesn't necessarily mean that the next automatic step is a marriage or a divorce.

Listening to things at 11 can also become desensitizing. That can be a real downside of psychedelics as too much of a standalone practice. If blasting the volume at 11 is the only way we hear important things, then in our non-medicine, daily lives the important things can actually become subjectively less salient, more drab.

In "I'm Free," Pete Townshend's Tommy maybe sings of something like this, the tendency to only notice things when the volume is cranked up; that we can miss the highest high because of its simplicity.

Working with the possible distortions and the desensitization of super charged salience is where some of the most crucial PAP integration work comes in. And this is another area where IFS can make some crucial contributions to PAP, in helping us be sensitive to the salience of the psychedelia of our daily lives.

Something akin to Webster's salience amplification hypothesis of psychedelics, as he points out, has been around in different forms since at least when Aldous Huxley famously quoted William Blake, "If the doors of perception were cleansed, everything would appear to man as it is, infinite."[114] And we can see overlap between Webster's salience hypothesis and some current theories of psychedelics, like Ido Hartogsohn's work on the "meaning-enhancing properties of psychedelics."[115]

But Webster points out that such work on meaning enhancing and psychedelics is *based* in salience but is several steps past it. That is, for making meaning, things must first become salient to us. Then, we can possibly make meaning from them or find meaning in them. This might seem like a ridiculously minor distinction, but it is an important one. As Webster argues, meaning enhancement can certainly come from medicine sessions, but with psychedelics there is a rich process at play between salience amplification and our *participation* in meaning making. In Webster's sense, set meanings do not automatically come from psychedelics. We participate in the meanings we take from medicine sessions; we are agents in the meanings. So this is a relational, hermeneutic sense of meanings from psychedelics, not a mechanical or computational "automatic" one.

We will soon see and discuss Webster elaborating his salience hypothesis of psychedelics as a relational and psychological theory, not as simply a neurological or mechanical theory. But before that, we should discuss some serious problems in current neurological

---

[114] William Blake, The Marriage of Heaven and Hell, quoted in Aldous Huxley, The Doors of Perception, 1st Perennial Library (New York: Harper, 1970).

[115] Ido Hartogsohn, "The Meaning Enhancing Properties of Psychedelics and Their Mediator Role in Psychedelic Therapy, Spirituality, and Creativity," Front. Neurosci. , 05 March 2018, Volume 12 - 2018

research on "brain-wide associational research." Many current psychedelic studies are based in brain-wide associational research, but there are big problems in such studies in terms of neurology and, most importantly, in terms of psychology.

Brain-wide associational research tries to find patterns of brain activity that are associated with something complex happening with people, like for instance a psychedelic trip. This is different from research looking at more simple activities, such as studying visual centers of the brain by research participants being in either light or dark while in an fMRI machine and studying corresponding patterns of activity in their brains.

Complex brain-wide associational research is currently in a crisis as a field. Scott Marek, a researcher at Washington University, and his team found that almost all brain-wide associational studies, not just psychedelic ones, are vastly statistically underpowered. The title of their paper sums up their findings, "Reproducible brain-wide association studies require thousands of individuals."[116] No brain-wide associational studies on psychedelics have anywhere near such a number of research participants.

That there isn't enough data to support the purported correlations is a huge problem, but it gets worse. In an interview, Marek further clarified that because of a well known potential pitfall in statistical analysis, "the winner's curse," "... it is the very findings that are most inflated by chance and least reliable that are most likely to be found 'statistically significant' and make it to publication."[117]

Pressing on with more problems in this research, Manoj Doss, a psychedelics researcher at Johns Hopkins University who frequently works with fMRI data in his research, explained that in most studies of brain activity and psychedelics, researchers have given people either a psychedelic or a placebo and placed them in an fMRI machine for hours. As Doss says, "... when people are

[116] Marek, S., Tervo-Clemmens, B., Calabro, F.J. et al. Reproducible brain-wide association studies require thousands of individuals. Nature 603, 654–660 (2022).

[117] RJ Mackenzie, "Stats Study Reveals Reason for Replication Crisis in Neuroscience" (technologynetworks.com, March 22, 2022),

on LSD or psilocybin, they move in the scanner — more so than when they're given a placebo. People fall asleep when they're on placebo when they're sitting in a scanner for 15 minutes! So what are you really comparing — is it people awake versus people asleep, or are you showing psychedelic effects?"[118]

All of this throws into deep doubt much of the current "your brain on psychedelics" research, including ideas such as psychedelics temporarily turning off the default mode network and the colorful images of a seemingly highly connected brain on psychedelics versus a less active, less connected brain not on psychedelics.

Things get even worse in terms of psychology. Even if we ran a thought experiment that supposed we were getting good neurological conclusions from neurological studies of psychedelics, there would still be massive psychological problems with highly neurological takes on psychedelics. To again quote Barry Magid's great image arguing against an overly neuropsychological framework: "Minds belong to people, not brains.... The mind is no more inside the brain than a dance is inside the muscles."[119] Unpacking that, we could say that even if we studied the muscle activity of thousands of dancers as they danced and found valid statistical correlations of muscle activity and dancing, that wouldn't take us far at all in really understanding and appreciating dance. It also wouldn't be totally irrelevant. Similarly, even if we imagined we had good data on brain activity correlations and psychedelics, that wouldn't help us understand what's most important about psychedelics. (And again, it also wouldn't be totally irrelevant.)

Here we can see Webster take up this theme in arguing against overly mechanical understandings of psychedelics:

---

[118] Jane Hu, "5 Questions for Manoj Doss" (The Microdose, November 22, 2021).

[119] Magid, Barry. (2020, February 14). "'Why I'm NOT a Neuroscientist' Thompson offers an incisive deeply informed critique of Buddhist modernism's mutual love affair with neuroscience." https://www.facebook.com/profile/804313867/search/?q=dance%20muscles%20brain

If one supposes that psychedelics "cause" the items in Masters & Houston's list [such as "the voyage inward... psyche and symbol... the world of the nonhuman... religious and mystical experience"[120]], he then confirms from yet another dubious perspective Francis Crick's "Astonishing Hypothesis": the mind and its experiences cannot be anything but states of the brain's neurons, and thus "our most cherished beliefs about God, value, meaning, purpose, culture and morality are shown to be without foundation."

If consciousness, free will, et al., can be trivialized or eliminated by radical scientific naturalism, the "hard science" advocates, the "nothing-but-us-objects-here" crowd, then the idea that a mere "drug effect", such as that of LSD, is "all that is really behind" the items on Masters & Houston's list, fits perfectly with their outlook: Even psychedelic experience, in all its disguises, would be in the final analysis just another state of the brain's neurons. How disappointing. And how bland an outlook for one studying the mysterious, the unpredictable, the ineffable...

But if in actuality, LSD causes only a measurable, definable amplification of a neurocognitive operation (as per the present essay) which the person then uses and builds upon voluntarily to enter the great range of psychedelic effects, his humanity is restored, as well as that of the researcher who recognizes where the mystery lies... It is surprising that so many psychedelic researchers seem to support the stultifying scientism of the

---

[120] Masters, Robert E. L., Houston, Jean. The Varieties of Psychedelic Experience. United Kingdom: Holt, Rinehart and Winston, 1966.

nothing-but-crowd, for that is precisely the attitude that is shown to be mistaken by the psychedelic experience itself.[121]

Which, I think, leads us into Martin Buber's work on I-Thou relationships.

MARTIN BUBER'S I-THOU RELATIONSHIPS

I want to say a little about Martin Buber biographically and historically before getting into his work directly. Buber was not a psychologist or a therapist. He was both a philosopher and a devout Jew. He had a long career that surfed a creative tension or inhabited a rich ecotone between the religious and the secular. He grew up in Vienna and Ukraine and moved to Jerusalem when the Nazis came to power in Germany. He was a professor for much of his career at the Hebrew University in Jerusalem and he was a frequent visiting professor at the University of Chicago.

Buber possibly had a paradigm shifting and undersung influence on psychotherapy. He may have planted some of the most important seeds that would become humanistic and relational psychotherapy. He was great friends and a long term collaborator with Carl Rogers, of Client Centered Therapy fame. Buber may have also influenced Heinz Kohut in Kohut laying the groundwork for what would become relational psychoanalysis, a shift that revitalized and humanized psychoanalysis. Buber, Rogers, and Kohut were all at the University of Chicago in the 1950's and were the most prominent lights in psychology there.

Buber's masterwork is his book *I and Thou*, first published in German in 1923 and in English in 1937. It is a strange and wonderful book. I'm not sure if it's philosophy, poetry, prophecy, or rant.[122]

Buber's main terms in the book are the compound words I-Thou and I-it, which, to put it briefly, describe relationships.

---

[121] KOSMOS: A theory of psychedelic experience, available at https://www.psychedelic-library.org/

[122] Buber, Martin. I And Thou. India: Free Press, 1970.

Let's unpack these terms more. As I think we will see, they are very important to our topic.

By an I-Thou relationship, Buber meant that if we are relating to someone (or I'll go ahead and say something) as a Thou, then we are relating to them as a full, real being.

In an I-it relationship, if we are relating to someone or something as an "it," then we are not relating to them as a full, real being, as someone who is fully worthy of respect. If we show up in a relationship in an I-it way, then we will be relating to the other mostly as something that is a resource to us, an obstacle to us, or something that is irrelevant and ignorable.

The same goes for how others relate to us: they could relate to us as a Thou, in an I-Thou relationship of respect. Or they could relate to us as an it in an I-it relationship, as just an object to use, manage, or ignore.

I-it relationships, I-Thou relationships. That's the heart of Buber's work.

But this also gets more profound — and more poetic and hard to follow. Let's look at an excerpt from *I and Thou*.

> The primary words are not single words but word combinations.
> One primary word is the word combination I-Thou.
> The other primary word is the word combination I-it....
> Thus the I of [humanity] is also twofold.
> For the I of the primary word I-Thou is different from that of the primary word I-it....
> Primary words do not signify things, but they intimate relations.
> Primary words do not describe something that might exist independently of them, but being spoken they bring about existence.
> Primary words are spoken from being.

If Thou is said, the I of the combination I-Thou is said along with it.
If it is said, the I of the combination I-it is said along with it.
The primary word I-Thou can only be spoken with the whole being.
The primary word I-it can never be spoken with the whole being.
There is no I taken in itself, but only the I of the primary word. [123]

I want to bring in IFS to look at this.

Let's look at Buber's lines, "Thus the I of [humanity] is also twofold./ For the I of the primary word I-Thou is different from that of the primary word I-it." By this, when we are relating to a part of ourselves or of the world as a Thou — as a real being, fully worthy of respect — then we are the I of an I-Thou relationship. I think we might say we are then our Self. When we are relating to a part of ourselves or of the world as an it, as primarily a resource for us or an obstacle to us, not primarily as a being, then we are the I of an I-it relationship. I think we could say we are then blended with a burdened part of ourselves. We can feel these differences experientially and we can watch them play out in IFS clinical work. Clinically, when our patient is blended with a burdened part of themselves, then the relationships with their parts don't go very far in a good direction. However, clinical relationships of Self, of I-Thou, can be profoundly healing, growthful, and are deeply satisfying for all involved.

Buber goes further, "There is no I taken in itself, but only the I of the primary word." This is a radically — meaning, "to the root" — relational take on I. I only exists as part of a relationship. There is no I without a Thou or an it.

---

[123] This translation is a personal mashup I did of Ronald Gregor Smith's and Walter Kaufmann's English translations and consulting German dictionaries. Buber, Martin. I And Thou. India: Free Press, 1970. Buber, Martin. I and Thou. Japan: Scribner, 2000.

If we extend this to IFS, I think this can argue that Self is radically relational, is only relational. No relationship, no I. And we are always in relationship. So, no Thou related to, no Self. By this, Self is not a reified, separately existing, standalone "thing." By this, Self is 100% relational, Self only manifests in relationships.

We will return to this theme in the clinical chapters, where I think we will see this fully relational sense of Self being active and clinically crucial in the case material of both PAP and standard IFS.

Buber does not highlight this, but I think it can be important to highlight the two-way relationship of I-Thou relationships and I-it relationships. That is, not just how someone relates to us, but how we relate to ourselves in relationships.

When someone is relating to us as a Thou, it is easier for us to know, at some level, that we are a real, worthy being, a Self. And when someone is relating to us as an it, it is easier for burdened parts of us to blend with us, with their burdens of perhaps unworthiness or defectiveness, and to then see ourselves as an it. This obviously has important clinical implications.

By this two-way sense, we always have the right to claim ourselves as a Thou, as a Self. I think we will see this sense of being able to claim and assert our worthiness and right to be respected become very important clinically, especially in some of the challenging times of medicine sessions, in the clinical material in Part II.

We should say more about I-it relationships in light of "the twofold I of humanity."

I think we might see that when we relate to someone or something as an it, we are not seeing that they are a Self. This also applies when someone relates to us as an it; they are then not seeing us as a Self. As far as they are concerned, they are the only supposed real being in the encounter — but they are then the I of an I-it relationship, a different I.

I-it relationships are central to so much human to human trauma and deprivation. Martin Luther King, Jr helps us profoundly understand this in racism. Here is King from his "I Have a Dream" speech: "We can never be satisfied as long as our children are stripped of their selfhood and robbed of their dignity by signs stating: for whites only."[124] The racist, abusive, I-it relationship that overtly or unstatedly signifies certain things as "for whites only" is an attack on the selfhood of Black children. But it strips the selfhood of the racist abuser, because they are then the I of an I-it relationship. "The primary word I-it can never be spoken with the whole being." Buber writes of what happens to us when we are too much the I of I-it relationships: "When man lets it [I-it relationship] have its way, the continually growing world of it grows over him like weeds and robs him of the reality of his own I, until the incubus over him and the phantom inside him exchange the whispered confession of their need for redemption."[125]

The I of I-it relationships is a ghostly existence.

I want to point out that there is far more than a coincidental overlap of Buber's work and King's. King and Buber were friends and they collaborated on working for respect and against racism in the United States, apartheid South Africa, and in the Middle East.

BRINGING WEBSTER AND BUBER TOGETHER IN IFS AND PAP

We can now start to bring Webster and Buber's work together. This leads us back to a simple and crucial axiom of this book: that PAP and IFS each heal and grow through living relationships of mutual respect. For that to happen, our relationships, inner and outer, need to become salient. That is, we need to be able to notice them and see that they matter. Then, in relationships of Self, in I-Thou relationships, we can help one another, befriend one another, inner parts and outer world. From there, healing and growth and satisfaction can come.

---

[124] King, Martin Luther, Jr. 2018. Letter from Birmingham Jail. Penguin Modern. London, England: Penguin Classics.
[125] Buber, Martin. I And Thou. India: Free Press, 1970.

That is pretty much the theoretical "map view" proposed and assumed here. As the great cliché says, it's all about relationships.

SOME POSSIBLE OBJECTIONS TO PAP FOLLOWING FROM THIS READING OF WEBSTER AND BUBER'S WORK

I can hear a possible legitimate objection to what I've laid out here about the health bringing power of salience and of I-Thou relationships: that it is so simple and grounded that it doesn't need psychedelics. It doesn't need the complication, "side effects," or the "weirdness" of psychedelics.

There is great truth to this objection. I want to amplify it. It's fully true that this same simple, fully relational healing, growth, and satisfaction of I-Thou relationships applies to so many things: to regular IFS, to many schools of psychotherapy, to healthy schools, workplaces, families, friendships, cultures, towns, neighborhoods, healthy religious communities, art, music, ecology.

Here's a relevant story buttressing this objection. Steven Beyer, a psychedelicist, researcher, and author of *Singing to the Plants: A Guide to Mestizo Shamanism in the Upper Amazon*, wrote, "Shaman's Drum magazine published a report of an informal mycological field trip to Kamchatka, which speaks of meeting an eighty-two-year-old shaman, Tatiana Urkachan. The shaman was willing to lecture her visitors on the correct use of fly agaric for healing and intoxication, but she insisted — tellingly — that she never ingested the mushroom herself, for she was too powerful a shaman to need it."[126]

I think she was saying that she can work in a fully psychedelic way — souls or minds manifesting — without needing mushrooms.

But just because this simplicity of healing is not dependent on psychedelics doesn't mean it follows to throw out psychedelics. In practicality, I don't think any of this needs psychedelics, except when it does. They seem to be necessary for some people at some point. This fits with the clinical data of the many, many people

---

[126] Stephen Beyer, "Hallucinogens in Siberia" (singingtothelpants.com, February 18, 2008).

who had been through just about all the standard treatments and only found some real relief with the help of psychedelics.

And as we will see in the Integration Work chapter, this very simplicity and groundedness is exactly what makes real PAP integration possible. If psychedelics were about "other worlds" then they would result in a nasty dualism, a half life in one world, a half life in another. This would result in a very problematic dis-integration.

Here's a relevant and great integration question for even the weirdest, most otherworldly, and perhaps most difficult experiences in a medicine session: "Have you felt this way in your life before?" Major, grounded trailheads can open up.[127]

Yes, there are "side effects," risks, and complications to PAP. These are important considerations in PAP. But I don't think that means we reject a valuable clinical option. It is a truism that there are no "perfect" treatments. If we only allowed perfect treatments, we'd have no treatments at all. Our patients, and we as clinicians, need all the good ways of healing that we can find.

---

[127] Personal communication, Rainer Scheurenbrand.

Introduction to Part II

Part II is the clinical heart of this book, on IFS in psychedelic preparation work, medicine sessions, and integration work, one chapter on each.

I am obviously using the common grouping of psychedelic work into prep work, medicine sessions, and integration work. Although these distinctions are quite useful in helping us organize our practice and our thinking about PAP, I think these distinctions should be held lightly and seen as fuzzy. I would recommend considering the three chapters to follow as really about one living thing: psychedelic assisted healing. Like in biology, if we separate a living thing too much, it is no longer alive!

For example, we will see in these chapters, and I think in our clinical work, that preparation work is healing work itself. Medicine sessions might be experiences of great healing; or they might primarily inform healing to come in integration work. And integration work can naturally become preparation work for future medicine sessions. And so on, lines blurred and crossed.

I am happy to say that there is quite a bit of diverse case material in these chapters. Some of this is from my patients and our work together, and some is from several masters of PAP, including Richard Schwartz, Michael and Annie Mithoefer, Bill Richards, Rick Doblin, and Robert Grant. Very notably, not all this work was within an IFS framework at all, but IFS still somehow fits excellently.

Some sections in these chapters will get into pretty technical "deep dives." I do this so that therapists who already have a good background in both PAP and IFS can see some very concrete suggestions on combining PAP and IFS. I hope that these deep dives are also helpful for therapists in training. But for some readers, some of these discussions might seem pretty weird and indecipherable. My apologies for that. But hey — psychedelics! Sometimes weird and indecipherable can ultimately be useful?

CHAPTER FIVE

PREPARATION WORK

"The well-prepared person" — Bill Richards

Like in house painting and gardening, good preparation work in PAP can make everything that follows smoother, more enjoyable, more effective, and longer lasting. In PAP, good preparatory work can also make what's to come more humane and safer.

The main term of this chapter is a beautiful and simple one from Bill Richards, "the well-prepared person." Richards is a true elder in this field. Richards stresses that trust and safety are foundational to good preparation work.

Here is Richards from his book *Sacred Knowledge*:

> The bottom line with a well-prepared person is to trust one's own mind, one's grounding with the guide beside him or her, the safety of the physical surroundings, and, if religious perspectives permit, God or another sacred symbol for ultimate reality.[128]

An axiom of this chapter is that all preparation work towards trust and safety is relational and dialogical. In this chapter, we will explore many preparatory dialogues – that is, preparatory relationships – towards our patient possibly becoming "a well-prepared person."

---

[128] Richards, William A., Sacred Knowledge: Psychedelics and Religious Experiences. United States: Columbia University Press, 2015.

A crucial part of the preparatory dialogues and relationships of this chapter will be about consent from all parts of our patient to do any medicine session. And in prep work, we don't always get to consent from all parts to do a medicine session. Fully respecting parts means that any part has the right to veto a possible upcoming medicine session.

We will also see that preparatory dialogues can lead to far deeper and richer collaboration from all our patient's parts in preparing for a possible medicine session. Such collaboration can deepen, guide, and smooth out medicine sessions quite a bit.

The relationships of prep work are not only inner, so in this chapter we will also discuss "in the room" relational prep work. That is, overt dialogue about the relationships of our patient and their parts with us as therapist.

And prep work also isn't just for our patient! A major theme here will be some preparation work we can do as therapists. Specifically, a major focus here will be on therapist unblending. That is, on us being Self well enough in PAP work.

We will also start to discuss prep work for possible psychotherapy in an upcoming medicine session. Psychotherapy in medicine sessions is a crucial, complex, and often controversial topic. It will be a major focus in the Medicine Session chapter as well.

We will also explore here a way to bring IFS to topics of general PAP preparation work, like discussing getting to and from the bathroom safely. This can be as easy and as crucial as adding on a great IFS question to the topics of general prep work: "… and all parts of you?" This can make general PAP prep work far richer and more grounded and therefore lead to greater safety and efficacy.

And a crucial topic here is that I think we will see that prep work for a medicine session is fully healing work. Prep work is not just instrumental to the supposed "main event" of the medicine session.

For case material, we are very fortunate to have a full session of prep work. This is from the work a patient and I did together. It is also fictionalized and amalgamated to cover more topics and to protect confidentiality. We will draw on this session throughout the chapter and we will review it and discuss it in its entirety. I am very grateful to "Claire" for agreeing to share her process here as a way of helping others.

Let's jump in with specific topics on prep work. We'll start with the crucial topic of consent, or not, from parts for a medicine session.

DIALOGUE WITH ALL PARTS ABOUT CONSENT FOR THE MEDICINE SESSION

We might say that respect is foundational to IFS. That is because respect is essential to relationships of Self. If we recognize the autonomy and ontology of parts, that is, their "beingness," then they naturally deserve respect. And this respect is all the more important and real if we consider parts as being the children of our patient's inner family.

So, parts need to be in consent for a medicine session. This is for both clinical and ethical reasons. There are risks in PAP of traumatizing patients. It is not clinically or ethically good enough to just take the medicine, "trust the medicine," and go from there. There is some data in one psychedelic study, that does not reach statistical significance, that found that for some people there can be increased suicidality in the period after medicine sessions.[129] Very notably, this study had a protocol of a thin "psychological support" (their term)[130] as opposed to a rich psychotherapy, where all parts can be considered, dialogued with, and respected.

When we engage with all parts about possible consent and collaboration in prep work, and parts do come to true agreement for the medicine session, they then don't feel as victimized if things get very weird or challenging in the medicine session. Medicine

---

[129] Goodwin, Guy M et al. "Single-Dose Psilocybin for a Treatment-Resistant Episode of Major Depression." The New England journal of medicine vol. 387,18 (2022): 1637-1648.
[130] Ibid.

sessions can be quite powerful, and part of that is that they can be quite difficult. Parts need to be in informed consent for this before each medicine session. We don't want to have to try to negotiate with parts for consent for a rocket ride as the rocket hits "lift off." That's probably not going to be fair to them, and it's probably too late then.

By these respectful, Self to part dialogues with all parts, IFS can help us prevent *needless* suffering in medicine sessions. As we'll see, medicine sessions can often somehow have protector parts become far less active or even seemingly not aware at all, and then exiles can manifest *profoundly*, maybe more so than they have since the initial trauma or deprivation. This is one of the greatest healing opportunities of PAP, but it can also be harrowing. Burdened exiles are not carrying pretty burdens. If parts were not consulted beforehand about all these possibilities and did not come to informed consent for the medicine session and its possible intensities, then these experiences risk being significantly traumatizing or retraumatizing ones for parts and for our patient.

I want to underline that we only need good enough consent from all parts to do a medicine session. Robert Grant, as usual, puts this wonderfully and clearly when he teaches that we don't have to get a "Hell, yes!" from all parts about a medicine session.[131] As we'll see in the example preparation session, parts' consent for a medicine session can be conditional, negotiated, time limited, or experimental. For instance, it can be truly good enough consent for a part who has worries about an upcoming medicine session to agree to try one medicine session as an experiment and then re-evaluate from there. I've found parts, both protectors and exiles, often really like this "experimental" frame, that they don't have to make a permanent decision, yes or no, about medicine sessions.

When there is good enough consent in place from prep work, then during intense times in a medicine session parts can "say,"

---

[131] Robert Grant, "Level 1 IFS class for psychedelic practitioners," 2023

implicitly or explicitly, "Okay, we talked about this. I can do this." Because they are in informed consent for such intensity, parts might be more willing to go "there." And once "there," they might more richly receive the crucial healing they need.

Parts can also get to a negotiated, good enough consent when a part says to Self or other parts something to the effect of, "I don't want to do the medicine session, but it seems like you really do. I'll just stand back and won't be involved, but you go ahead." I've been amazed that this works, but it really seems to. That part then doesn't feel victimized by what's going on in the medicine session. And again, this sort of simple collaboration and teamwork — "You go for it, I'll hang back" — might help Self or other parts then go places they might not otherwise have been able to get to and to be there more stably, and to get crucial healing and growth that they need.

So a crucial part of technique here is that early in prep work we make it clear to our patient that if all their parts are not in real, good enough agreement to do the medicine session, then we don't think we should do the medicine session.

When we state this to our patient, this is some direct access: we as therapist, as our Self well enough, being in relationship with our patients' parts.

When we put our stance on consent on the table, I think it's safe to assume that all parts of our patient will be listening. Just hearing this commitment from us can be deeply reassuring to our patient and to all their parts and can help create some real safety and trust for them.

Hearing such a respectful stance from us can even be directly healing for our patient and their parts, perhaps as a sort of *in vivo* "do over" or corrective emotional experience. Our patient and their parts may have rarely, if ever, been respected and consulted like this.

Here is an example of this from the prep session with Claire. In this excerpt, I state my position to her and all her parts that

I don't want to do a medicine session until and unless all of her parts are on board:

> Therapist: .... so now your psychiatrist has recommended that you maybe look into ketamine. What do you think about that?
>
> Patient: I don't know, she wanted me to come talk to you. And I had all these questions, and I have mixed feelings about it. I'm nervous. I mean, I keep hearing all these great things, but I don't — I don't know, I've never done anything like it. It's making me nervous.
>
> Therapist: Okay. And I think it's really important that you don't force yourself to do this. You don't have to do it because your psychiatrist wants you to do it. And honestly, I don't want to do it unless your whole complex self is good enough on board, good enough in agreement for it. So what about some of these, some of the nervousness?

Collaboration with parts as central to prep work

As we open up dialogue with all parts of our patient about a possible medicine session, this can also lead to parts collaborating on planning the medicine session. Parts have a lot of wisdom. They may want to be part of the discussion about an intention, an ask, or a prayer for the medicine session. They may have things about the room or the "setting" that they want or don't want. They often know important things that they need or that other parts need for healing or safety. So it can increase the efficacy and smoothness of a medicine session to ask and listen to all parts in preparation work.

We will follow up on this topic throughout this chapter.

Common fears and concerns of parts about a medicine session

As part of informed consent and collaboration from parts for a medicine session, we also need to get specific about possible fears or concerns parts might have about a medicine session. We could ask something like, "Do you or any parts of you have any concerns or questions or hesitancy about possibly doing the medicine session?"

This could lead to dialogues that take a handful of minutes or to important work in therapy for months before any medicine session.

In the example session, parts of my patient started sharing some of their fears:

> Patient: I mean, I have a lot of health anxiety, so I worry that something bad could happen to me. I worry that like, it'll stop my heart, or I've heard weird stories, or I worry that, like, I'll go even more crazy and like, I've never even used an anesthetic. I've never used a, you know, hallucinogenic, even for fun or recreation. In college, I never did anything like that, so I never tripped. And you know what? What if I stay that way?

It could happen that in response to our questions about fears that no parts seem to have any concerns or questions. I think it can be important to then press on a bit. It could be that a protector who really wants to do the medicine session is blocking other parts. We might ask something like, "Could you check if maybe a protector part is blocking other parts from sharing?"

If our patient finds there doesn't seem to be a protector blocking other parts, I think we can still press on more. We could ask something like, "Are there any quiet or hidden voices or reactions in you that would like a chance to talk about any worries or questions about the possible medicine session?" We could also ask our patient to just pause and spend some time with their body, to take a few breaths and feel the breaths all through their body, their mind, and emotions. And then ask them to check if anything seems to be "up," if anything seems to be active in them.

This can be some implicit direct access (that is, we as therapist talking directly with parts, but we haven't made that explicit with our patient). By pressing on in these dialogues, we're really letting parts know that we sincerely want to hear from them even if they have doubts or objections about the medicine session or psychedelics. Perhaps our patient or parts of them think that we as therapist are "very into the whole psychedelic thing" and they don't want us to judge them for not being "totally into it." So we want to make it clear to such parts that we really want to hear from them about whatever they're thinking or feeling, that this isn't us trying to impose any "groupthink" stance.

If parts of our patient do have concerns, questions, hesitancies, objections, or asks about the medicine session, we can then offer some standard IFS. That is, offering to our patient that they find the part, check on how they feel towards that part, and so on until they are optimally in Self to part relationship. Excellent preparatory dialogues can then naturally come from there.

These preparatory dialogues aren't necessarily about doing full healing for any of these parts. The "contract" for these dialogues is more about just discussing the possible medicine session. But very important parts might, of course, come up in these preparatory dialogues. Perhaps a part in such a dialogue eventually helps our patient shape an intention for the medicine session, like getting healing for that part.

Direct access will probably become prominent at some point in these discussions with parts about fears. Parts will want to hear from us directly. Our patient might literally say something like, "They want to hear from you. They have questions for you."

When we are doing direct access, we are then the primary Self in the relationship with that part of our patient, so it's important that we are Self enough! So again, therapist unblending to Self will be a major focus later in this chapter.

In an excerpt from the example prep session, we'll soon see direct access becoming important.

Some common fears of parts about a possible medicine session are "bad trips;" that psychedelics will make our patient go insane or psychotic permanently; and concerns about medical issues. We saw those come up in the vignette earlier.

If any fears like these come up, it is important that within the scope of our practice we talk honestly about such risks, however rare.

I'm not a medical person and I try to be careful to not let a little knowledge be a dangerous thing. So for me, if a patient has a medical concern, I will probably either refer back to conversations they probably already had with their prescriber or encourage them to ask their prescriber.

In discussing fears that parts might have about a "bad trip," I tend to talk about how medicine sessions can be a temporary, intense shift of perspective, which is a great opportunity, but that it can be hard as well. I discuss that the prep work we are doing is partially to help prevent something like a bad trip.

Like we've discussed, a lot of bad trips can be from parts feeling victimized by being in a medicine session. Again, parts might find a medicine session quite intense or challenging at times, but if they came to true, informed consent for the medicine session beforehand, then they don't have to try to stop what's going on or try to get out of it somehow. They can then more be with whatever is going on in the medicine session, to have some real acceptance, because they had choice and agency in being there.

In terms of fears of "going crazy" in a long term way, I tend to discuss what is currently being called hallucinogen-persisting perception disorder (HPPD). Something like that can be when some emotional or otherwise psychological part of a medicine session can go on for days or weeks or months after a medicine session. Something like that can be, quite understandably, very disturbing for someone.

I tend to talk about this as quite rare and discuss that there seem to be certain risk factors that we will *not* be doing, like extremely high doses, inadequate preparation work, and working with psychedelics too much in isolation, without adequate, ongoing support.[132] I explain that my sense with HPPD is that it is from parts who, because of those inadequacies in the process, got overwhelmed in a medicine session. I also explain that the preparation work we are doing specifically seems to help prevent that kind of overwhelm. And I underline that we will only be working with doses prescribed by an expert prescriber.

I've found that parts very much appreciate hearing from me directly and honestly in discussing these risks and then they are far more ready to consent freely to the medicine session.

Let's now look at Claire and me discussing her fears of "going crazy" and of bad trips.

In this part of the session, I worked with my patient's part's fears and questions in implicit direct access. I partially chose to do implicit direct access instead of helping set up Self to part dialogues because this was our first session, Claire was totally new to IFS, and it felt like there was a lot of Self to part and Self to Self relationship going on in the relationship between my patient and me. I had the hunch that her parts really needed to hear from me about their concerns. So I went ahead with implicit direct access. It went quite well.

---

[132] Evans J, Robinson OC, Argyri EK, Suseelan S, Murphy-Beiner A, McAlpine R, et al. (2023) Extended difficulties following the use of psychedelic drugs: A mixed methods study. PLoS ONE 18(10).

Patient: What about the, like, going crazy and never coming back?

Therapist: Yeah, about going crazy. Have you ever had any kind of — do you feel like you've ever had any kind of experience like that? Like, I don't know, psychosis? Anything from any of the medicines? You've ever had anything like that?

[-- Checking for concrete experiences and history that might be very concerning to this part who is worried about her going crazy. Also, checking for myself on her history with psychosis, even in reaction to medications.]

Patient: No.

Therapist: Okay. Yeah. And it can be very intense during the experience.

[-- She doesn't have a history of psychosis. So moving on to dialogue about this fear more generally. Validating that the part might be right in a way, a ketamine session can be a temporary substantial to profound shift of mind.]

Patient: Like, what's that like?

Therapist: It can be very disorienting. And that can be really an opportunity. You know, one way of looking at it is that you can really look at things from a different perspective, because things can get pretty different, pretty jumbled. And it can feel like you're going crazy.

[-- Helping this part and any other parts listening be fully informed so that they can have real consent, or not. And starting to give some sense of "flight instructions," that a medicine session can be quite challenging, but that those are useful challenges, directly related to why she would do the medicine session: for psychological healing and well-being.]

Patient: That sounds terrible.

Therapist: Yeah. It can be very challenging. And that's exactly why the preparation work is exactly to help prevent that from being really a needlessly painful experience. And I've never heard it with ketamine — I have heard it with some of the other psychedelics, that sometimes people for a number of weeks, maybe a handful of months, can have some pretty disorienting stuff going on. But yeah, like I said, I've never heard that with ketamine. But even with other psychedelics it's rare. And it tends to be extremely high doses, like really into overdose territory. And when people don't have preparation and they're maybe doing it too much alone. They're doing it with friends who don't know how to support them. So exactly what we're doing now, that if your whole self feels on board and is informed about what might happen and you're taking medically safe, medically prescribed doses, then, yeah, we're preventing that, that stuff. But we absolutely need to talk about any of the nervousness because you don't want to go into this feeling like you have to fight it or like you're at risk.

[-- Again, validating that part about fears of something like HPPD, providing expertise and guidance around that, and continuing to provide a sense of flight instructions and meaningfulness of the challenges that might arise.]

Patient: So what is the prep work like then?

Therapist: Well, we're doing it now. I want to hear from your whole self about any concerns, any questions, any collaboration, any asks that you might have about a possible ketamine session.

A parts map as part of preparatory work

So far, we've been talking about prep work as mostly happening in open ended dialogue. We can also bring some important structure to prep work with a parts map.

A parts map is a standard IFS exercise, and it can be very helpful in PAP prep work. A parts map can help us and our patient identify many of the relevant parts and many of the relevant inner relationships early in the prep work. This can be of great value for the prep work and the whole therapy.

Robert Falconer described doing a parts map in psychedelic prep work like this in a class on IFS and PAP:

> You ask the person, "What part of you comes up when you think about doing psychedelics?" Find a simple way to represent that on a piece of paper…. Then have them step back, wait for a body change, see what other parts come up in relation to that, and then put that on the paper. And then keep working with that until you get a whole map… maybe six to eight parts….
>
> And then you ask, "How do you feel towards each of these parts that are on the paper?" And if you get anything less than a Self quality, that's another part and that needs to go there too. Then you ask, "Are there allies? Or certain of these parts working well together?" Draw a nice smooth line between them. "Are there antagonisms, fighting?" Draw jagged lines between them.

Now you've got a whole map. "Which of these parts
should we start working with?"[133]

We can then help our patient into Self to part dialogue with
that part, or maybe that dialogue seems to need direct access, or
maybe some of both. These dialogues can go in lots of directions.
And again, for the "contract" of prep work, this doesn't have to be
about full healing for the parts involved. We can let parts know
that we can come back to focus on them more in further sessions
or perhaps in the medicine session.

Regardless of where these dialogues initially go, it's important
that we eventually return to the parts map and make sure we
check in with and hear from any parts who had concerns, worries,
questions, or objections about the medicine session.

All these prep work dialogues don't need to rush towards a
decision of consent or no consent for the medicine session in one
therapy session. Eventually, in the prep work we do need to get
specific and clear on that. But I think respect of parts means that
they have at least two sessions, and the time in between them, to
think about consenting or not for the medicine session.

We will return to discussing finalizing any agreement and
consent, yea or nay, about a medicine session towards the end
of this chapter.

DOING A FULL SESSION OF STANDARD IFS AS PART OF PREPARATION WORK

Robert Grant makes the excellent recommendation that at some
point in the prep work we do a "full IFS session" with our patient.
That is, IFS work all the way through finding an exile, helping and
healing that exile, helping any relevant protectors integrate with
the now healed exile, and helping the relevant parts integrate
with each other and into our patient's daily life.

---

[133] Robert Falconer, "IFS and psychedelics class," 2021

Such a session can give our patient and their whole psyche a real taste of what might be coming in a psychedelic medicine session. Again, there is a lot of overlap between standard IFS healing and psychedelic healing. By a standard session of IFS, our patient might get a sense of what real healing is. They might also get an embodied, experiential sense of possible uncomfortable aspects of psychedelic healing and how such difficult parts of a healing process can ultimately be part of a crucial healing process. They might get a sense of how they might navigate such difficult aspects of a healing process, maybe with some acceptance, now that they see they are meaningful.

If we're doing PAP with a patient who we've already been working with in IFS therapy, then this "full session" as part of prep work won't be as necessary, but in a "bubble model," this is important to prioritize in the prep work.

PREVENTING AND WORKING WITH POTENTIAL COLLUSIONS WITH PARTS

One possible big pitfall of not doing IFS PAP preparation work is that we as therapist could then wind up colluding with one part of our patient against another part. Such a collusion could happen because in a "mono mind" model maybe we'd only be hearing from one part of our patient, the one who is currently blended with them. That part might want to do the psychedelic medicine session to try to get rid of other parts of our patient, possibly an exile or another protector. So without something like IFS, we might naturally get sucked into that part's agenda. And even with IFS therapy, there are of course great risks that we as therapist could unwittingly collude with one part of our patient against other parts of them, like against a depressed part or an angry part.

A common dynamic can be that protector parts can be quite attracted to the power of psychedelics to try to "super charge" the exiling of an exile or of another protector who they're in a contentious polarity with. If we as therapist get wrapped up in a collusion with such a protector, we might wind up pejoratively diagnosing or demonizing the exile or the other protector. This can make for a nasty dead end in the therapy or cause other problems in the therapy, at least until the collusion is recognized and worked with.

Just having a framework that recognizes the multiplicity of the psyche helps us a ton in working with possible collusions. We can then wonder something like, "Okay, I've maybe heard from one part of my patient. I wonder what other parts of them there are, and I wonder about their relationships."

We as therapist having a "parts detector" going can be very helpful in preventing potential collusions with just one part, and can be helpful in so many other ways. So let's discuss a "parts detector."

Parts detector

A "parts detector" is a half joking term for a sense we can get that there is a part or parts present in our patient. For instance, if our patient is blended with a protector, they might tell us forcefully that they want to use the medicine session to get rid of the anger or despair or confusion that plagues them. Then, with our parts detector, we might also "see" other parts as our patient talks, like our patient flashing a tear in their eye or their lips quivering as they say all this. Perhaps we are then seeing exiled parts or parts who are worried about the extreme agenda of this one protector?

Our parts detector mostly raises questions. No one's parts detector is perfect, but a parts detector can very helpfully let us wonder about possible parts that are present, even subtly.

If we guesstimate that we might be hearing from just one part to the exclusion of others, we can check on that with our patient. We might say something like, "Okay, so one way of looking at this is that there is a part of you that really, really wants to help you by getting rid of that despair that has caused you so much trouble. Does that sound right?"

Just positing the possibility that we're hearing from one part can help our patient start to see their internal relationships clearer. Our patient might then naturally unblend some and start to get into richer Self to parts relationships. We can support that by asking if they'd like to spend some time with the part of them who can go into despair (or feel so angry or get stuck in confusion, whatever part was being exiled earlier).

A parts map can be *very* helpful in terms of working with possible collusions. They can help both us as therapist and our patient, as Self and all their parts, see that there are many diverse parts and that they are in living relationships. From that perspective, the relationships between these parts can be worked with directly.

Whether we get there through our own curiosity and compassion for all of our patient's parts, a parts map, our parts detector, or all of the above, the center of gravity of the work can then shift out from just one part having a clear voice, towards a community of parts together, even a teamwork of parts. Perhaps we and our patient together discover a polarity of protectors and then through Self to part dialogue and relationship those protectors eventually come to the conclusion that they're willing to allow a part who they've been exiling to be more free during the medicine session. That exile, more clearly seen, might then be held by the protector or protectors in compassion instead of contempt. Then, instead of us as therapist and a protector part of our patient colluding against that exile, a great inner collaboration and teamwork might be in place for the medicine session and beyond.

This is again primary healing work directly in the preparation work.

MAKING OURSELVES EASILY KNOWN, EASILY "MENTALIZED;" MORE ON DIRECT ACCESS

As we've mentioned, in prep work, very often parts will want to hear directly from us as therapist. That is, they will want direct access with us.

One important way this can come up is parts just wanting to get to know us, to get a fairly clear sense of who we are, and, importantly, how trustworthy we are. Going into a medicine session with someone is an intense relationship and a very vulnerable one. I think parts are right to want to get to know us.

I don't think we really need to "work at" being easily known by parts. Like so much of this, if we're just Self enough, if we're just unblended, then parts will probably naturally get to know us because we'll be connected to our patient. It's just a relationship.

Some of our patient and their parts getting to know us might happen in explicit direct access, some might happen in implicit direct access. And some of this might happen in super implicit direct access, when neither we as therapist nor our patient know we're relating with a particular part of our patient, but it's happening anyway! All of these can work very well.

We can also explicitly ask our patient and all their parts about getting to know us better. We might ask something like, "Is there anything you or any parts of you would like to know about me? Going into a medicine session is an intense relationship, I want you and your parts to know well enough who they'll be doing that with."

When we respond to any questions they may have, again, we are then doing direct access. So I like to check myself for blending before responding, and if necessary, unblend.

If some of my patient getting to know me better might get into them hearing about parts of me, I always check with my own parts before sharing about them or speaking for them with a patient (or anyone). Our own our inner children as therapists matter, and need to be respected. If parts of me do not want me to speak about them, I have not found this to be a limitation at all in the therapy. I wonder if my patient and their parts sense my respect and care for my own parts and might then feel more reassured and trusting in me.

We might think about "making ourselves easily known" as "mentalization," a term from Peter Fonagy's work in relational psychoanalytic therapy. Mentalization roughly means being able to look into or at least wonder about each other's minds and our own mind. Other ways of putting it could be psychological mindedness or psychological awareness. In his work and research, Fonagy discusses that for many of our patients, especially those dealing with complex PTSD issues, the people in their lives who initially abused or deprived them probably had minds that were very difficult or very dangerous for our patients to mentalize. That is, it might have not been safe or possible for our patient to see clearly into the other person's mind because of the sadism, rage, or chaos there.[134]

Again, for many of our patients, part of what can make trauma and deprivation so psychologically difficult is the wrongful *relational* aloneness it happened in. That can very much include the fraught mentalization of the relationships in which it happened.

So, making ourselves easily known or mentalized can be a relational healing act in itself. This can again be an *in vivo* "do over" or corrective emotional experience for our patient. By our being easy to be known, our patient and their parts might have a rare and important chance to look into another's mind safely.

From there, when those of us who have been through relational trauma or deprivation can safely mentalize another in a safe and caring relationship, we can often then become far more able and willing to mentalize ourselves. That is, we can then feel far freer and safer to look into our own minds in a safe and caring way.

---

[134] Bateman, A. and Fonagy, P. (2010), Mentalization based treatment for borderline personality disorder. World Psychiatry, 9: 11-15.

All parts of us, as they are, welcome into relationship. This can be a powerful healing.

As part of this "making ourselves easily known," at some point in the prep work I think it can be helpful and respectful to overtly let our patient and all their parts know what we will be doing during the medicine session. This can build more safety and trust for our patient. If we let our patient and their parts know directly what we'll be doing during the medicine session, then they don't need to spin their wheels unnecessarily during the medicine session trying to guess or surmise what we're up to.

Personally, I'll often tell my patients that the main things I'll be doing during the medicine session are being present, trusting them, and trusting the medicine.

Stating this not only helps my patient get to know my mind better and what I'll be doing during the medicine session, it can also be empowering to my patient and all their parts. It directly communicates my trust in them.

"BEING WITH, BREATHING WITH" AS PART OF PREPARATION WORK

Michael and Annie Mithoefer have done some of the seminal work in studies of MDMA assisted psychotherapy for treatment resistant PTSD. They also lead trainings for MAPS in MDMA assisted psychotherapy.

They recommend a very simple and very rich practice as part of prep work, a practice that our patients can then bring into the medicine session. A practice of "being with and breathing with." This can be one idea for "flight instructions," for what our patient might do at times during the medicine session, especially during challenging times. Here's how Michael Mithoefer describes "being with, breathing with" in the treatment manual for the MAPS' MDMA studies:

... if anxiety or any other intense emotion comes up, rather than trying to relax, it is often most helpful to use the breath to "breathe into" the experience and stay as present with it as possible in order to fully experience, process, and move through it.

... healing often comes as a result of bringing conscious attention to difficult feelings, memories or body sensations, and staying present during these challenging experiences rather than attempting to avoid or escape from them.[135]

I read this to my patients during prep work and give them a copy of it.

This is a deeply relational practice, and as such, it is very much an IFS practice. One way of looking at it is that it can be a very simple and very natural Self to part or Self to Self relationship.

But with most of my patients, I don't label it as that. It's so simple and unencumbered that I think it's best left simple.

On first hearing of this, many patients will think of this being with and breathing into as a relaxation exercise, but that's not really what it is, so we might need to offer some clarification. In relaxation exercises, we try to use breathing to change distress, maybe to take the edge off it, to shift it, or to get it to go away. But this "being with and breathing with" is something different. It is an exercise in relationship with what is present, not necessarily changing at all what is present.

The Mithoefers do recommend a distinct, separate relaxation exercise for the early part of an MDMA session. Early in an MDMA session there can be physically tense, "speedy," anxious side effects going on. Doing some relaxation exercises with that can be helpful. But once our patient is past that initial, tense stage,

---

[135] Michael Mithoefer, A Manual for MDMA-Assisted Psychotherapy in the Treatment of Posttraumatic Stress Disorder (Santa Cruz, CA: MAPS, 2015).

they are in the journey. It's no longer about relaxing anything away. It's about being with.

And as is well known, relaxation exercises probably wouldn't even work well in the full intensities of a medicine session, which could then lead to more distress.

To further clarify "being with, breathing with," it is also not "rubbing your nose" in the distress. It's not trying to amplify or exaggerate the distress. It's just being with it as it is, and breathing with it or into it.

Especially if my patient has a background in DBT, I'll sometimes half jokingly call this a form of "radical acknowledgment," a play on "radical acceptance."

Once we've introduced and explained this practice, we can ask our patient if they would like to do it right there in the prep session. We can explain that like in the medicine session, they can do this practice with whatever might be there with them in the therapy session at the moment. It might be comforts or discomforts. It might be what's going on in their body, their emotions, their thoughts. It might be awareness of a part or parts. It might be what's going on in the room or the external situation; what's going on with their imagination; with whatever "realms" might be present; with anything unnamable, but still there, however inchoate. Whatever.

I like to cast a wide net on this exercise because quite a lot of different "stuff" can come up in a medicine session, so for this exercise in prep work it's good to be open to a very wide and diverse range of feelings or experiences or relationships.

If they would like to, our patient can then do this "being with, breathing with" in the session, for a few breaths to a few minutes, the timing being up to them.

If our patient finds value in this practice or they are just willing to give it a try, we can recommend that during the preparation phase they do this practice from time to time during their daily lives. They can do this with anything they experience or feel.

But before doing a medicine session, it can be good to have some practice doing this with discomforts or upsets of one kind or another. I ask my patients to make this something of a drill, that during the prep period they look for one thing or so a day that they find uncomfortable or distressing and be with it and breathe with it for maybe a half breath, maybe a few breaths, or as long as it seems to fit the situation. Before we get to the medicine session, we want this turning towards, being with, and breathing with to become something of a habit, especially for distressing things.

Here's how "being with, breathing with" came up in the example prep session with Claire:

> Therapist: And, you know, I think it can also be really helpful that, if things do get weird and do get challenging [in the medicine session], my sense is that that can be partially what's helpful. It's maybe like you kind of throw the cards in the air and then they can be rearranged in ways that you might not have been able to get to before. But with some of those challenging experiences, I think one thing that can be really important is to just, as best you can, stay with whatever comes up, and breathe with it. That would be part of the prep work.
>
> Patient: Mhm.
>
> Therapist: Sometimes we might find that some of the most challenging things wind up being some of the most helpful things.
>
> Patient: That's for sure.
>
> Therapist: Being present with things, and breathing into them or sharing your breath with them, that's something that, if we're going to do this, would be really important that we practice in our sessions

and you start practicing in your daily life, before any kind of ketamine session, so that it becomes almost maybe a bit of a habit, or you see some value in it before you even go into the ketamine session.

Patient: Uhm. I can for sure try. Meditation has always been hard for me.

Therapist: Yeah, and it is a kind of meditation, but you don't have to sit still.

Patient: Mhm.

Therapist: You don't have to set a timer.

Patient: Mhm.

Therapist: It's just anything that's going on in your life — Have you done any DBT?

Patient: I mean, I was in partial once and I did.

Therapist: Yeah, yeah, there are a lot of kind-of DBT programs out there. Did you come across the term radical acceptance?

Patient: Yes.

Therapist: I sometimes half jokingly talk about this as just radical acknowledgement.

Patient: Mm hmm.

Therapist: Then just acknowledge whatever, and then maybe share your breath with it. Or you can breathe into it. You can do that while you're washing the dishes. You can do that if you get upset about something with your kids, or even if in your daily life you start seeing some of that hopelessness poking through. Can you maybe just acknowledge it and share your breath with it? Or that protective move comes in. You can just acknowledge it and share your breath with it. Even just half a breath, maybe three breaths.

Patient: Mhm. Yeah.

We can then come back to this practice in subsequent prep sessions and ask our patient if they'd like to do it together a little bit in the session.

If our patient can work with this "being with, breathing with" in their daily life here and there, joys and discomforts and in between, for a week or more before the medicine session, then I think they will be able to bring it quite naturally into the medicine session. I think they will be able to more readily get into relationship with all that comes up in the medicine session: parts of themself, visions, their body, their emotions, us as therapist, whatever "realms," whatever else.

We will see this practice become very important in the case material in the Medicine Session chapter. It will also be of central importance in the Integration Work chapter.

As we just saw in the case vignette, I personally shy away from labeling this as a meditation exercise. Often, people will interpret it as a meditation exercise, as Claire seemed to. Personally, I find the word "meditation" has become so loaded up with different meanings that it's become a problematic term. It can have so many different connotations, often of doing some technique right or wrong or getting into some good or bad "state." That all can become quite unrelational, which is of course not what we're after here. So again, I tend not to use the word meditation in describing this "being with, breathing with."

Again, I think this practice is best left simple, just being with and breathing with.

This practice did remind me of meditation when I first learned about it in my training with the Mithoefers. During a break, I went up to them and asked them where they got it from, if it was some kind of meditation exercise. They both burst into delightful grins and Annie exclaimed, "We don't know! It's just what Stan did!" The Mithoefers had trained in Holotropic Breathwork with Stanislav Grof and had long experience in leading those workshops. Who knows where Grof got it from, I just left it at that.

"CONTRACTING" AROUND EXPLICIT THERAPY, OR NOT, IN MEDICINE SESSIONS

If we are going to possibly offer therapy in the medicine session, it is very important that we discuss that with our patient as part of prep work. As we'll discuss much more in the Medicine Session chapter, doing or trying to do therapy in a medicine session can go off the rails quickly! Prep work around consent or no consent for therapy, and coming to a "contract" for therapy in the medicine session, are crucial to help any possible therapy in the medicine session be a healing experience, not a derailing one.

Sometimes people might have sought us out specifically to do IFS therapy as part of medicine sessions, but we still need to have specific dialogues, all parts included, about consent and contract around possible IFS therapy in the medicine session.

It could also be that, for whatever reasons, we as therapist might not want to offer IFS therapy in a medicine session. We might not prefer to work that way in medicine sessions, or we might not feel that that is within our current capabilities. It's important that we are then clear with our patient that the contract is that we won't be doing explicit therapy in the medicine session.

If we think therapy in the medicine session might be a good option to have and one that we are comfortable providing, then we can simply put that option on the table for discussion.

So in prep work, we might say something like:

> One option is that we could do some explicit therapy in the medicine session. We'd have to be mindful

about the timing and dosing on this. There are times in a medicine session when it just might be too hard or annoying or distracting to do anything like typical therapy. And any therapy we might do would probably be brief.

Medicine sessions can be a great time for some specific therapy. We might be open to things that are hard to get to otherwise.

Does any of this sound interesting and useful to you or any parts of you? We can decide what options we might want for the medicine session.

If our patient does have some interest or curiosity about therapy as an option in the medicine session, we can dialogue on that further. I tend to tell my patients that we can't "steer" the medicine session very well and that is maybe part of why medicine sessions can be so helpful. So I will recommend to my patients that we don't go into the medicine session with any big, specific plans, but that we can prepare for the possibility of therapy in the medicine session.

Identifying parts for possible therapy in the medicine session

If our patient does want to have the possibility of doing IFS therapy in the medicine session, then it can be good to start identifying parts who might want or need that kind of help. This could be an open ended discussion. And the original parts map or a fresh one could be helpful here. Our patient's "chief complaints" could also importantly inform this discussion.

In the Medicine Session chapter, we will look at and discuss an example of a session of IFS therapy in a low dose ketamine session. We will see there the great pragmatic benefits of having done this prep work, of having come to consent, contract, and identifying parts for possible therapy in the medicine session.

We will continue discussing therapy in medicine sessions in the Medicine Session Chapter.

RELIGIOUS OR SPIRITUAL ASPECTS OF PREPARATORY WORK; "GUIDES"

Psychospiritual, religious, or spiritual factors can be of central importance to the healings in PAP work. I say "can be" because for some patients, they are not relevant or not wanted.

But such things often seem to come with the terrain of PAP. There is research indicating that participants in PAP studies who had more "complete" and strong "mystical experiences" in their PAP had better mental health outcomes.[136] From this research, we see that not only can mystical, religious, or spiritual aspects of a medicine session be of great clinical importance in PAP, but they also appear to be pretty common.

We may even be under reporting religious or spiritual aspects of PAP. Almost all of the current PAP outcome research is gathering data on the religious or spiritual aspects of medicine sessions using either the Mystical Experience Questionnaire (MEQ-30)[137] or the Mysticism Scale (M scale)[138]. Both of these are heavily focused on "mystical experiences" as experiences of "oneness." Neither gather much if any data on divinity or relationships with divinities, which are of course very common varieties of religious or spiritual experiences. Both instruments seem strongly influenced by Aldous Huxley's *The Perennial Philosophy*[139] and similar work, a movement which highly emphasizes mystical experiences as experiences of oneness. So a broadened and more diverse sense of religious or spiritual aspects of PAP might show that they are even more common than the current data show and might be of even greater clinical importance.

---

[136] Kangaslampi, S. (2023). Association between mystical-type experiences under psychedelics and improvements in well-being or mental health – A comprehensive review of the evidence. Journal of Psychedelic Studies, 7(1), 18-28.

[137] MacLean, K. A., Leoutsakos, J.-M. S., Johnson, M. W., & Griffiths, R. R. (2012). Revised Mystical Experience Questionnaire (MEQ) [Database record]. APA PsycTests.

[138] Hood, R. W. (1975). The construction and preliminary validation of a measure of reported mystical experience. Journal for the Scientific Study of Religion, 14(1), 29–41.

[139] Huxley, Aldous. The Perennial Philosophy: An Interpretation of the Great Mystics, East and West. United Kingdom: HarperCollins, 2012.

So, there are serious holes in our current data on the psychospiritual in PAP. This is an important area for further research.

Regardless, I think it is clear that to serve many of our patients well, good Western PAP is going to need to find good ways to have *options* for including the psychospiritual in PAP. Again, I say the *option* of including the psychospiritual in PAP because for some patients the psychospiritual can be of the utmost importance to their PAP, while for other patients such including things would be a horrible intrusion on their PAP.

We can see this in Bill Richards' prep work where he includes, but makes optional, the spiritual or religious. We see this in his quote opening this chapter: "*if* [emphasis mine] religious perspectives permit, [trust in] God or another sacred symbol for ultimate reality" can be central to helping our patient become well prepared for a medicine session. If such trust is available, that's a lot of trust! But such things can also be a horrible intrusion in their PAP for some patients.

Pragmatically, in prep work we need to at least put on the table the topic of possible mystical, religious, spiritual, or psychospiritual aspects of the medicine session, and open some dialogue on that, all parts welcome.

This is all quite complex and quite important. Luckily, IFS has some great strengths to bring here. One great strength is that in IFS work, we as therapist don't have to be "the knower" about these matters, one way or another. We don't have to determine whether religious perspectives will be or won't be important to the PAP. We, of course, will have our particular beliefs or disbeliefs or questions or leanings. It's not that we need to be or can be some perspective-less blank figure. Everyone has some sort of perspective, that's just natural. It's just that our patient's perspectives, beliefs, disbeliefs, questions, and leanings are of great importance, not ours. So, in one of the great IFS truisms, in psychospiritual prep work we can just ask our patient. This gives IFS a huge flexibility.

In contrast, many schools of psychotherapy unfortunately have somewhat "baked in" prejudices about spiritual matters, for or against or ignoring them. Such prejudices can either impinge badly on our patients or leave them too alone in these matters.

Many schools of psychotherapy are very attached to some flavor of a Modernist, materialist, purely secular worldview. And some schools of therapy are rooted in a specific religious or spiritual worldview. Either stance can become clinically problematic in standard therapy, and these problems can become, like so many things, far more intensified in psychedelic assisted therapy.

With overly attached Modernist schools, if religious or spiritual relationships were to show up in the PAP, too often the therapy wouldn't be able to bridge to that, so it ignores it, leaving our patient too alone. Or it might impinge badly on our patient's experience, often by offering an interpretation of a possible psychospiritual manifestation that tells the patient, "What's *really* happening is..." and then imposes the therapist's view on the matter, which might be a highly reductionistic one and therefore highly invalidating to some patients.

Or, with schools of therapy that are overly attached to a specific spiritual or religious perspective, if religious or spiritual phenomena that fit the therapists' preconceptions of what's important or helpful don't show up in the PAP, the patient or the therapist could feel a sense of failure in the PAP or a deficit in the patient. These purported "true" experiences of "real spirituality" or religion could be experiences of "oneness;" an experience of a particular divinity; of "guides;" of a particular experience of nature; of "ego death;" or whatever a particular school of therapy or psychospiritual healing holds as "real" spirituality.

Or, in such a therapy with set beliefs on what is "real spirituality," if psychospiritual elements come up in the PAP but don't exactly fit that school of therapy's religious or spiritual perspective, they might be ignored as weird or confusing or again badly impinged on by the therapist imposing an interpretation of them, again possibly badly invalidating the patient. Stated or unstated, there can be a stance from the therapist that the "correct" or "real" religious or spiritual experience didn't happen.

Again, as Western mental healthcare becomes more psychedelic, it is going to need to grow richer options for the psychospiritual. As we transition to that as a field, I think we very much want to be aware of and avoid any Procrustean beds.

In the old Greek stories, Procrustes was a monster who lived, shockingly enough, along the pilgrimage road from Athens to Eleusis, where the likely psychedelic Eleusinian Mysteries were held. On cold, rainy nights, Procrustes would offer travelers to spend the night in his home. He would be the consummate host, lending them warm, dry clothes. He would feed them a hot meal by his fire. He would then show them to their private guest bed and help his guest get settled. But once in bed, if he found that his guest was too tall to fit the bed, was "too much" for his guest bed, Procrustes would cut off parts of his guest until they fit (and died). Or if his guest was too short to fill the bed, "not enough," Procrustes would mechanically stretch their body until they fit the bed (and died).

We of course don't want therapy to be a Procrustean bed. And again, IFS therapy has particular strengths by favoring our patient as Self and favoring our patient's experiential relationships of the religious or spiritual or lack thereof. This experiential, relational flexibility is very helpful so the therapy can fit our patient, not our patient having to fit the therapy.

So in prep work, we could ask our patient something along the lines of, "This may or may not apply, but I should ask. Is there any kind of religious or spiritual help or support that you or any parts of you might want for the medicine session? That you or any parts of you might possibly find helpful for your healing or help you feel safer in the medicine session? Or maybe none of this applies to you or any parts of you." We could then offer our patient some time to check in with their whole, complex self around this.

I think it's important to ask *all* our patients about this sort of thing. I've found I'm bad at guessing who might or might not find religious or spiritual perspectives valuable! Sometimes, assuming my patient will have no interest in such possibilities or even a disgust in them, I've hemmed and hawed in bringing up this topic in prep work and my patient has interrupted me and said something like, "Oh yeah, totally. I was hoping we could talk about something like that."

Other times, I've been surprised in the other direction. Patients who I guessed would have a real interest in such matters might, in fact, be vehemently opposed to anything religious or spiritual and want them to be in no way part of their PAP work.

Sometimes, patients will say they don't have strong beliefs or feelings about these topics one way or another, but that they are open to whatever help is available. Many people with treatment resistant conditions might understandably say that and mean it.

So having asked our patient and their parts, we can just go from there. If our patient or any part of them is interested in such help in the medicine session, we can help them dialogue, Self to part, about what those parts might need or want so that they can feel and be safest and freest in the medicine session.

This could go in a lot of directions. Parts might want images or rituals or prayers or asks. They might want to include figures, forces, allies, or religious or spiritual helpers. These might be known clearly to them, or they might be more "agnostic," inchoate and hard to name, but felt as powerful and helping figures. Or again, there might be a simple and pragmatic openness to *any* good help that might be available.

Part of these dialogues might be that if we as therapist have spiritually or religiously meaningful art or figures in our office, parts of our patient might want to dialogue with us about those and possibly ask us to remove them for the medicine session.

The same might go for any sort of "rituals" we might want to do before or during the medicine session, such as "smudgings," "calling in" of any spiritual helpers, playing religiously or spiritually meaningful music, and so on. It's not necessarily that we cannot do any of those or use any of those in the medicine session, it's that they need to be honestly and adequately discussed with our patient and all their parts in prep work. Like so much prep work, this ultimately comes down to respectful, real consent from our patient and their parts, because that ultimately comes down to safety, trust, and agency for our patient and their parts.

These discussions might lead to us removing figures from our office or the space for the medicine session. They might also lead to us or our patient bringing in figures or art to the space for the medicine session. Or they might lead to clarity and greater intimacy between us and our patient around any figures in our office.

Here's a personal example of such a discussion. My therapist has a beautiful Virgin of Guadalupe figure in her office. I am Catholic. I knew my therapist was not Catholic or Christian. So as Self I needed to speak up for young parts of me and ask her what that figure meant to her. She explained that it is a very important Goddess or divine feminine figure for her. My parts and I liked that quite a bit. That figure became a meeting place for my therapist and me, a place of intimacy and connection for us and has been for years now. But we had to discuss it, all parts welcome, for that to happen.

I'm also a Buddhist (I have a busy religious life…). So if a therapist had a Buddha figure in a space where I was going to do a medicine session, I would probably need to speak up for parts of me about what that figure meant to the therapist.

Through IFS dialogues about the psychospiritual, or lack thereof, we can come to a customized, respectful, and relational set up for the psychospiritual in the PAP work. Again, this is a huge strength of IFS PAP prep work.

These discussions, by being respectful of our patient and all their parts, can be healing discussions themselves. They are very much not traumatic or depriving discussions.

I want to mention that there are, of course, very specific and overt psychedelic religious and spiritual traditions. They have views and rituals around the religious or spiritual in psychedelic practice and how that relates to healing or worship. But those sorts of traditions are outside our topic here, which is PAP in a Western clinical mental healthcare context. So we won't focus on such traditions here, but that isn't meant to indicate that they aren't important.

Specifically asking for help from any seeming "helpers"

If our patient or parts of them are in fact interested in possible spiritual or religious aspects of the upcoming medicine session, we might offer them the recommendation that in the medicine session they have the agency to ask for that kind of help. In a way, a "prayer" is simply an old fashioned word for an "ask," as in maybe a meal at an English dinner table way back when: "Pray thee pass the butter."

We can also recommend to our patient that as part of any such psychospiritual ask for help, they can also decide how much help they might want at any given moment, including that they can to pass on any seemingly offered spiritual help. I think it is important to affirm to our patient that they are an agent, a Self, even in relationships with the possible divine.

Along these lines, Robert Falconer makes a crucial observation that we can share with our patient. Falconer observes that seeming spiritual "helpers" can be so incredibly respectful that they will not even intrude on us to heal us unless they are explicitly asked.

So by this train of thought, it can be quite pragmatically helpful for our patient to make *very* explicit asks for such help. And again, our patient can customize those asks how they and their parts feel ready to.

In the Medicine Session chapter we will return to possible psychospiritual aspects of healing in PAP.

SOME THERAPIST PREP WORK

Prep work isn't just for our patient. As is often observed about psychotherapy, the therapist is often the "rate limiting step" of a particular therapy. There are some old truisms about that: we can't help someone with stuff we haven't been through ourselves at least in some way. And "countertransference" and the therapy relationship – that is, the therapist's parts and Self – affect a therapy greatly.

So we'll now discuss two crucial elements of therapist prep work: therapists having experience as patients with the psychedelic medicines that they use in their practices, and therapist blending and unblending.

Therapists having experience themselves, as patients, in medicine sessions with the medicines they work with

There can be some controversy around the idea of therapists needing to have their own experience with the medicines they work with. But it's pretty much a given that if we were going into challenging mountain terrain, that we'd want a mountain guide who had traveled and lived in such terrain, not someone who had just read books and watched videos about mountains. As therapists in PAP, as companions or guides on "trips," I think it is optimal that we have "been there" ourselves.

I think it's telling that just about every psychedelic helping tradition besides the current Western one is an apprenticeship model of at least several years.

This doesn't mean that we as therapists have to break laws or spend a lot of money traveling to countries where we can legally work with certain medicines. The main medicine that most of us can work with in our practices now is ketamine, and for most of us that is pretty accessible to work with.

PAP training programs have generally recognized the value and need for therapist experience with the medicines. But I would recommend going beyond a single training experiential session or short retreat and actually engaging in an IFS PAP treatment as a patient, as one who, in an ongoing helping relationship, presents their suffering and seeks relief. That can be one of the most powerful ways to learn this work.

Therapist unblending

As I've already stated, I personally think of unblending as maybe the most astounding contribution IFS has made to psychotherapy. That is because by unblending, we get to Self, and then in Self to part relationship some of the most important and real healing can happen.

So here we will look in detail at unblending as a great contribution that IFS can make to therapist prep work for PAP.

A lot of different traditions and schools of therapy recognize something like therapist blending, but then they don't often have much concrete to help with that. For instance, the often cited advice for therapists in PAP to "W.A.I.T." — to ask themselves, "Why Am I Talking?" That can help us be aware that maybe we don't need to be saying what we're saying, that maybe we're blended with a part of ourselves. But it leaves us little to go forward with from there.

Understanding therapist blending can help us greatly with this. We can see that if we as therapist are largely blended with a part, burdened or not, then at that moment that part is running the therapy! Burdened or not, nothing against parts, but if they're running the therapy, it's probably not going to go great, even if it goes fine. Parts are inner children. It's not fair to our patient or to our young parts for them to try to do therapy, psychedelic or standard. So we can work on unblending.

Let's start looking at that in detail.

One important bottom line with unblending is that, as the term pretty much states, unblending is a process of subtraction, not addition. We don't get to Self by adding *anything* to ourselves, no matter how great the attempted "add" might be. Not love, not presence, not compassion, and so on. Unblending isn't about trying to pump up more Self in ourselves or trying to find more Self somewhere out there and hitch a ride. Such efforts could very much risk inviting "Self-like" parts to blend with us. "Self-like parts" are probably protector parts who have an agenda to be, for example, *really courageous, really compassionate,* or *really present.* That sense of italics, that intense agenda, even an agenda to be like Self, can be a possible tell of a still burdened part.

This isn't to rip on Self-like parts. They are wonderful and they are trying so hard to help. But they are in an extreme role. We can ask them to unblend from us, and when the time is right, we can offer them and the parts they are in relationship with a chance for healing. There's probably a lot there, I can attest.

When parts are healed (or were never burdened) they can have tons of compassion, presence, curiosity, playfulness, and so on, but they don't have an anxious or intense agenda to do or be those things. It's just that, as healthy parts, they are Selves, so all their great qualities are natural to them. They can then be powerful teammates and helpers for us in the therapy.

Healed or never burdened parts also don't often try to blend with us so intensely. They might blend with us here and there, often bringing their great qualities, and that can be great.

So the discussion here will mainly focus on parts of ourselves who are still burdened.

The first step with unblending is maybe the trickiest: knowing that one of our still-burdened parts has blended with us! When we're very blended with a burdened part, we think with its mind, we feel its emotions as ours, we even feel its bodily sensations. And all that seems totally natural to us and not really worth reflecting on. So we tend not to notice the part and we don't notice we're blended.

Because we may not notice we're blended, it's important that we check ourselves every so often throughout our work to see if we're blended or not. In PAP this is particularly important before any direct access and before proposing or doing any therapy in a medicine session.

One of my favorite ways to check myself for blending is an excellent checking question I learned from Robert Grant: "Do I have an agenda?" If we have an agenda, it's likely that we are blended with a part, a part in some kind of extreme role, hence its intense agenda. It could be a part who wants us to do "extreme therapy." Or it could be a protector who wants to protect us from an exiled part, an exile who carries burdens of shame or inadequacy about our abilities in our work. Those are both common parts for therapists.

An assumption around this checking question, "Do I have an agenda?", is that when we're Self with our patient, we are of course compassionate, curious, caring, and so on, but that those don't come with a big to-do list, not even a healing to-do list. Not a set agenda even to retrieve and heal an exile. Not specific outcome goals, such as, "My patient will be less depressed or suicidal," or, "My patient will be happier in their daily life from this PAP work."

Sometimes the best treatment plan is to put the treatment plan in the drawer for the time being, to ask it to unblend from us.

If we're bringing too much of a script into a relationship at a particular moment, even with excellent intentions, I think that would still be what Buber might call an I-it encounter. In contrast, I-Thou encounters don't have a big agenda. They can't. When there are two full beings present, a full Thou and full I, there is too much autonomy, too much wisdom, and too much creativity present for a big pre-planned agenda to work.

There's an old Zen *koan* about compassion, about *Kuan Yin*, the Bodhisattva of Compassion, the One Who Hears the Cries of the World, who has 10,000 arms of compassion. Someone asked their teacher what she *does* with all those arms of compassion. The teacher responded, "It's like someone fumbling for their pillow in the middle of the night." She simply reaches out and does the next thing. And then maybe rests.[140]

With the compassion, curiosity, and caring of Self, we might wind up with quite a bit of not knowing: not sure what's going to be co-created next, if anything. We might just mostly be present there together with our patient and their part or parts. And open to being surprised and learning. We might find that then we can go ahead, with our patient and their parts, with the therapy in ways that seem quite appropriate, including all the IFS "steps."

Besides that great checking question, "Do I have an agenda?", there are myriad other ways that we can get a sense of whether we're blended with a part or not. Burdened parts pretty much by definition are in extreme roles. If we can notice that we're having something of an extreme reaction, even just on the inside, that can be a big "tell" that maybe we're blended.

Physical senses or sensations can be great "tells" that we're blended. Sometimes in medicine sessions and in standard IFS, I'll physically feel a little crowded, like there isn't enough space around me for my body, like I'm in a crowd. I'll notice I'm getting a little constricted, that I'm not breathing fully, my ribs trying to fit into what feels like a constricted space. This can all be a good tell for me that maybe a part or parts are trying to blend with me or have blended with me. I find that when I do get to unblending, that then I can literally take up more physical space and breathe

---

[140] Yuanwu., Cleary, T. F., & Cleary, J. C. (1992). *The blue cliff record*. Shambhala Publications. Case 89.

more fully and easily, a good tell for me that they've unblended from me.

We might also get tells from our thoughts. When a burdened part has blended with us, we might hear certain thoughts, maybe excited thoughts, maybe self-attacking thoughts, maybe thoughts of a certain tenor, tone, or demeanor. Maybe we've come to know those thoughts, those voices, those tones pretty well over the years. That awareness can help us reflect that maybe a part of ourself is trying to blend with us or has blended with us.

I've found that another powerful tell that I'm blended is when I find that things aren't going forward well in a therapy. It might feel like the wheels are spinning in a rut or otherwise kind of "off." We might then ask a possible part that we don't "see" in any way, but that we guesstimate is there, "Are you blended with me?"

One more of my favorite ways of checking on blending is asking, "How do I feel towards my patient right now?" Or, "How do I feel towards this part of my patient right now?" This is pretty much the same checking question that we use all the time with our patients. And just like then, if we get anything but qualities of Self, we know we're blended with a part.

Whether we notice spontaneously that we might be blended, or we check and find that we seem to be blended, we can then work towards unblending.

It's important that we find our own ways of unblending. Working towards unblending is ultimately entirely of our own relationships with our own parts. There is no mechanical way to do it, like there is no mechanical way to "do" any real relationship.

Unblending is something that a part freely agrees to do, not something that we "get" the part to do. That would be from another part of us in an extreme role who is blended with us.

Unblending usually centers on a respectful, clear request from Self to the part to unblend. So, if we find we're feeling towards the part of us qualities of Self (well enough), then we can go ahead and ask the part to unblend from us. We might say something like, "Hey, would you let me be here with my patient? I think that will go best and we both want that." Or, "Would you please unblend from me? I think I got this." We might add something like, "I'd like to come back and spend time with you later and try to help you and any other parts you're around."

Or maybe we find we're not feeling qualities of Self towards the part. Just like we help our patients do, we can then ask *those* parts to unblend from us. And so on.

If we can't unblend from a part or parts during our work, whether in medicine sessions or in standard therapy, then that is a great thing to bring into our own IFS therapy or consultation. Such situations tend to be very powerful trailheads to our own healing.

Unblending doesn't have to be a part leaving the room or agreeing to go quietly into a corner of the room, although it can be those. The bottom line is we just need the part to agree to really let us be there. Robert Falconer talks beautifully in his teaching about offering to hold close, maybe nuzzled under our arm, a part who we found had blended with us.[141] That can be part of a powerful unblending.

One of my personal favorite ways of unblending is to turn towards a part that's gotten very active, that is trying to blend with me entirely or is seriously crowding me, and ask it, with real sincerity, because I mean it, "Do you have any wisdom for me?" Through long and deep experience, often forged in medicine sessions, I've come to trust and value my parts greatly – that they can very helpfully answer that question. I often find that parts try to blend with me when I haven't been paying enough respectful attention to them, when I haven't been listening to their wisdom, so they've gotten very loud and extreme to try to get me to listen. Children can be like that, thankfully. Our parts can invade our very minds if we're not listening to them enough! When they can share their wisdom with me, and I really take it

---

[141] Robert Falconer, "IFS and psychedelics class," 2021.

into full, respectful consideration, they very often relax and find a space that's comfortable for them and naturally give me more space. I can then be much more present with my patient and their parts, and I have the benefit of my part's wisdom.

Just like we do with our patients, even if we think that a part has unblended from us, it can be wise to check again. Maybe that part got quiet but didn't unblend. Or maybe it sincerely unblended from us, but another part popped in and blended with us. So we need to check freshly until we're clear that no part is blended with us. We might use the same checking questions, "Do I have an agenda?", "How do I feel towards my patient or this part of my patient?" Or any other way that we've found is good for us to check on blending.

Therapist unblending can take a while to write about and discuss, but it doesn't have to take long in actual practice! With some practice, we can check on our blending and, if need be, do some unblending right in a session. It might just take a moment or so, about as long as a normal conversational pause.

If we think we might need a longer time to check on our blending or to unblend, if it doesn't seem like it would be too disruptive to our patient, we could ask our patient, "Could you give me a minute?"

Asked for or not, in a medicine session (or a regular therapy session) most of the time people will just naturally accept our pause. We might think about ourselves as patients. If our own therapist paused for a handful of seconds or asked for a moment, most of us would be fine with that. Speaking for myself, I even appreciate it. I can guess that my therapist is taking some time with something important, and I appreciate her care in what we're doing. I also like seeing that she has to work as well, that she's not "on point" 24/7. That can help me be more accepting and loving of myself and others in my life. I think many of our patients would have similar reactions.

Let's now turn to some more possible "flight instructions." We've already discussed "being with, breathing with" as a form of "flight instructions." I'd like to look at another take on flight instructions that I find very useful and that is compatible with IFS: being a *flaneur*.

SOME "FLIGHT INSTRUCTIONS," BEING A FLANEUR

Flaneur is a great word for trips. *Flaneur* is a word with layers of historical meanings. By *flaneur*, we might mean a traveler in a foreign land who wanders at the intersection of what's there, chance, and interest. Like being on a trip in a new city: waking up, leaving the hotel, and hitting the street. Looking both ways, "Left or right? Which way looks more interesting?" Making a choice and then going. The day has begun. Walking a while, being with what's there, including oneself. Eventually again: "Left or right?" And so on.

In prep work, I half jokingly and half seriously discuss with my patients being a *flaneur* as one option for what they might do in their journey.

Henry James, the great travel writer (and interestingly, the brother of William James) writes of being a *flaneur* on a trip, on his first day in Rome:

> The first day of my stay in Rome... I spent in wandering at random through the city, with accident for my *valet-de-place* [guide]. It served me to perfection and introduced me to the best things; among others to an immediate happy relation with Santa Maria Maggiore [a Roman Church]... I remember, of my coming uninformed and unprepared into the place of worship... only that I sat for half an hour on the edge of the base of one of the marble columns of the beautiful nave and enjoyed a perfect revel of — what shall I call it? —

taste, intelligence, fancy, perceptive emotion? The place proved so endlessly suggestive that perception became a throbbing confusion of images, and I departed with a sense of knowing a good deal that is not set down in Murray [his guidebook].[142]

James would go on to have a lifelong, evolving relationship with Santa Maria Maggiore.

Here in PAP, we might add that one can journey not just out of curiosity and interest, but also out of need.

This *flaneur* sense of "flight instructions" for a medicine session is highly compatible with IFS. It leaves the door wide open for our patient as Self and for their Self leadership: for their compassion, connectedness, clarity, confidence, curiosity, creativity, presence, persistence, playfulness, patience, perspective. Them as Self.

And this is not a Self alone as a monad. It is also entirely compatible with IFS in that it is fully relational: it is our patient being there and being with. This is not a Self alone; this is a Self always in relationships.

This *flaneur* sense of flight instructions can be different from some other common flight instructions that might implicitly or explicitly downplay or reject our patient's agency, and therefore them as Self and their relationality in medicine sessions. Such flight instructions can recommend a passivity of self or of "losing one's self" or a simplistic "letting go" as the goal of the medicine session.

At the same time, this sense of being a *flaneur* in a medicine session doesn't obviate any possibilities, including true, legitimate surrender. Henry James seemed to get to surrender in his "perfect revel" in his relationship with Santa Maria Maggiore. But this surrender was by his agency and relationality: it was done by him, with what was there.

In a recent conference presentation, Sunny Strasburg, a close colleague of Richard Schwartz's in their ketamine assisted IFS

---

[142] James, Henry. Italian Hours. United Kingdom: William Heinemann, 1909.

retreats, highlighted our patients' creativity. She said that she recommends to her clients that they take the medicine session as a creative possibility, as a canvas that they can create with for their healing.[143]

Crucially, this sense of our patient as a *flaneur* in their trip also affirms our patient as a Thou of two-way I-Thou relationships. That is, both our patient being respectful to the Thous who they meet on their journey, *and* our patient knowing that they deserve to be treated as a Thou, as always deserving respect in all the relationships that manifest in the medicine session.

I think it's also notable that this *flaneur* sense of flight instructions is also highly compatible with and can be informed by Jung's therapeutic process of "active imagination." The Jungian analyst Robert Johnson writes of active imagination in his great book *Inner Work*, "It is this awareness, this conscious participation in the imaginal event, that transforms it from mere passive fantasy to Active Imagination."[144]

We will see this sense of patients' agency and participation in medicine sessions come up repeatedly and crucially in the case material in the Medicine Session chapter.

AN EXAMPLE PREPARATION SESSION

Let's now look at a full example session of prep work. We will have a transcript of the session interspersed with some commentary from me on what I was thinking or doing in the session and what I thought was going on.

There will be some repetition as we go through the session here because we have already viewed parts of this session as vignettes in this chapter. The bad news is the repetition. The good news is that we now get to see those vignettes in their full context.

---

[143] Sunny Strasburg, IFS conference presentation, Denver, 2023

[144] Johnson, Robert A.. Inner Work: Using Dreams and Active Imagination for Personal Growth. United States: HarperCollins, 2009.

This is the first therapy session with a woman referred to my practice by her psychiatrist to possibly work with ketamine for treatment resistant depression. Again, I'll call her Claire here. She is 48 years old, white, married to a man, and has two young kids at home. She has a long history of depression, including postpartum depression, and she has had various treatments, but never with much relief. She is naive to psychedelics and to IFS.

This isn't meant to be a perfect or complete session of prep work. I think it went quite well, but it is one 45 minute session, with the particular zigs and zags that came up in the meeting of this woman and her parts and me and my parts.

I can't remember the times when I did my own unblending, but it was several times throughout this session. "Do I have an agenda?" "How do I feel towards my patient or this part of her?" And if I found I was blended, asking that part if it would unblend from me and let me be with my patient. And then maybe not quite knowing what's up or where things might go but being present and connected with Claire. Good things can be co-created from there. I think they were in this session.

And once again, my great thanks to "Claire."

Transcript of Claire's first preparation session, with commentary

Patient: My God, I feel like I've tried everything.

Therapist: Okay, and then your psychiatrist thought that maybe ketamine might be helpful?

Patient: You know, in my 20s, I tried an SSRI, when I was in college, but I had side effects and it didn't really help. I was anxious, but then I was like really depressed. But then I got pregnant, and I had really bad postpartum depression. That was a fucking nightmare. Then I could not get off of it and that freaked me out. And then my psychiatrist added Lamictal, and I'm not bipolar at all. But she said maybe it might help with some of my, like, ups and downs and like my history of trauma and, you know, in terms of intrusive thoughts. And it was kind of helpful, but I really did not ever get into feeling the way I wanted to feel.

Therapist: All right.

Patient: And then they suggested an atypical antipsychotic and she put me on Abilify. It didn't work.

Therapist: Okay, I'm sorry to hear that. Sounds like you've really tried. And you've really been suffering.

Patient: I have been. Suffering.

Therapist: I'm really sorry to hear that. And so now your psychiatrist has recommended that you maybe look into ketamine. What do you think about that?

[-- Here I'm trying to start the prep work of hearing from different parts of her about their feelings, thoughts, and reactions to possibly working with ketamine.]

Patient: I don't know, she wanted me to come talk to you. And I had all these questions, and I have mixed feelings about it. I'm nervous. I mean, I keep hearing all these great things, but I don't — I don't know, I've never done anything like it. It's making me nervous.

[-- We could say we're starting to hear from different parts. We're in it.]

Therapist: Okay, and I think it's really important that you don't force yourself to do this. You don't have to do it because your psychiatrist wants you to do it. And honestly, I don't want to do it unless your whole complex self is good enough on board, good enough in agreement for it. So what about some of these, some of the nervousness?

[-- Making it clear to her and all her parts the frame here, that we won't do a ketamine session unless they are all on board. Having established that, starting to hear from a part or parts, the nervousness.]

Patient: I mean, I have a lot of health anxiety, so I worry that something bad could happen to me. I worry that like, it'll stop my heart, or I've heard weird stories, or I worry that, like, I'll go even more crazy and like, I've never even used an anesthetic. I've never used a, you know, hallucinogenic, even for fun or recreation. In college, I never did anything like that, so I never tripped. And you know what? What If I stay that way?

[-- Really typical fears in prep work that need to be heard and dialogued with: that something bad medically will happen. And a fear that she'll lose her mind, and with that, that Self will be lost or impinged on, for the long term, or forever, by working with psychedelics.]

Therapist: Yeah, yeah. Have you talked to your psychiatrist about any of these fears? Like especially the medical fears. Like with your heart?

[-- Trying to bring her medical provider into the dialogue because I don't have medical training.]

Patient: Yeah.

Therapist: What did she say?

Patient: She said theoretically, there was no issue.

Therapist: Do you know why she said that? Do you feel like you have an understanding of why she's saying that's so? She's saying it's medically safe for you. Is that right?

[-- Checking with parts that they understood and were satisfied with the answers from her psychiatrist. If they haven't really been reassured around medical safety, they probably need more dialogue with her psychiatrist.]

Patient: She indicated that.

Therapist: All right. Well, I know her. And she has a very good background on working with ketamine. And I know she takes your welfare very seriously. But it sounds to me like you maybe need to really talk with her about some of your medical fears in more detail. What do you think about that?

[-- Providing some general reassurance to these parts that I can offer because I respect my colleague a lot.]

Patient: Isn't that what I'm here to do with you today?

Therapist: Well, I don't have medical training. I'm just not the right person to talk with about that. I try to read the research, but, you know, you don't want medical advice from me! I have a master's degree in psychology. I never heard of any cardiac problems. Ketamine was created specifically to be a safe anesthesia that medics could use in combat in Vietnam. So that, you know, medics with not a lot of medical training could give anesthesia to wounded soldiers. And they didn't have to worry about respiratory problems or cardiac problems, like you might with a lot of anesthetics. And I've talked with anesthesiologists who love ketamine. They love to use it in their practice partially because it is so safe. And ER doctors love it, from some I've talked to, because someone can come into the ER and they're like, "Yeah, we can give them ketamine because it's safe."

[-- Clarifying roles, that I am not a physician. But also providing the expertise and background that I ethically can within my scope of practice.]

Patient: Oh, interesting.

Therapist: But yeah, I think you should talk with your psychiatrist more about the medical stuff. But she wouldn't have recommended it to you. She knows your medical history. She knows about your health anxiety and any kind of cardiac vulnerabilities you have.

[-- A path forward will be more dialogue with her psychiatrist.]

Patient: What about the, like, going crazy and never coming back?

[-- Another part returns to that fear, wanting dialogue on that.]

Therapist: Yeah, about going crazy. Have you ever had any kind of — do you feel like you've ever had any kind of experience like that? Like, I don't know, psychosis? Anything from any of the medicines? You've ever had anything like that?

[-- Checking for concrete experiences and history that might be very concerning to this part who is worried about her going crazy. Also, checking for myself on her history with psychosis, even in reaction to medications.]

Patient: No.

Therapist: Okay, yeah. And it can be very intense during the experience.

[-- She doesn't have a history of psychosis. So moving on to dialogue about this fear more generally. Validating that the part might be right in a way, a ketamine session can be a temporary substantial to profound shift of mind.]

Patient: Like, what's that like?

Therapist: It can be very disorienting. And that can be really an opportunity. You know, one way of looking at it is that you can really look at things from a different perspective, because things can get pretty different, pretty jumbled. And it can feel like you're going crazy.

[-- Helping this part and any other parts listening be fully informed so that they can give real consent or not. And giving a sense of some "flight instructions" — knowing the lay of the land of a medicine session and that it can be quite challenging, but these are useful challenges, directly related to why she would do the medicine session, for psychological healing and well being.]

Patient: That sounds terrible.

Therapist: Yeah, it can be very challenging. And that's exactly why the preparation work is exactly to help prevent that from being really a needlessly painful experience. And I've never heard it with ketamine — I have heard it with some of the other psychedelics that sometimes people for a number of weeks, maybe a handful of months, can have some pretty disorienting stuff going on. But yeah, like I said, I've never heard that with ketamine. But even with other psychedelics, it's rare. And it tends to be extremely high doses, like really into like overdose territory. And when people don't have preparation and they're maybe doing it too much alone. They're doing it with friends who don't know how to support them. So exactly what we're doing now, if your whole self feels on board and is informed about what might happen and you're taking medically safe, medically prescribed doses, then, yeah, we're preventing that, that stuff. But we absolutely need to talk about any of the nervousness because you don't want to go into this feeling like you have to fight it or like you're at risk.

[-- Again, validating that part about fears of something like HPPD, providing expertise and guidance around that, and continuing to provide a sense of flight instructions and meaningfulness of the challenges that might arise.]

Patient: So what is the prep work like then?

Therapist: Well, we're doing it now. I want to hear from your whole self about any concerns, any questions, any collaboration, any asks that you might have about a possible ketamine session.

[-- Clarifying what we're doing here. Continuing to invite parts to come into dialogue, so far mostly in implicit direct access. As discussed earlier, direct access can be particularly important in prep work because parts want to get to know the therapist directly.]

Patient: Well, yeah. I mean, what's the deal I hear from, you know, friends who've done like the IV ketamine, it's just like in some clinic with an anesthesiologist. But there's no therapy there. Is that different than what you're talking about?

[-- A rightful fear of being too alone in the ketamine session.]

Therapist: Yeah, yeah. And I think that can go really well. And there's a lot of research that it goes really well, and I'm glad it goes well for people. But yeah, we want to be more respectful of your emotions and your whole complex self, including the parts of you that are nervous about this. I see them as like the children of your inner family, and they have to be on board with this. So it's really important that we hear from them. And they might want to ask for things about the session, and that can really make it better. They might ask for things they need. So if you check in with the nervousness now, can you find that part of you right now?

[-- Being honest that solo ketamine sessions can be helpful but validating and reassuring that part that I would be there for the session. Continuing to invite all parts into the dialogue. Starting to work in more Self to part relationship with the part who is feeling nervous.]

Patient: About getting children on board with things. I think that's very hard with my kids.

[-- Maybe she is concerned that she won't be able to get all her parts in line.]

Therapist: Huh. Yeah, and they only have to be well enough on board. One of my colleagues talks about how it doesn't have to be a "Hell yes!" It might be that they just say, you know, "Okay, this seems like it's safe enough to maybe try once and then evaluate from there."

[-- Clarifying with her and with her parts that there is a wide range of truly good enough consent. There are options here, there is flexibility.]

Patient: I mean, I'm very curious and, you know, hopeful that something could work because I feel like I've tried a lot of things. And I'm not getting anywhere, and I guess — you know, one of my fears is that it won't work. And it's just like the last ditch effort. I haven't done ECT or anything. But, you know, everyone kind of touts ketamine and all the psychedelic stuff as lifesaving.

[-- Starting to hear from the part.]

Therapist: Right? What if it doesn't work, right? So there can be a part of you that's afraid. If this doesn't help you, then it can feel that there's little to nothing that might help you.

[-- Validating that part.]

Patient: Yeah, yeah.

Therapist: Would you be interested and willing to try and spend a little time with that part of yourself right now?

[-- Proposing to bring this dialogue into a Self to part relationship.]

Patient: Mhm.

Therapist: All right, so just see if you can find it right now, maybe in your body and your emotions.

[-- Starting to find the part.]

Patient: You mean that hopeless part of me? Mhm. Mhm.

[-- She identifies this part as feeling hopeless.]

Therapist: Yeah, that this might not be helpful.

Patient: Mhm.

Therapist: All right, where do you find it now? In your body and your emotions and your mind?

[-- Helping her find it.]

Patient: I mean, I guess I'm finding it in my gut.

[-- She's with it.]

Therapist: Yeah. Okay, so just stay with it there. Notice it there. And how are you feeling towards it right now as you're noticing it there in your gut?

[-- A brief "Fleshing out." Then checking if she's in Self to part relationship with the part.]

Patient: I feel sorry for it. All right, yeah.

[-- Seems like some Self to part relationship there, but I'm not sure, so I try to clarify:]

Therapist: Do you feel open to getting to know it better?

[-- Another way of checking on Self to part relationship, like we saw in Richard Schwartz's demo session from the overview chapter of IFS.]

Patient: Well — I'm supposed to say yes.

Therapist: But are you?

[-- This doesn't sound like Self; Self doesn't do things by template, because "I'm supposed to."]

Patient: I think I protected myself from that part. I could be open to it, I suppose, if it'll be helpful.

[-- Sounds like a protector has blended with her. Maybe it is afraid that things could go badly if she was with the hopeless one. So I switch the dialogue to be with this protector.]

Therapist: But there's maybe a part of you that has tried to protect you by not seeing that part of you, not being with that part of you?

Patient: Sure, yeah, yeah.

Therapist: Can you ask that part of you what it's afraid of? If you're with this hopeless part of you, if you acknowledge this hopeless part of you, what's that protective part of you afraid of?

[-- Seeing if this protector will help her and me get to know it better, and get to know itself better, by exploring its fears.]

Patient: I mean, I'm afraid of letting it out.

Therapist: Yeah. And what might happen to you then, if you just ask that part to play it out? Worst case scenario? What might happen to you then?

[-- Trying to really clarify the specific fears this protector has.]

Patient: Yeah, I would kill myself.

[-- The specific fear.]

Therapist: Yeah, that's a big fear.

[-- Validating the fear and important role of that protector.]

Patient: Yeah, yeah. Um, yeah.

[-- Maybe she's in some Self to part relationship with that part, validating it as well. Or maybe that's that protector validating itself, being seen and understood.]

Therapist: Has anything like that happened? Like where you felt really suicidal or maybe, you know, maybe you even acted on that.

[-- Seeing if this protector has specific experience that informs their role.]

Patient: Definitely felt like it. I know, a long time ago. Okay, technically I acted on it, but I, you know, it was very much kind of explained away just like that I was like looking for attention or whatever for my parents, but, mhm. Yeah. But sure, I mean, yeah, off and on, throughout the years, I've had thoughts.

Therapist: Yeah. And it's really been there. And you've acted on it. Yeah, that's a grave risk.

[-- Validating the role and work of that protector.]

Patient: I spent a long time like kind of girding myself. From the source, distracting myself with family and work and trying to, you know, substitute some meaning so as to distract myself from it. But those thoughts...

[-- The protector seems to explain itself more. And explain that they don't succeed in their job perfectly and that that's hard for them.]

Therapist: They're still there. Yeah, and so part of that protective move is to distract yourself, build, bring good things, positive things into your life.

[-- Clarifying and validating the specific work of this protector and that it doesn't succeed perfectly.]

Patient: Yeah.

Therapist: So it'd be a huge move, for that protective part of you to let you be with, with this part of you that can feel so, so hopeless.

[-- Validating the fear of that protector and acknowledging that it would be a big deal for them to allow access to the hopeless one.]

Patient: Yes. Yeah, um.

Therapist: You know, I've got to say, it seems like that's been maybe the status quo. And maybe you see where that gets you, which is maybe it's done you some real good.

[-- Validating that the protector has brought her real good, but her whole self is also stuck in a tense and difficult status quo.]

Patient: But be alive.

Therapist: Yeah, right, right. Which is huge. Can you maybe, can you thank that protective part of you?

[-- Seeing if we can bring in some Self to part relationship with this protector.]

Patient: Mm, sure. You mean, like, I say it out loud?

Therapist: Whatever. If you want to, you don't have to do it out loud. It's just, it's most important that it's between you and these parts of you, your own self.

[-- Clarifying how we might work in therapy.]

Patient: [Silent for a moment.]

Therapist: How does it react to you thanking it?

Patient: It's like mortified. Embarrassed.

[-- There's some Self to part relationship established, which, if possible, is often far more powerful and far faster than direct access.]

Therapist: Do you know why it's embarrassed? Do you get that?

[-- I couldn't understand why that protector would feel embarrassed, so partially I'm checking if Self does, which is more important, and partially I'm trying to understand for myself so that I can stay with her and these parts better.]

Patient: It did not want to be recognized. Or even acknowledged. Oh.

Therapist: Can you ask it? Or do you know why it's afraid of being acknowledged, recognized? Maybe ask it, see if it'll share with you. Help you understand that better.

[-- Again, trying to facilitate Self to part relationship and for my own understanding of this part.]

Patient: I mean, it's just embarrassed. It's embarrassed of, feeling like a loser. Like you can't get it together to enjoy all the clearly good stuff that's going on.

[-- The part helps her, and me, understand it.]

Therapist: So it feels like it's not really doing a great job in your life. But it's been helping keep you alive, huh?

[-- Validating the part.]

Patient: I guess you could say that. Well...

Therapist: How do you feel towards that protective part of you right now?

[-- Now that she knows the part better, checking on and maybe deepening the Self to part relationship.]

Patient: I mean, I want to say I feel like grateful and impressed by it, but I also feel annoyed that, that it has to be here.

[-- It seems like another part blended with her, a part who is annoyed.]

Therapist: So there's a part of you – maybe one way of looking at it – is that there's a part of you that's annoyed that it has to be here. Annoyed at the protective part, or maybe annoyed at the hopeless part, or both?

[-- Clarifying the relationships, who is the annoyed one annoyed at?]

Patient: It's probably more the latter.

[-- It seems the annoyed one is in a fraught relationship with the hopeless part.]

Therapist: Yeah. So it's been really hard to have a, a hopeless part of yourself and then a part of you that tries to distract you, but maybe doesn't let you really enjoy and really maybe let you live richly.

[-- Checking on the role of the annoyed one and validating them.]

Patient: Yeah, totally.

Therapist: Well, so do you see where that annoyed one is coming from?

Patient: Uh, do I see where it's coming from?

Therapist: Do you feel like you understand its annoyance?

Patient: I mean, yeah.

[-- Facilitating some Self to part relationship.]

Therapist: Now could you ask it, what would it like for you?

[-- The goal for this session isn't a full IFS healing. The goal is prep work for a possible ketamine session. So now that we've gotten to see and know some of the parts that are active around the ketamine session and their relationships with each other, I shift to seeing if they can start to explore collaborating together on a possible ketamine session.]

Patient: The annoyed one?

Therapist: The annoyed one, yeah. What would that annoyed one want for you? Can you ask it that?

Patient: I mean, it would want me to just be myself. To live fully. To not need the protective part. Because the hopeless part would be exorcised. Mm.

Therapist: What do you mean, like "The Exorcist?"

Patient: Mhm. Yeah, yeah.

[-- We can start to get to some of the hopes of these parts, something of a "hope merchant" move, by letting the part share their hopes, if they have some. This can get into intention setting and, again, collaboration of all these parts in the IFS PAP work. But the annoyed one seems to want some exiling to happen, so I clarify:]

Therapist: Far be it for me to say, but I think a lot of times psychedelics can somehow or another help these parts of ourselves, not have to get rid of them, but can help them. Or that's been my experience, it's my trust. It's why I do this. What if the ketamine could help that hopeless part of you, even somewhat, and that could then help the protective part of you not have to do its job so intensely? Wouldn't have to do its job all the time.

[-- I don't like to try to speak for psychedelics. But I do want to provide some psychoeducation about healing versus exiling and how ketamine might help with that.]

Patient: Um, well, I think that would be pretty great. Yeah. So you're saying it wouldn't get exorcised, but it would just help that part?

Therapist: Yeah, maybe more like, again, like an inner child who's just been suffering and maybe get some help, get some connection. Get some peace. Get some friends, find some wellbeing.

[-- Providing some psychoeducation on what Self to part relationships and healing for parts can be like.]

Patient: Like parenting, right?

[-- Very cool association she had! She's probably in Self a lot as a mom.]

Therapist: Yeah. But again, that would be a big risk to even hope for that.

[-- I don't want to push on her parts a simplistically happy vision of our work, so in implicit direct access, I return to acknowledging and validating the fears of the protector, that having hope can be quite a risk because of possible disappointment. Then, the hopeless one could be hurt further and break out and could lead to more suicidality.]

Patient: Sure, yeah.

Therapist: Can you ask these parts, the hopeless part, the protective part that tries to distract you from the hopeless part. The annoyed part that's annoyed that all this has to go on in your life.

Patient: Uhm.

Therapist: What do they think about? Maybe give this a try, maybe just giving it one try?

[-- Having explored hopes and fears, where do these parts stand on free consent for a ketamine session at this point?]

Patient: Yeah, they're tired. Yeah. Yeah.

Therapist: Yeah. What might they each want from this? If they could make an ask for themselves or for these other parts of yourself? For you? That's a big question.

[-- This is getting towards possible intention setting and rich collaboration of her whole self in the PAP.]

Patient: These parts don't understand how it might happen, what they might want.

Therapist: Yeah, yeah. And I don't understand how it might happen either. But honestly, I've just seen it over and over and yeah, there's lots of good outcome research.

[-- I've often seen that people seem to want to understand the possible mechanisms of psychedelics and then try to tailor their hopes to fit those mechanisms. I can honestly say to them that I don't get the "mechanisms" of psychedelics and I think no one does. This can help them set aside pinning hopes to specific possible mechanisms and instead let them and their parts just find and speak their hearts.]

Patient: Yeah, I mean, obviously the hopeless part, I mean, ideally would want hope, but if not, like what you just said earlier, it would like to at least be soothed. The annoyed part, would like to not have to do its job. So I could just chill. Yeah.

[-- We hear from these parts.]

Therapist: Yeah, and we don't have to come to any decision, you know, sign any permanent contract now. But yeah, one option is that they could agree to maybe try this once and then evaluate from there. And again, I couldn't personally go ahead with this unless they were really in good enough agreement to go ahead with it.

[-- This is the first session, I don't want to rush consent. Rushed consent is not free enough. Parts should have time to change their minds and to explore other fears and questions.]

Patient: So would you be there?

[-- This gets back to the legitimate concern of parts of her of being alone in a purely medical IV ketamine clinic. I think it also gets to the connection that she and I and her parts and I have formed.]

Therapist: Right. Yeah, so I would be there. You would be there. Probably all these parts of you would be there. And the medicine would be there.

[-- I validate that I will be there and with her. And I suggest expanding the relational frame to include her parts, her as Self, all their relationships and collaborations, and the medicine itself. Including the medicine can increase a feeling of trust with the medicine, which is so important to prep work, and can open doors to far richer collaboration with the medicine.]

Patient: Yeah, I mean, I think I can agree to at least once to see how it goes. Does it usually help after just one time?

[-- Free consent is forming. But also some concern and wanting information about what she might expect.]

Therapist: Honestly, yeah, from what I've seen. And the research goes along with this too. It can help for a fairly short time.

[-- Providing some clear expertise.]

Patient: Um.

Therapist: But I think, again, far be it for me to say, but I think ketamine can kind of specialize a bit in giving us options on how to see things. So you might wind up with more of a menu of options on how to look at things, like maybe hopelessness could be an option, but maybe you'd see you have some other options. And the protective move could be an option, but you might have more of a freedom to, that part of you might have more of a freedom to say, "Okay, you know, maybe there are some other options." I think that that can really kind of stick. But I think the sort of automatic wellbeing, that's maybe biochemical in some way, that can be pretty short lived.

[-- Again, I hate to speak for psychedelics, but giving her and her parts some psychoeducation on possible outcomes.]

Patient: Mhm, mhm. So it can be repeated? And we can also be working on the changes that you're talking about?

[-- She clarifies our therapeutic relationship and contract.]

Therapist: Yeah, yeah.

[-- I agree that I'm on board with that therapeutic relationship and contract.]

Patient: One ketamine session, that sounds fair.

Therapist: Okay. But what about the fears of going crazy?

[-- I've been holding the part of her in my mind that had that fear of going crazy, and I think their fear hasn't been fully dialogued on, so I advocate for that part and bring it up.]

Patient: Well, you know, I just never really experimented with any quote-unquote drugs besides alcohol. And, you know, the thought of losing control in some way is, you know, anxiety provoking, I guess.

Therapist: Mm, yeah.

Patient: If it's not going well, I have to wait for how long before it feels more normal again?

[-- A part, maybe that same part, asking for some understanding about worst case scenario for just the session, as we already came to some clarity about fears of HPPD.]

Therapist: Right. Just to cover a good range, maybe 1 to 3 hours.

[-- Providing some expertise.]

Patient: Mhm, um.

Therapist: And, you know, I think it can also be really helpful that, if things do get weird and do get challenging, my sense is that that can be partially what's helpful. It's maybe like you kind of throw the cards in the air and then they can be rearranged in ways that you might not have been able to get to before. But with some of those challenging experiences, I think one thing that can be really important is to just, as best you can, stay with whatever comes up and, and breathe with it. That would be part of the prep work.

[-- Providing some psychoeducation about challenging times in medicine sessions and their possible value and, because consent seems to be forming, starting to move forward in the prep work into some flight instructions on "being with, breathing with."]

Patient: Mhm.

Therapist: Sometimes, we might find that some of the most challenging things wind up being some of the most helpful things.

Patient: That's for sure.

Therapist: Being present with things, and breathing into them or sharing your breath with them, that's something that, if we're going to do this, would be really important that we practice in our sessions and you start practicing in your daily life.

Patient: Uhm.

Therapist: ...before any kind of ketamine session so that it becomes almost maybe a bit of a habit, or you see some value in it before you even go into the ketamine session.

Patient: I can for sure try. Meditation has always been hard for me.

Therapist: Yeah, and it is a kind of meditation, but you don't have to sit still.

Patient: Mhm.

Therapist: You don't have to set a timer.

[-- As discussed earlier, very often patients take "being with, breathing with" as a meditation exercise, very understandably. I think that is a legitimate frame on "being with, breathing with," but again, "meditation" has also become a very crowded and complex word in our culture, so I like to distance from that frame and make this more simple, more everyday.]

Patient: Mhm.

Therapist: It's just anything that's going on in your life — Have you done any DBT?

Patient: I mean, I was in partial once and I did.

Therapist: Yeah, yeah, there are a lot of kind-of DBT programs out there. Did you come across the term radical acceptance?

Patient: Yes.

Therapist: I sometimes like half jokingly talk about this as just radical acknowledgement.

Patient: Mm hmm.

Therapist: Then just acknowledge whatever and then maybe share your breath with it. Or you can breathe into it. You can do that while you're washing the dishes. You can do that if you get upset about something with your kids. Or, even if in your daily life you start seeing some of that hopelessness poking through. Can you maybe just acknowledge it and share your breath with it? Or that protective move comes in. You can just acknowledge it and share your breath with it. Even just half a breath, maybe three breaths.

Patient: Mhm, yeah.

Therapist: And that can really help a lot with what a lot of times people talk about as bad trips. Because I think a lot of what goes on in what people talk about as bad trips is like when parts of themselves did not agree to go into something maybe as intense and as weird as a ketamine session, and they don't want to be there. Understandably, they didn't sign up for it, right? And then they may be angry and scared and they want to get out.

[-- Returning to the fears of that part about going crazy and tying the prep work we are doing into those fears.]

Patient: Um.

Therapist: And when things get weird, they want to — they want out. They want it to stop. They want to get away from it. But, you know, if your whole self is on board even in this kind of experimental frame, you know, maybe try it once. And your whole self has agreed to, you know, acknowledge what comes up and maybe just breathe with it, then it doesn't maybe feel as victimizing.

[-- Validating the agency of the parts, if that is how they freely decide they want to use their agency.]

Patient: Mhm, oh.

Therapist: All right, we can keep talking about all this. There's no contract on the table right now.

Patient: Okay, thank you.

Therapist: So maybe talk with your psychiatrist more about any medical fears so those parts of you really feel informed about what's going on. And maybe try just being with and breathing with things in your life here and there, but especially try it a bit when you're feeling upset.

Patient: Okay.

That's it for this example prep session. We'll now shift to exploring more topics in prep work.

ADDING IFS TO PAP PREP WORK GENERALLY

There are many topics of general PAP prep work that aren't discussed in this book because we are just focusing on some contributions of IFS to PAP work. But there is a pretty easy and effective way to add IFS to just about any general PAP prep work. As mentioned previously, we can simply add on, "… and all parts of you?" to the discussions of general PAP prep work. This could be very helpful in dialogue on many PAP preparation questions and topics, such as discussing eyeshades, food, any involvement of family or friends, setting up the room or space for the medicine session, and music.

I'd like to look at two examples of adding this great IFS question to two important general prep work topics. We'll look at the relational, "in the room" work of asking our patient about any questions or reactions they or their parts might have towards us as the therapist. And we'll look at discussing with our patient and their parts any reactions or concerns they might have about safety with us as therapist, particularly if there are important differences in social roles between us as therapist and our patient.

Prep work around parts' reactions towards the therapist

Just asking, just inviting our patient to share reactions towards us as therapist can be a relational healing act itself. It communicates a lot. There is an implicit respect in such a question, that we value hearing from our patient and from all of their parts.

We could ask something like, "I think it might be helpful as part of this prep work if we can spend some time discussing any reactions you or any parts of you might have towards me. Would you like to do that?"

Assuming our patient does want to do that, we could suggest, "Maybe just check with yourself if you or any parts of you have any reactions about me, or questions about me that might be helpful to bring up."

Being able to talk about a relationship directly might be a rare or new experience for our patient, another possible "do over" or corrective emotional experience. For example. our patient or their parts might want to share positive things about us or the therapy process. This can be very important. Being able to talk about even positive things can be an important type of relational sharing that our patient may have been denied or shamed about in important past relationships. Those past relational experiences could have caused parts carrying warmth and closeness to need to be exiled.

By this kind of asking, we are implicitly putting on the table that down the road we are willing to communicate openly about reactions to us and the therapy process. Having such pathways of communication opened early in prep work can allow for important safety and agency for our patient and all their parts, that they might be able to talk about the relationship with us and not have to be alone or exiled. This can, of course, also be crucial in the upcoming medicine session and the whole therapy.

Preparation work around safety in unequal social roles between therapist and patient

Again, so much prep work is about trust, about our patient being and feeling safe. And this is very unfortunately a very messed up world in many ways, with some people far less safe and valued than others because of nothing but social roles. Given these realities, some dialogue on social roles, all parts welcome, can be simply necessary for good clinical practice.

If there are power inequalities in the societal roles between therapist and patient, especially if the patient is from a more socially oppressed group than the therapist, then that becomes a crucial aspect of explicit relational preparatory work. This is, of course, usually about differences in race, sex, class, gender identity, and sexual orientation.

This type of prep work is going to be particularly important when the therapist is white or male because — white guy here — let's face it, white and male have been and are the social roles that have been the most dangerous to the most people.

It can also be important to do this relational prep work if we as therapist are a white man and our patient is a white man. White male patients also often carry traumas and fears of other white men.

So for me, as a white, straight man, especially if my patient is female, Black, brown, or queer, if it hasn't come up already, I explicitly ask about reactions to me around my social roles. I might ask something like, "It's very important that you and all your parts are and feel safe enough in the medicine session, including with me. For part of that, I'm wondering if you or any parts of you have reactions or concerns or questions about doing the medicine session with me as a white, straight man. Would you like to check in with yourself and all your parts about that?"

Once again, this is important in any therapy, but since we're adding the power of psychedelics into the mix, this relational work in terms of social roles is all the more important before any medicine session. Dr. Robert Strayhan, a Black psychiatrist active in PAP and someone I was fortunate enough to study with, discussed an example vignette with a group of trainees: A Black patient is in a psychedelic session with a white therapist. The patient becomes all the more psychologically sensitive and vulnerable thanks to the psychedelic medicine and at the same time is physically stuck alone in a room with the therapist for many hours. What is then coming up in the session for this Black patient might not just be what brought them into therapy (such as depression, anxiety, or PTSD) but also the added levels of societal and cultural vulnerability and trauma. This situation could get much harder for the patient if the white therapist does or says oppressive or culturally insensitive things. And all this can then be far harder for the patient if they are uncertain whether they can talk with the therapist about what is going on, about what the therapist is doing and how it is affecting them.[145]

So in prep work, having some good dialogue about social roles, and inviting all parts of our patient into that dialogue, can help such situations immensely. It won't preclude therapists from socially favored groups from being unaware and making missteps. But it can help patients from socially oppressed groups and their parts feel safer that they maybe don't have to be exiled from the therapy relationship and can talk with the therapist about what has happened and what's going on with them.

This discussion can again bring up important psychological work that some of us therapists can do for both increasing our effectiveness as clinicians and for our own healing. Richard Schwartz has done great work in focusing the wisdom of IFS on

---

[145] Robert Strayhan, personal communication, 2021.

the intrapsychic levels of racism and other oppressions. I highly recommend his article "Working with our Internalized Racism."[146]

Even with such good preparatory dialogue on unequal social roles and safety, there might not be enough safety for a patient to do a medicine session with a particular therapist. It can then be necessary to discuss with our patient referring out to or bringing in as a co-therapist a therapist with a similar background to our patient. I took a class from MaryEllen Baker, a Native counselor and healer of the Lac Courte Oreilles Ojibwe people, on doing psychotherapy with Native patients. As I remember it, she said that the history of Native genocide, abuse, and deprivation, and the present racism, was so horrible that the necessary trust for therapy probably could not be established between a white therapist and a Native patient. She therefore recommended, if possible, for white therapists to try to refer Native patients to a Native therapist. But sometimes it is hard to find such referrals in part exactly because of systemic racism. Hopefully, this situation will improve, and rapidly.[147]

Even if a patient declines such an offer to refer out to or include a co-therapist with a similar background to theirs, the offer can possibly lead to our patient and their parts feeling safer with the therapist, and to our patient and their parts feeling more able to talk about the therapy relationship directly including any issues around social roles.

DOING PREPARATION WORK BEFORE EACH MEDICINE SESSION

Even if our patient is quite experienced with psychedelics, it's important that we still do prep work with them, including checking with their parts about consent for the possible upcoming medicine session. This might seem counterintuitive, that the horse has already left the barn, that it's unnecessary or too late for such questions or dialogues. But the prep work and dialogues with

---

[146] Richard Schwartz, "Working With Internalized Racism" (Psychotherapy Networker, October 2020), https://www.psychotherapynetworker.org/article/working-internalized-racism/.
[147] MaryEllen Baker, "Therapy with Native clients class," American Indian Center of Chicago, 2014

parts around consent and collaboration for an upcoming medicine session can be just as helpful and necessary for patients very experienced with psychedelics as they are for someone preparing for their first medicine session.

Along these lines, it's important to do this same basic preparation work, especially checking with all parts for consent and collaboration, before each medicine session. Parts deserve such dialogue and respect, and doing prep work before each medicine session can make the medicine sessions safer and more effective.

This might get quite hard to schedule if people are doing multiple ketamine sessions over a short period of time like in many protocols of ketamine assisted psychotherapy. The good news is that the check-in with parts for subsequent medicine sessions might be quite brief and simple, but it's still important. Or it might open up into longer and very important dialogues about consent and collaboration.

STRUCTURES OF PREPARATORY SESSIONS

As discussed in the Overview of PAP chapter, we might think of two basic models of PAP: a more short-term, "bubble model" and a more open ended "long form model." Structuring prep work is going to be different between the two.

In bubble work, it can be a good idea to think about at least three preparatory sessions. The first preparatory session might be mostly an intake type of session, but might also get into some important prep work. We saw some of this in the example prep session with Claire. The second session might involve a full IFS healing session. And by the third prep session, we might be finalizing if there is consent or not from all parts to do the medicine session.

In a long form model, or if PAP is being introduced to an already established therapy relationship, then it might still be good to think about at least three prep sessions. Again, it can be good for our patient and their parts to have plenty of time to mull over the important and maybe novel questions and considerations that a possible medicine session can bring up. Those sessions might not be just on prep work. Prep work might become one of several important topics in the ongoing therapy.

In an ongoing therapy, if free and good enough consent for a medicine session is not present after a few prep sessions, but our patient is still interested in psychedelic work, then prep work might become something of an ongoing topic with our patient and their parts.

When this sort of situation has come up in my practice, I've been able to very honestly tell my patients that I think we are doing psychedelic work. I explain that I see IFS work as fully psychedelic, and that just seriously discussing the topic of a possible medicine session often seems to bring awareness of parts who might otherwise not have become part of the therapy. Through the prep work, our patient's psyche is manifesting just fine.

This ongoing work on prep work might not lead to a medicine session for weeks or months, or it might never lead to a medicine session.

I've also shared with patients in these situations that I see standard IFS as even having some advantages over medicine sessions in that it can be less rushed, more everyday, and not get into distortions that can happen when the volume is at 11 with psychedelics, as we discussed in Chapter 4.

In a bubble model therapy, if true, good enough consent for a medicine session hasn't happened after a few sessions, then it would be important to be able to offer standard therapy oneself or to make referrals for standard therapy.

FINALIZING THE AGREEMENT TO DO THE MEDICINE SESSION

If the dialogues around collaboration and consent for the medicine session are working out nicely, our patient might tell us that their parts seem satisfied, heard, and are quiet. Or the responses from our patient's parts might just start naturally slowing down. We as therapist and our patient might get a sense that we're done with this piece of work.

It's important then that we double check. We might ask something like, "Are there any other parts of you, anything else coming up in you, that might have questions or concerns or just want to be heard and seen about this possible upcoming medicine session?" If our patient isn't sure, we can ask them to just take a little time and share their breath with their body, their emotions, their thoughts, images, intuition, and see if anything comes up.

If the dialogues legitimately seem to be done, then it's important to explicitly finalize the agreement with parts to do the upcoming medicine session. We might ask something like, "Okay, so are you and your whole self, all parts of yourself, on board with this upcoming medicine session?" If our patient checks and can say "Yes" to that then we can let them know something like, "Okay, great. And just so you know, if you or any parts of you have further questions or concerns or asks or whatever about any of this, we can talk about that. Those dialogues can make this process better."

At that point, I think we can consider that our patient and all their parts have made good enough, free, and informed consent for the medicine session.

Optimally, I like to have one final preparation session the day before the medicine session. Nowadays, preparation sessions might be done remotely via video. But for the final prep session, if possible, I think it can be important to do it in person and to do it where the medicine session will happen.

During that session, at some point we can ask our patient again if they have any concerns, worries, or asks about the medicine session. We can ask them to check with their parts. We can particularly ask them if they and all their parts feel safe there with us as therapist and in the space of the medicine session, or if anything would help them be and feel safer.

In this final preparation session, if my patient and all their parts are still in consent to do the medicine session, I might offer to my patient that, if they'd like, they could imaginally "plant" their intention, ask, or prayer for the medicine session in the ground near where they will be for the medicine session. This can work even if their "intention" is to have no intention, no expectations; to be open to what happens, to be open to what they need.

I might then ask them to imaginally cover the "seed" of their intention with some warm, moist soil, and then to let it be. For about two weeks. Poking at a seed or digging it up to see how it's doing, in the medicine session and soon after, might not help it grow!

I let them know that I personally consider that once they've decided to do the medicine session and made their intention or ask or prayer, that the medicine session has begun. I ask them to pay particular attention to any dreams they might have that night or anything else that seems notable before we meet again the next day for the medicine session.

I like to start the medicine session early the next day, if possible. That can make for more continuity with the final prep session from the day before and less "day residue" going into the medicine session.

And then, some final preparation work can happen early in the medicine session, before taking the medicine. We might ask our patient to take some full, rich breaths, to feel their breaths all through their body. I might ask them to find some pleasure in their breaths, whatever those pleasures might be, in their body, mind, emotion, imagination, whatever. Partially, this is a relaxation exercise. But this is also a "being with," to help our patient become more present in their whole body and their whole complex self, implicitly or explicitly inviting all parts to be present and in relationship with them.

Then we might ask our patient to get up and move around some, to move their body. To move their joints, to feel their joints as they move, to move them however they might want to. To just explore their joints, muscles, skin; whatever they notice and find of their body as they move.

When that's done, they can sit down again.

This can all be quite nice and enjoyable, and again, it can also help our patient be more richly aware of their body and of their whole complex self. Again, psyche and soma, sides of one coin.

Then we can bring the medicine out. And riffing on Robert Falconer's great observation that "helpers" are often so respectful that they won't even enter to help unless they are asked, we could offer an option to our patient that whatever parts of them are fully or partially open to the medicine's help, or are not open to help from the medicine, that our patient and those parts could reflect on that now. And then our patient and their parts could explicitly welcome the medicine in to help them, to whatever extent they want to. Into their body, their mind, their emotions, their heart, their imagination, their memory; wherever it needs to go to help them.

At this point, I would consider that our patient is very much "a well-prepared person."

Then we can suggest, if they are in agreement, that they start with the medicine.

CHAPTER SIX

MEDICINE SESSIONS

And if you go
No one may follow
That path is for
Your steps alone

— Robert Hunter, "Ripple"[148]

This chapter will discuss some of the powerful contributions that IFS can make to medicine session work. As part of this, we will have the honor of following some very rich case material, including from the work of Michael and Annie Mithoefer, Richard Schwartz, Bill Richards, Robert Grant, and Rick Doblin. Notably, not all of this work was based in IFS at all, for the patient or for the therapist. But I think we will see that it still tracks amazingly well with IFS. This can again argue for the natural overlap of IFS and psychedelics.

This chapter will be in two sections, the first on low to medium dose medicine sessions and the second on high dose medicine sessions. Especially in the section on low to medium dose sessions we will look at psychotherapy in medicine sessions. Psychotherapy in medicine sessions can be controversial, both for excellent reasons and for not so good or even poor reasons. We will discuss these controversies and try to either learn from them or address them.

As part of our discussion of therapy in medicine sessions, we will closely follow and discuss a session of IFS therapy in a ketamine assisted psychotherapy that Richard Schwartz presented

---

[148] "Ripple," Robert Hunter, Jerry Garcia. Ice Nine Publishing Inc., November, 1970.

at the Psychedelic Science 2023 conference. We are very fortunate to have video available of the session.

Then in the second section of this chapter, on high dose medicine sessions, we will discuss how IFS can very helpfully inform "companioning" of our patient in the medicine session. We might say that companioning is when we as therapist are present with our patient, respecting and trusting them and any parts involved, and trusting the medicine. At many points in a high dose medicine session, that is about all we might be able to do. And I think we will find it is plenty and even decisive.

We will discuss "hyperblending," which is when, in the power of a medicine session, parts blend with our patient with a great intensity, a psychedelic intensity. This can be a great challenge for all involved, and it can be a great healing opportunity if worked with well, including in integration work.

We'll then have some discussion of what I'm calling here multiple Selves in the room in medicine sessions. This will get into some possible psychospiritual aspects of medicine sessions, which we also discussed in the Preparation Work chapter.

Then we will have the honor of following a very extensive case example of several weeks of a high dose MDMA assisted psychotherapy led by Michael and Annie Mithoefer.

And the last part of this chapter will be a discussion of working with difficult patches in medicine sessions. Difficult patches of a medicine session can often be crucial to some of the most important healing that happens in medicine sessions. And sometimes they seem to "hand off" some of the crucial healing work to the integration work.

Having made the distinction between low to medium dose and high dose medicine sessions, I want to clarify that I think it's important not to overestimate the differences between the two. Topics on low to moderate dose sessions might apply very importantly to high dose medicine sessions and vice versa.

Sometimes, a distinction has been made that low dose medicine sessions are of "personal" psychological work and high dose sessions are of "transpersonal" or "archetypal" work. I personally find that big, qualitative distinctions between low and high dose sessions, or between "personal" and "transpersonal" medicine sessions, confuse more than they illuminate. Instead, I think it can be important to be open to and aware of how any medicine session, of whatever dose, can be what might be called "personal" or "transpersonal," and often right at the same time. This can very much apply to being sensitive to how the sunset period of a medicine session or even the days following a medicine session can be profoundly "archetypal" or "transpersonal."

Medicine sessions are well described as trips.

Hopefully, as we set out on the trip, we and our patient are well prepared. We've done our due diligence, which is all we can do.

Then, we are in it, patient and therapist. Ups, downs, zigs, zags. Relationships. Discoveries. Neighborhoods. Byways. Ecosystems. Boredoms. Drudgeries, delights, dead ends. Back tracking. Getting stuck in a ditch. Meeting new friends. Getting a hand. Finding our own strengths, wisdoms, intelligences.

Being a *flaneur*. Being an agent. Making choices. Taking stands. Taking risks. Asking for help. Saying no. Exercising our free creativity.

Choosing to open to help. Being guided. Surrendering in trust. Being a patient.

Ultimately, growth, renewal, perspectives and relationships broadened. Maybe to put it mildly.

When we're done, our patient and we as therapist have separately and together walked a path that was ours alone, as the great Robert Hunter put it in the opening quote of this chapter.

LIGHT TOUCH AND SIMPLICITY IN **IFS** WORK IN MEDICINE SESSIONS

A lot can go on in a medicine session (*ahem*). As we discussed in Peter Webster's work on his salience hypothesis of psychedelics, it might be all the "same ole" stuff, but that stuff can become *way more SALIENT*.

Protectors might unblend and rest deeply, more than they have in standard IFS, maybe more than they ever have in our patient's life. This can help exiles then be far more salient and give our patient and their exiles unusually good opportunities to be together, with all the good that can come from that.

Our patient might be greatly there as Self. Our patient might find their agency far more freely and clearly than usual. They might have startlingly clear access to their compassion, to their connectedness, to their courage, to their creativity. They might be quite richly present with themselves, with their parts, with the people of their lives, with the world. They might be playful, they might be patient.

Again, maybe all this is nothing truly new. It might just be that because the "volume" is so much higher and clearer that it can feel extremely novel.

And louder can be qualitatively different. Healing can happen seemingly instantaneously, spontaneously. Parts, both exiles and protectors, can heal entirely with no seeming process happening. Or parts can seemingly quite naturally do "the steps" of healing, of being found, witnessed in caring relationship, helped in "do overs," updated, retrieved, unburdened, and claiming new roles or qualities. This can all bring great joy, great wisdom, as the power and qualities of the unburdened parts are now free in our patient and their life. Even "just" the power to rest, to have the quality of some real peace for maybe the first time in years, maybe the first time in any memory.

But of course, it's not always so simply nice. By the same token of "amplified salience," in medicine sessions protectors and exiles can also manifest *very* strongly, fully burdened. And protectors and exiles, of course, can be carrying *a lot*.

In the intensity of a medicine session they can hyperblend with our patient. Nowhere for our patient to hide from the parts and the hard, heavy burdens that they have been carrying alone for many years. This can, ultimately, be a very powerful form of witnessing and it can *eventually* become part of great healing. But it can be truly harrowing for a time, for our patient and for us as therapist. For what can seem like eternity, literally.

This can be a lot to be with, to breathe with, to be in relationship with — at least as best we can, both patient and therapist.

And not just all this "therapy" stuff, but a lot more can be going on in medicine sessions. Verbal and cognitive abilities coming and going, slowing down and speeding up. Bodies disappearing. Bodies suffering: tense, cold, hot, nauseous, gurgling, gaseous. Sounds forming. Movements needing to happen. Doing them. They feel good. Bodies feeling great: pain disappearing, pleasure suffusing. Straight up spiritual, religious, mystical experiences. Great, deep confusion. Dancing. Crying, for a long time.

And plenty can go on that doesn't fit into any of these boxes or any known box that our patient or we as therapist might have.

Given *all this*, simplicity can be an important part of any intervention we might offer in a medicine session. We are in a delicate, fecund ecosystem. And simplicity can be hard. It is often the mark of masters, as we will see in the case material to follow. But we are very lucky that IFS has something truly great to offer us here as therapists: therapist unblending. We don't need to "make" ourselves simple. We can unblend to ourselves as Self. That will likely be fully simple enough.

If we try to make ourselves simple, that is probably driven by a wonderful, eager to help part of ourselves. But that is a child trying to help possibly in an extreme, simplistic way. Some great news is that with that part there, right then we have an immediate path to being there as Self: if we're blended with a part or a part is trying to blend with us, asking that part to unblend from us could bring us right there to Self. Again, parts aren't obstacles to the path, parts are part of the path.

So, stated or unstated, therapist unblending – us being there as Self – is central to all we will discuss in this Medicine Session chapter.

Let's now turn to low to medium dose medicine sessions and a discussion of doing psychotherapy in medicine sessions.

LOW TO MODERATE DOSE MEDICINE SESSIONS

Psychotherapy in medicine sessions

I am shocked that this has become controversial, but unfortunately it needs saying: psychotherapy is crucial to PAP — to, as the name says, psychedelic assisted *psychotherapy*; including in medicine sessions.

Having said that, there are important nuances to therapy in medicine sessions: It's very important to be sensitive to considerations of dose and timing in the "arc" of a medicine session. The therapy in a medicine session is very probably best kept brief. Such therapy is best based in preparation work. The therapy might be of the art of simplicity, of less is more. And yes, therapist unblending is going to be key here in our discussion of therapy in medicine sessions.

Because there are complex considerations around therapy in medicine sessions, the goal here will be neither to automatically do therapy in medicine sessions nor to automatically not do therapy in medicine sessions.

We're back to good clinical judgment, and once again, to unblending. IFS can be extremely helpful here in terms of good clinical judgment: if we as therapist have a set agenda for or against therapy at any given moment in a medicine session, we are probably blended with a burdened part of ourselves. If we can unblend to Self, we can then enter into present relationship with our patient and their parts more richly, more humbly, and with more confidence. Then, we can naturally co-create with our patient, their parts, and the medicine where things go next, whether it's IFS psychotherapy of some sort, to some extent, or not.

It seems that often IFS work happens in medicine sessions whether IFS is being practiced in the PAP or not. This has been repeatedly astounding and uncanny to me. We will see this in a good bit of the case material to follow. I would posit that if IFS-type work is going to happen in medicine sessions anyway, then we best get good at it. This could very much include IFS helping us as therapist get out of the way in a more informed, skillful way, and letting our patient, their parts, and the medicine cook. As well, this could include some IFS therapy as part of a medicine session.

Because there are so many criticisms and attacks on therapy in medicine sessions in the field these days, we should address them or learn from them. We've already addressed one poor criticism of psychotherapy in PAP, in the policy discussion in the Overview of PAP chapter. That was in discussing possible business models seeking to limit or eliminate psychotherapy in PAP to minimize therapist labor costs and maximize return on investment for the owners and investors of psychedelic businesses. Again, as we discussed, these might be attempts to "Uber-ize" Western mental health treatment, to disrupt an "industry" so that labor is provided by mostly unprotected, undertrained, and low paid gig workers.

Such goals would obviously be very poor arguments against therapy in medicine sessions or in PAP more broadly.

There might also be reticence or opposition to therapy in medicine sessions from unwitting and unhelpful carryovers to general PAP practice from psychedelic randomized control trial research models. In the scientific model of a randomized control drug trial, and to the FDA and similar worldwide drug regulating agencies, adding therapy to drug research is mostly a confound nightmare. They simply want safety and efficacy data on a drug. So in such scientific and regulatory models, therapy needs to be minimized as much as possible. This again does not make for a great argument against therapy in general practice PAP.

Having said that, these psychedelic randomized control trials have produced very impressive results. This could tempt us into thinking we are done developing Western PAP, that we can just keep doing the RCT models in general practice. But even if these randomized control trial models are truly good models for PAP, as they appear to be, that doesn't mean they are the best models. And worse, as we've seen in important work like Suresh Muthukumaraswamy's, there are very likely huge placebo and expectancy responses at play in the current randomized control trial research that favor psychedelics. Crucially, such placebo and expectancy effects will likely not be active in general practice PAP to help boost the outcomes for our patients.[149] [150]

So again, a main assumption and impetus of this book is that in order to continue to help our patients well, in general practice, psychedelic assisted psychotherapy we will most likely need more and better therapy, more and better cultures of psychedelia, than has been available in the randomized control trials.

But there is an excellent critique of psychotherapy in medicine sessions that we will focus on here. This is from Raquel Bennett, a pioneer, practitioner, great advocate, and teacher of ketamine assisted psychotherapy. We will attempt to learn from her wisdom, experience, and great critical thinking.

Bennett warned in a class that I took from her that trying to do *too much* psychotherapy in a medicine session can get problematic fast.[151] Doing too much psychotherapy in a medicine session

---

[149] Muthukumaraswamy, Suresh D., et al. "Blinding and Expectancy Confounds in Psychedelic Randomized Controlled Trials." Expert Review of Clinical Pharmacology 14, no. 9 (2021): 1133–52.

[150] Haridy, Rich. "The Problem at the Heart of Modern Psychedelic Clinical Research." New Atlas. June 13, 2021.

[151] Raquel Bennett, "Ketamine assisted psychotherapy class," 2021.

can at best be uncomfortable for our patients and can make the medicine session a mess for our patient, at least for a while. In extreme cases, it can even get dangerous and traumatizing, for instance if a therapist keeps pushing therapy in the medicine session even against the turmoil it is causing in a patient.

Iatrogenic harm is a very real possibility in any treatment relationship, and once again, such dangers of harm in psychotherapy can be amped up by the intensity of psychedelics.

Bennett warned that what often seems to be at play in problematic attempts to do psychotherapy in medicine sessions is that therapists try to push for a big healing or a big breakthrough. My understanding is that Bennett is not arguing against all therapy in medicine sessions, but that she is warning against too much therapeutic ambition in therapy in medicine sessions.

I believe Bennett works from mostly a relational psychoanalytic perspective, and within that frame she seems to be recommending something like a supportive therapy stance in ketamine sessions. We might think about a supportive therapeutic stance as what we've briefly discussed as "companioning." (We'll discuss IFS companioning in more detail in the high dose medicine session section later in this chapter.)

Bennett taught in her class that a supportive, low ambition, less-is-more type of therapeutic stance in ketamine sessions seems to spontaneously lead to a sort of "consolidating of previous therapy."[152] That can be a great benefit of a medicine session.

I have seen Bennett's recommendations of a supportive therapeutic stance borne out in my practice, that companioning patients in an IFS informed way in ketamine sessions does seem to often lead to a sort of spontaneous, natural consolidating of previous therapy. Sometimes, I even wonder if the oft repeated experience of a medicine session being "better than five years of therapy" is at least partially that the last five years of therapy might have become consolidated in the medicine session.

---

[152] ibid.

I have also seen it that a supportive stance or companioning in medicine sessions can lead naturally to very helpful parts detecting. Companioning patients in medicine sessions can seem to help previously unknown parts come to the forefront and be seen, known, and named maybe for the first time, at least clearly. Then actually helping those parts and the parts who they interact with might mostly happen in the integration work and the regular therapy. I'm convinced that some parts who have come to the forefront in medicine sessions might never have come to awareness in just regular therapy.

I don't think any of these very good outcomes from a companioning or a supportive therapy stance in medicine sessions is a diminishment of the value of therapy in PAP. Companioning and supportive therapy are not "session monitoring." They *are* relational therapy, and they are part of a larger psychedelic assisted psychotherapy.

Returning to Bennett's warning about overly strong therapeutic ambition, in an IFS frame we might say that when we as therapist have overly strong therapeutic ambition, we are probably then blended with a part of us in an extreme role, maybe one of "therapizing." So again, therapist blending and unblending is going to be crucial here.

I've learned the hard way that Bennett is right in her warning about overly strong therapeutic ambition in medicine sessions. Even after taking her class, I fell into this problem myself. The first time I tried doing regular IFS in a low to moderate dose ketamine session, I was so excited — "What a healing opportunity!!" — that it went badly. No one was hurt, it just got painfully confusing for my patient for a period of time. Seeing his pained face and demeanor, I stepped back from my agenda, at least enough to shut my mouth more. I tried, but I just couldn't adequately unblend from my wonderful, excited parts during that session. So I chose a "plan B" to just talk little. The session wound up going fine as a sort of companioning medicine session.

When my patient and I debriefed that session in the following integration session, he reported finding the medicine session very useful. I asked him about the period of confusion, and he remembered it, but he said he wasn't particularly bothered by it. I briefly explained what had happened with me and my excitement. I apologized that I had made that period difficult for him. He accepted that and appreciated me doing that work myself and sharing it with him directly. And we moved on.

Mistakes happen. Hopefully, they're not too egregious and we can repair. Our mistakes can even be crucial healing opportunities for our patients. If we can acknowledge our mistake directly and apologize, this can be a powerful corrective emotional experience, an *in vivo* "do over." In important relationships, many people have been unrightfully denied such acknowledgement of mistakes and apology, over and over and over. Also, our patient might then see that we're ordinary humans like they are and come to be more compassionate and accepting of themself and others. As well, maybe in the temporary disruption with us, they find resources within themself or their lives that they didn't know they had.

After this session, for a while before each medicine session I would take maybe five to ten minutes of personal time to try to relate with and ultimately unblend from my therapeutically excited parts.

I now just check in with those parts briefly before and during medicine sessions. Through my own work, very much including working with them in my IFS consultation and therapy, most of those parts are now healed parts — Selves themselves. They are not burdened with extreme roles, beliefs, or emotions. They don't try to blend with me in medicine sessions. They're now great friends and helpers. They now quietly help me to be simply present with my patients and whatever is going on with them in medicine sessions.

Having said that, I still get blended with "therapist parts" sometimes. Like a lot of therapists, I seem to have a lot of them! But they more readily unblend from me in medicine sessions these days and I continue to offer them, and therefore myself, healing. These parts wouldn't be trying to do extreme roles without real reasons, and I respect them.

I am very grateful to Bennett for her excellent criticisms of therapy in medicine sessions and they inform this whole chapter. I think the bottom line that we can take from her critique is that therapist unblending and helping our "therapist parts" are crucial to therapy in medicine sessions.

Another legitimate criticism of doing therapy in medicine sessions is that most kinds of therapy just don't seem to fit in medicine sessions. For instance, I very much like and use some CBT in my regular psychotherapy practice (we could think of "cognitive distortions" as the utterances of parts in extreme roles). But I can't imagine trying to do much, if any CBT in a medicine session! I just don't think it's experiential, relational, and flexible enough to be a good match. It would be, as far as I can see, a "round hole, square peg" situation. Similarly, I can't imagine trying to implement a DBT skills approach in medicine sessions, except maybe some DBT mindfulness.

However, many somatic based therapies seem to fit quite well with medicine sessions. They are flexible and experiential enough, and optimally relational enough, to partner very well with much of what comes up in a medicine session. But as mentioned in the first chapter, somatic schools of therapy often need an add on to work with the multifaceted, non-somatic manifestations of the psyche and the medicine session. That "add on" could very fruitfully be IFS. Again, IFS can be deeply somatic and in a fully relational way.

So I think it's a pretty good rule and criticism that most existing psychotherapies just don't fit in with psychedelic medicine sessions. But IFS therapy seems to be an exception that proves the rule.

Again, I think we'll see in the case material of this chapter that the fit between PAP and IFS is so natural that something very much like an IFS healing process seems to happen quite commonly and naturally in medicine sessions, whether or not the therapist or patient have a background or interest in IFS.

Let's now get very concrete in looking at how IFS therapy in medicine sessions can work by looking at a session of IFS therapy in a low dose ketamine session. This is from the work of Richard Schwartz.

Example session of therapy in a low dose ketamine session

Richard Schwartz presented excerpts of this session at MAPS' Psychedelic Science 2023 conference, so video of the session is available online, making it a very helpful resource. I am very thankful to the participants in the video for so richly helping therapists get better at helping people.

We will follow a transcript of the session. And video of the session is available on the website for the Psychedelic Science 2023 conference. The video is not free to watch, but MAPS has generously made videos of the conference presentations available on a "pay what you can" model that supports the crucial and relevant mission of MAPS' work. I highly recommend watching the video. There is so much in the tone and demeanor of all involved that is quite important, powerful, and beautiful.

Here is a link to the video: https://tinyurl.com/IFSPAPsesh

This session was done during a short-term residential IFS KAP retreat for couples.

I'll call the participant here "Ann." In her prep work before the session, Ann had identified four parts of herself who she might want to work with in her session.

She had received a 5 mg intramuscular (IM) injection of ketamine shortly before the therapy session. This dose was calculated specifically for therapy during the medicine session, a low dose that would hopefully put her squarely "in the neighborhood" of ketamine while also keeping her present and her verbal ability pretty good. From my sense of the session, this dosing seemed to have been quite optimal for psychotherapy during the medicine session.

Again, this was a couples retreat. Often, couples can get stuck in self-reinforcing dynamics of just each other's protector parts relating with one another and exiled parts getting further and further alone. This, of course, can become badly frustrating and unsatisfying. As is common in IFS couples work, in this session both members of the couple were present together for the session. Part of the idea with this is that one member of the couple does some IFS work on something relevant to their relationship while the other stays present with them and their process. Then they switch roles. This can help bring far greater awareness to each other of who they are and who their exiles and protectors are, and that can increase the richness of their relationship, getting well beyond just protector battles.

Ann's husband had also received an IM dose of ketamine at the same time as Ann. Video of her husband doing his session was not in Schwartz's presentation. I'll call him "Gerry" here.

It's also important to note that this session was done in a "fish bowl" style where the other participants in the retreat and the other retreat staff were sitting attentively in a circle around the couple and the therapist as they did their therapy. This is a typical style of IFS group work. As we'll discuss in a section to come, having "multiple Selves" in the room can make for deeper work and more healing. So besides the helping power of the regular IFS therapy and the help of ketamine, the help of the Selves of the other retreat participants were also arguably active in this session.

Very notably, this session is 10 minutes. Just 10 minutes. This is focused, simple, deep therapy, not drawn out or complicated or wandering. Good, therapeutic prep work is essential to this therapy being able to be so focused and relatively brief. Like Bennett's warnings, too long is probably way too much for a medicine session!

We'll follow the whole session and then discuss it.

If you are following along on the video from Psychedelic Science 2023, the section we will look at starts at about 14:38 and goes to about 25:00.

Therapist: So we named four maybe? Is there one you want to start with?

Participant: Abandonment.

Therapist: Abandonment. So, that's probably the exile. Before going to the exile, just see if you have any fear about doing any of this in front of the group or doing it in front of Gerry.

Participant: Feels like if I close my eyes it feels good. My belly feels shaky.

Therapist: Yes, just maybe check with your belly.

Participant: Okay.

Therapist: Is that where that abandonment is, or is that a different part?

Participant: Yeah, it feels like that's the abandonment.

Therapist: Okay. Does it feel like we have permission to work with it in this context?

Participant: Yeah.

Therapist: Okay. Alright, so, as you notice it down there, how do you feel toward it?

Participant: I feel soft.

Therapist: So let it know.

Participant: Yeah, feels soft.

Therapist: Yeah. Do you feel open to getting to know it also?

Participant: Umh-hm. Yeah.

Therapist: So maybe just ask it more about itself. How it gets triggered by Gerry. And whatever it wants you to know about itself.

Participant: Hm. [very vulnerable, quiet whisper] It feels very alone.

Therapist: Feels very alone. Yeah.

Participant: [vulnerable, pleading, quiet whisper] It's very alone.

Therapist: Very alone. Yeah. So let it know you get that.

Participant: [sighs]

Therapist: How are you feeling toward it now?

Participant: [whisper] Really sorry.

Therapist: Really sorry for it. So let it know that too.

Participant: [whispers] Sorry. [starts crying]

Therapist: And how is it reacting to your compassion?

Participant: [crying, but stronger] It's starting more energy in my heart.

Therapist: Good.

Participant: Yeah, feels brighter.

Therapist: Feels brighter.

Participant: And, like I have more space in my core.

Therapist: Okay.

Participant: Yeah, feels like I'm more connected now, in my core.

Therapist: Good.

Participant: Yeah. Yeah.

Therapist: And how does that abandonment part feel?

Participant: Connected.

Therapist: Feels connected to you? To you?

Participant: Yeah.

Therapist: That's great. Just ask if it trusts that you care about it.

Participant: It does now. But that feels new.

Therapist: That's new, right?

Participant: Yeah.

Therapist: Okay, good. Okay, ask it to really let you know where it got this abandonment feeling in the past.

Participant: Can you ask that again?

Therapist: Yeah. Ask it to really let you feel and see what happened to make you feel so abandoned in the past.

Participant: [whispering, crying] Yeah. Yeah, I know.

Therapist: You know?

Participant: Yeah.

Therapist: Does it believe you, do you get it all? Or is there more? Just ask it that, if it does agree that you know.

Participant: Okay. [long silence] Yeah, I believe the part. The part believes me.

Therapist: Part believes you?

Participant: Yeah.

Therapist: And just ask if that's everything it wants you to get about it.

Participant: [long silence] Yeah.

Therapist: Okay. So does it feel fully witnessed?

Participant: Yeah.

Therapist: Okay. Are you ready to get it out of there?

Participant: Yeah.

Therapist: Okay. So go into that scene and be with that one, in the way — I'm assuming it's a she, but I could be wrong.

Participant: It is.

Therapist: Okay, in the way she needed somebody.

Participant: Can you say that again?

Therapist: Yeah, go into that scene and be with her in the way she needed somebody.

Participant: Yeah! I'm doing that.

Therapist: And how is she reacting to you being there?

Participant: She's shocked.

Therapist: Yeah, she's shocked to have you there?

Participant: She was always alone.

Therapist: She's always been alone. [pause] Just let her know she's not alone now, and she's not going to be alone anymore.

Participant: [crying] I'm here.

Therapist: You're here, that's right.

Participant: [whispering] I'm picking her up.

Therapist: You're picking her up. Good.

Participant: [whispering very quietly and simply] I know the way out.

Therapist: [leaning in] "I know," what?

Participant: [strong, clear] I know the way out.

Therapist: Good. Yeah. Before we take her out, see if there's anything she needs you to do for her or with her back there? [pause] She might just want to leave, which would be fine.

Participant: She wants to shine light out of her eyes. I don't know what that means.

Therapist: Okay. Can you help her do that, though? Even though you don't know what it means?

Participant: Yeah — I'm holding her and she's just shining light out of her eyes.

Therapist: That's great. [pause] At you or just —

Participant: Around the room.

Therapist: Around the room, that's great. That's great. [long silence] Anything else she needs, or is she ready to leave with you?

Participant: She feels ready. She's like, "Can we go up the green stairs."

Therapist: Okay, so let's take her out of the green stairs. And does she want to come here, to you here, or to a fantasy place?

Participant: She'd love to come here.

Therapist: Let's bring her here.

Participant: To green trees!

Therapist: With the green trees? Yeah. There's lots of green stuff. And just tell me when she's here with you.

Participant: [emphatic] Yeah...

Therapist: And just tell me when she's here with you.

Participant: [silence] Yeah, she's here.

Therapist: How does she like being here?

Participant: Free.

Therapist: She feels free? That's right. [long silence] And tell her she never has to go back there and you're going to be taking care of her now.

Participant: [whisper, strong and gentle, directly to the part] You never have to go back there. I got you.

Therapist: How does she react?

Participant: Her heart hurts. Because she's never heard that before.

Therapist: She's never heard that before?

Participant: Right. Yeah.

Therapist: Okay. [silence] Ask her now if she's ready to unload the feelings and beliefs she got back there.

Participant: [emphatic] Yeah...

Therapist: And where does she carry all that? In her body, in her —

Participant: In her heart.

Therapist: And what would she like to give it all up to?

Participant: The air.

Therapist: So tell her, whenever she's ready she can let that all go into the air. Let the air take it.

Participant: [long silence, big sigh] It's like ashes, it's like maybe there was fire involved. But it just looks like ashes, just go up in the air.

Therapist: That's good. That's really good.

Participant: [silence, sigh]

Therapist: Keep it going until it's all out.

Participant: [more long, big breaths] Yeah — yeah.

Therapist: How's she doing now?

Participant: She feels really clean inside.

Therapist: Good.

Participant: Yeah.

Therapist: And tell her if she'd like she can invite qualities into her body — she'd like to have.

Participant: [long, searching silence]. Yep. Magic. Freedom. Creative power.

Therapist: Nice. So how is she feeling now?

Participant: It's time.

Therapist: Right, that's right. [long pause] Okay, so now let's bring in all the parts that have been protecting her, or reacting to her, to come in and see she's okay.

Participant: Okay.

Therapist: And see how they react.

Participant: [deep breaths, silence, sniffles, then calms] They're surprised. They're still. They're also — there's this sense, uhm — [silence] — It's like a very quiet joy. Yeah.

Therapist: That's great.

Participant: [long silence; she opens her eyes and looks directly and calmly at Schwartz]

Therapist: Before we shift to Gerry, just imagine he's in that shutdown part or he's reaching out to other people and just see how it feels now.

Participant: [pause] It's okay.

Therapist: It's okay, right?

Participant: It's okay. He comes back.

Therapist: He comes back, right?

Participant: Yeah.

[End of the session.]

This is *all* just IFS. This is all covered and practiced in every Level 1 training. None of this is a secret, "next level" IFS that Schwartz and some inner circle have squirreled away. But this is refined and deep IFS. Part of this is because, to quote a wry joke from Sunny Strasburg, Schwartz's partner in this retreat, Richard Schwartz "… is really good at IFS!"

But some of the power and clarity of this session is because the medicine is helping. Ketamine is an amazing psychedelic. There is a truly profound collaboration going on here, between Schwartz, the participant, all her parts, and the ketamine.

The participant, herself as Self and herself as all her parts, manifests so fully, so simply, and with so much togetherness, so much connection. We can scarcely imagine a clearer example of the refrain of this book, that in Self to part relationship some of the profoundest healing happens. Heck, Schwartz, and we as observers, don't even know much about what's going on between her and her parts. And we don't need to know. It's between her and her parts and it goes profoundly well.

This session is so complete that it's hard to add anything to it. So I will just underline, as Schwartz does later in his conference presentation, that the completeness and depth of this work would have probably taken a lot longer in standard IFS.

And really, I wonder if that completeness and depth might not have happened at all in regular IFS. Again, some of us just seem to need the help of psychedelics.

If there needs to be more arguments in favor of at least the option of psychotherapy in medicine sessions, I think this session just about seals it.

Yes, a counter argument could be made that this participant may have had a profound healing experience if she had just had an IM dose of ketamine and laid back alone on a couch with eyeshades and a playlist. But that healing experience would likely have been different and it likely would not have been so targeted and relevant to her purposes in being on a couples retreat.

Again, we see here that psychedelics and IFS can be truly great partners.

Crucially, this session was likely not the end of this participant's journey with abandonment. She likely had a complicated and real path ahead of her. As we'll see in the next chapter, IFS is also excellent in psychedelic integration work.

Schwartz started the relational integration work right there in the medicine session. He asked the participant to "bring in all the parts that have been protecting her [the former exile who had been burdened with abandonment], or reacting to her, to come in and see she's okay." That way, the other parts can start shifting their roles and relationships with each other and in Ann's life.

Schwartz presses on with the integration work, helping to start integrating the healing right into her daily life, even as they're sitting there in the ketamine session. Schwartz asks her to, "imagine Gerry is in that shutdown part or he's reaching out to other people, and just see how it feels now." She and her parts, the formerly exiled part and that part's former protectors, found, "It's okay." They are healed. They have each other. They know her husband comes back.

These are inner relationships, and like all relationships, she will need to maintain them in one way or another for them to remain vital, to live on, as we will discuss much more in the Integration Work chapter.

Again, this integration work further cements the argument: psychotherapy is not superfluous or optional to PAP. It is essential to PAP. Taking a medicine and laying back alone will likely do little to nothing for such exact, powerful, and necessary day to day integration of the healing. Without this integration psychotherapy, even profound healings can wither badly, like any plant or any relationship that is left too much alone.

This session is greatly inspiring and touching. But to return to Bennett's criticism, this session would likely have been something of a mess except for three things: the participant had done very good and clear prep work, including her and her parts coming to real consent for the medicine session and for IFS therapy in the medicine session; there was good dosing and timing of the therapy in the medicine session; and that Schwartz was well unblended, that he was Self there enough with "Ann" and all her parts.

With these, the session went truly great.

Some pragmatic recommendations on doing IFS therapy in in-office ketamine sessions and around medicalized ketamine sessions

Not all of us have the excellent setting and medical support that was available in the retreat session we just discussed. Many of us will be trying to do IFS ketamine assisted psychotherapy with patients who are working with purely medicalized ketamine or Spravato treatments, such as ketamine or Spravato clinics that do not focus much on therapy.

Or, because of simple logistics, many of us will often be doing ketamine sessions with our patients in our offices via sublingual delivery of ketamine, that is, with troches (lozenges). Because of the wide range of bioavailability of sublingual ketamine, we really don't know what dose our patient is getting in a given sublingual session. This can make doing therapy in these medicine sessions tricky, which we'll continue to discuss.

And if we are not prescribers ourselves and we aren't collaborating with a prescriber who is dosing for psychotherapy, we may then be working with fairly high doses of ketamine. This can be daunting for IFS therapy. For much of a high dose ketamine session, the verbal and cognitive state of our patient can just not be compatible with therapy.

In a class, Robert Grant had some great suggestions for doing IFS therapy in these situations.

For in-office, high dose sublingual ketamine sessions, Grant suggested that we could companion our patient in the onset and peak phases of the session, maybe the first hour. And then somewhere in the second hour there might be a good "sweet spot" for therapy, of good verbal and cognitive ability for our patient while they are still squarely "in the neighborhood" of ketamine. That can be a very good time for doing some brief IFS therapy.[153]

And again, it is important that we have done good prep work before this, including that we discussed and reached a contract on possible therapy in the medicine session and identified specific parts who might be good for therapy in the medicine session and who are in consent for that.

Even then, it's important that before we start doing any therapy in the second hour of the medicine session that we check in with our patient and be sensitive to their parts about if they are in fact interested in doing therapy at the time. Often, they are not. A high dose ketamine session can be plenty for anyone in one day!

---

[153] Robert Grant, "Advanced KAP: IFS in ketamine assisted psychotherapy class," 2021.

This is one downside of this hybrid, high-dose-and-then therapy model. Doing a medicine session that is specifically framed and dosed for therapy is definitely preferable for therapy, as we just saw in the demo session.

Therapist unblending is again very important here. If we are blended with therapist parts in extreme roles, we might be disappointed if our patient declines therapy in that second hour. If we are unblended enough, then we are just connected, present, and in compassion with our patient and their parts regardless of what they are up for in the second hour.

And like all therapy in medicine sessions, if we do wind up doing some IFS therapy during that second hour, it is very likely best that it is brief and focused, working with primarily one part, and for no more than about 10 to 15 minutes.

We can also do good IFS psychedelic assisted psychotherapy when our patient is doing ketamine or Spravato treatments where we can't physically be with them, like in a specialized clinic that we don't work in. Grant suggested that we can then schedule to meet with our patient later the same day, as soon as *reasonably* possible after the ketamine or Spravato session — no one wants to be rushing somewhere right after a medicine session! This can also work quite well. When we then meet with our patient, they can still be in enough of a "sweet spot" for some focused IFS therapy assisted by ketamine.

I very much like to do medicine sessions in person, but for combining a visit to a medical clinic with a therapy visit later in the same day, I have found video to have some real advantages and sometimes to simply be necessary. Again, a high dose ketamine session is a lot for anyone in one day. After a high dose ketamine session, many people will just want to get home and get settled, not commute again to our office and then have to commute home again after their therapy session. So we can meet with our patient via video once they've got home and settled in.

Sessions like this can wind up being a nice combination of some brief, specific IFS therapy and some integration work from the ketamine session earlier in the day.

Let's now move to the second part of this chapter, which focuses on IFS in high dose medicine sessions.

IFS WORK IN HIGH DOSE MEDICINE SESSIONS

IFS companioning in medicine sessions

Companioning is a word I borrow from my IFS colleague Ted Cation. It is maybe the most basic and important thing that IFS can help us as therapists do in medicine sessions. We briefly started discussing companioning earlier, but here is a working definition of companioning: To be present with our patient; to trust them and all their parts, whatever they are going through. And in IFS in medicine sessions, to also trust the medicine.

Sometimes companioning is all that's really possible or appropriate for us to do in a medicine session.

And we are fully doing IFS then. As Richard Schwartz wrote, "... I believe that anytime you relate to the client from your Self, and you keep in mind her system of parts, with or without using parts language, you are doing IFS."[154]

We might think of companioning in medicine sessions as us as therapist staying present with our patient, but also staying a step back. When we do that, we're clearly not "leading" the journey. We are respecting our patient's whole self and allowing a free space where their Self to part relationships can happen.

Many of our patients may have never been in such a free space. For many people who seek us out for therapy, much of their early life was wrapped up in problematic relational impingements of "too much" from some or almost all of the important people in

---

[154] Martha Sweezy, ed., Chapter 1 in Internal Family Systems Therapy: New Dimensions (New York: Routledge, 2013).

their life. These could have been problematic relationship patterns of enmeshment; of being cajoled into being a narcissistic extension; of their parents fostering inappropriate dependencies; of anxious hovering by parents; of on-going disdainful dislike and distrust of them by their parents; and so on.

When we companion our patient respectfully in a medicine session, that might be a rare and crucial experience for them of being together with another person in an important way while not being impinged on by the other.

Companioning dovetails wonderfully with what the child and family psychoanalyst D.W. Winnicott wrote about as "play space" or "transitional space." Winnicott meant these as literal physical spaces as well as inner, psychological spaces where children and adolescents could be free to have opportunities to be themselves, alone or with others. To play, with some real freedom, and to "play" at different possibilities, and thereby come to find themselves, others, and the world more and more.[155] Adult patients who did not get enough play space or transitional space growing up can really need it in their therapy. Medicine sessions can be an amazing time for that crucial developmental need to finally happen.

By our respectful companioning and the play space of a medicine session, our patient might find themself as Self far more and trust their parts far more, and bring all that more into their day to day life. In the medicine session, I think we can trust that our patient will find or choose what they need. Through that, they might find that they can be real agents in their own health and healing. This can be a tremendous boost to our patient's trust in themself, in both their inner worlds and outer worlds.

Companioning is pretty much the same thing as what I tell my patients I'll be doing during the medicine session: being present with them, trusting them and all their parts, and trusting the

---

[155] Winnicott, D. W. (1971). Transitional objects and transitional phenomena. In Playing and Reality.

medicine. Companioning is a relationship of presence and of trust and care.

Companioning is highly relevant to our next topic, hyperblending. Often, when our patient is hyperblended in a medicine session, an IFS informed companioning of them is about all we really can do. And it can be decisive.

Hyperblending and useful blending in medicine sessions

Hyperblending isn't a standard IFS term, but I think it can be a useful term for medicine sessions. As we began discussing earlier, hyperblending can mean the *incredibly* intense blending that can happen in medicine sessions. Hyperblending can be excruciating for a patient and it can feel literally unending. And one possibility is that hyperblending is part of a needed healing path.

A similar non-standard IFS term from non-psychedelic IFS is "useful blending," which is when sometimes blending winds up being very useful as a crucial form of witnessing. It may be the only way our patient can really get to know and understand a burdened part and what it's been through, where it's been stuck living, and what it's been carrying and doing all these years.

Hyperblending in a medicine session can sometimes seem to be just about the only way — *with that much power* — that a very deep exile can come to be with Self at all. To be witnessed, to finally not be alone. Hyperwitnessed, for a time.[156]

When we are understanding the stories and experiences of exiles and protectors, they usually do not have happy stories to tell. In hyperblending, our patients don't hear and understand these stories at a remove, they simply become the part for a while, with all that it has been through and all that it carries. This can be a lot, a whole lot, for our patients to go through.

Psychedelic medicines often don't seem to help and heal by bliss alone. "To fathom Hell or soar Angelic, / just take a pinch of

---

[156] Heather Smith, an IFS therapist who works extensively in PAP, has also been a great champion of the ideas of hyperblending and useful blending. Our conversations on this have been gratifying and bolstering to me.

psychedelic," the psychiatrist Humphry Osmond wrote when he first coined the term psychedelic.[157] Sometimes, witnessing means witnessing hell. Trauma and deprivation and their sequelae are sometimes truly horrible.

Again, this can all be part of a healing path. And very good preparation work is important here. As we discussed in the Preparation Work chapter, when parts have made informed consent to be in the medicine session, even given this possible intensity, they can then feel less victimized by it, even if the medicine session still feels quite challenging or harrowing at times.

Understandably, when our patient is going through hyperblending, that can be very challenging for us as therapist as well. Parts of us can want to blend with us to try to protect us or to try to protect our patient in ways that are "too much," of trying to fix or stop the distress our patient is going through. When our patient is hyperblending, this can be an important time to check our own blending and, if need be, ask those parts to unblend, and then go from there.

When our patient is hyperblending with an exile, again, it often seems to act as a very powerful form of witnessing. We as therapist might trust that at some point that part will not only be witnessed, but will be fully helped and healed. But that might not happen until much later in the medicine session or in the integration work.

Sometimes it just seems there might not be any healing path for that part that doesn't include the hyperwitnessing of hyperblending.

When our patient is hyperblending with a protector, a possibility is that that can be a sort of "prescribing the symptom": the protector gets the mic for an hour with the volume on the PA system *all the way up*, and it cannot leave the stage and it cannot stop sharing. Everyone — all parts, the shreds of Self there, the protector itself

---

[157] Nick Fetty, "The Origin of the Term 'Psychedelic'" (The New York Academy of Sciences, April 4, 2024).

— gets to see and hear, *ad nauseum*, the protector's jobs and its fears, which are its key burdens.

This might become part of an unburdening for that protector. The protector might wear through its burdens and be more willing to put them down.

By that, the protector might then unblend from our patient more, take a rare rest, and allow access to a deep exile it protects and protects from. Then that exile can become available for relationship and healing in the medicine session or in the integration work.

In hyperblending in a high dose medicine session, it might be impossible to get anything like unblending to happen. The "point" can seem to be full volume for a while. If we as therapist get blended with a part of ourselves in an extreme role, we might try too hard to help our patient unblend. That just might not be in the cards.

If we're blended with a burdened part of ourselves who wants to push our patient to unblend, then we are not there as Self as much. Then our patient and their parts are more alone as they go through hyperblending. This can, of course, make a hard experience even harder for our patient. So again, our own unblending, our own being there as Self well enough, can make a huge difference.

As Self, we may be able to offer some very simple interventions to our patient in hyperblending. If we can say it sincerely, we could offer some reassuring presence and support to our patient. Maybe, "You're doing great."

We may even be able to offer to our patient a suggestion for some possible Self to part relationship with the part who is hyperblending. Maybe something like, "Can you ask them to show you in another way, a way you can understand better?" (I'm indebted to Jose Stevens, a very psychedelically astute therapist and practitioner, for this suggestion.[158]) Maybe that goes somewhere, maybe it doesn't.

But ultimately in hyperblending, we might best just try to stay with our patient; to trust our patient, their parts, and the medicine; to check on our own blending and do our own unblending if need be; and to have done very good preparation work.

Often, the path beyond a trauma or deprivation is through it. But not going through it alone. Our patients need us as companions.

Multiple Selves in the room in medicine sessions

Again, the chorus of this book: in IFS, Self to part relationships are where the most real healing happens. Very often, that is optimally our patient as Self in relationship with their own parts. But sometimes it needs to be the Self of the therapist in relationship with their patient's parts. That is, in direct access. So in standard IFS we have at least two Selves available to help our patient's burdened parts: our patient as Self and the therapist as Self.

One idea is that in medicine sessions we may have more Selves available. This can get squarely into the spiritual side of psychospiritual work, like into full-on religious, spiritual, or mystical aspects of medicine sessions, of seeming divine or non-human helpers.

In the case material later in this chapter, we will see at least a couple prominent instances of what, at least by face value, could be called something like divine helpers, guides, or other Selves. As we discussed in the Preparation Work chapter, this often just seems like it is part of the psychedelic terrain.

For our discussion here, I'll call this sort of thing "multiple Selves" or "other Selves," as in Selves in addition to the patient as Self and the therapist as Self.

---

[158] Jose Stevens, personal communication, 2014

What sense we as therapist or our patient make of such figures or events or experiences can be a complicated story. We have options. Are "other Selves" just inner? Or are they outer?

Are they inner projections from the patient's own psyche, a helpful, but simply psychological manifestation of what, in the MAPS training, is called an "inner healing intelligence?" Or a sort of hyperimaginal active placebo?

Or, are they part of the world, do they have ontology? That is, are they beings? If they were part of the world, that could lead, from a Modernist stance, to a Copernican level revolution. But from other, non-Modern perspectives, that would simply get us in the main flow of the global diversity of cultures and the historical record of cultures. A sense of "helpers" like this is not even far removed from many modern Westerners. Such a discussion or supposition wouldn't even merit a pause in conversation from much of my Sicilian-American and Irish-American Catholic family. They'd just want to get to the important part of the conversation, "Yeah, what are you praying to them for?"

Or maybe we just want to keep it pragmatic, with a primary focus on "what works." As we discussed in the Preparation Work chapter, some patients will simply gladly take what help is seemingly available and not worry too much about big questions about it. They're just happy for the help.

And to briefly repeat a previous discussion, regardless of what sense we as therapist make of "other Selves," it's best if therapy, psychedelic or otherwise, doesn't become a Procrustean bed. All of this about multiple Selves probably best comes down to just our patient's relationships and experiences, or lack thereof, and whatever sense they make of them. It would be a big problem to try to cut down our patient's sense of things to fit our sense of things, or to try to stretch our patient's understanding to fit ours.

Let's go ahead and look at some ways in medicine sessions that we might help our patient work with seeming "multiple Selves."

One thing that is important here is that we've done good preparation work with our patient and their parts around possible spiritual aspects of a medicine session. That way, if some sense of multiple Selves seems to show up in the medicine session, at least it's been on the table in the relationship between us. We don't want to necessarily have to broach that topic for the first time in the midst of a very intense period of a medicine session.

If what seems like a helper or an other Self comes up in the medicine session, it's pretty common that our patient might express some hesitancy or confusion about such a figure or force. Again, prep work can be crucial here. If our patient was interested in the possible spiritual, religious, or mystical stuff in the prep work, we might have offered our patient some relevant flight instructions: of our patient having the option of negotiating and dialoguing with such a seeming helper. This can help orient our patient in what might be an intense experience. It can highlight their agency. And it can make the experience of multiple Selves in a medicine session far more healing.

As we'll see in one of the case vignettes to follow, a research participant, as part of a dialogue or negotiation with such a figure, demands before accepting any help from them, "If we do this I want my body returned to me in at least as good a shape as it is in now."[159] That negotiation being accepted, she could then feel safe to profoundly let herself open to the help and healing available.

Again, our patient and their parts can choose to open up to help from such helpers to *whatever* extent they are open to such possible help at the time. Self and each part can make that call for themselves. This can be dialogued on, negotiated, and "jerry-mandered" in whatever ways our patient as Self and their parts want.

If our patient has come to a sense that they sincerely want to accept some level of help from such a seeming helper, then we might suggest to them that they explicitly ask for and welcome

---

[159] Richards, William A., Sacred Knowledge: Psychedelics and Religious Experiences. United States: Columbia University Press, 2015.

in the help of that figure or force as fully and deeply as they feel safe and ready to do at the time.

Our patient could also take a pass on any seemingly spiritual help offered or available. Our patient and their parts have agency in the medicine session. They do not need to accept even seemingly divine help or healing. They also do not need to be pushed or cajoled into accepting any such seeming help by anyone, including their therapist! If a therapist did that, it could obviate the patient as a Self, as an agent. That would likely bring a wound with any healing that might come.

And, like everything in the medicine session, if our patient is unsure about what to do with any apparent helper or multiple Self in the medicine session, we could suggest to them that they could simply be with and breathe with such a figure or presence *and* with their uncertainty. Who knows what follows that?

I want to point out an important distinction around other Selves, "guides," and religious or spiritual healing that Richard Schwartz has talked about. If the healing in a medicine session (or elsewhere) is primarily or totally coming from an "outer Self," and our patient as Self is not at least central to the healing, then what's happening is not IFS. That's not to say that whatever is happening is bad, it's just not IFS. IFS can partner very well with many, many forms of healing, including what might be widely termed "shamanistic," spiritual, or religious healing practices, but our patient as Self has to be there and be central to the healing for this work to be legitimately called IFS.

Let's now turn to case material of high dose medicine sessions.

We will start with an extensive and close following of some of the work of Michael and Annie Mithoefer with Nick, a research participant in a MAPS study of MDMA assisted psychotherapy for treatment resistant PTSD.

This material is so richly available through Nick's service and compassion. He wanted to make his therapy process widely available so that therapists could better learn how to help people who had been hurt like he had been.

He has succeeded greatly.

Case example: Nick and Annie and Michael Mithoefer's work

Many readers might be aware of Nick's work from MAPS' training or from Tom Shroder's excellent book *Acid Test: LSD, Ecstasy, and the Power to Heal.* I will quote and reference this material extensively, so you won't be at a big disadvantage if you haven't read *Acid Test* or done MAPS training with the Mithoefers.

But I would like to make a plug for reading *Acid Test*, even if you've done the MAPS training with the Mithoefers. Through Shroder and Nick's excellent interviews in *Acid Test*, we get to go "behind the eyeshades" with Nick in his sessions, to understand what he was experiencing during the medicine sessions. This was, of course, not captured in the videos used in the MAPS training! Let's jump in.

Under the protocol for this study, Nick received three medicine sessions. Here we will follow his first two medicine sessions and a period of integration between them.

A note on Nick's dosing of MDMA: Nick was randomized to receive 75 mg of oral MDMA in his medicine sessions. This seems to be an optimal dose of MDMA for PAP. I say that because from this same study there is data that 75 mg of MDMA had better psychological outcomes than 125 mg.[160] This could be because at 125 mg the anxious and tense effects of MDMA, which we will see shortly in Nick's first session, are often much stronger, while 125 mg does not seem to lead to increased improvement in outcome

---

[160] Mithoefer, Michael C et al. "3,4-methylenedioxymethamphetamine (MDMA)-assisted psychotherapy for post-traumatic stress disorder in military veterans, firefighters, and police officers: a randomised, double-blind, dose-response, phase 2 clinical trial." The Lancet. Psychiatry vol. 5,6 (2018): 486-497.

measures. This data on dosing seems to be independent of the patient's body weight and gender.[161]

The Mithoefers also offered a 37.5 mg booster dose mid-session, which I believe Nick decided to take in each of his medicine sessions. The boosters seem to prolong the working time with the MDMA rather than increase the intensity of the MDMA.

Michael Mithoefer was the principal investigator of this study as well as a study therapist. Michael is dual boarded in emergency medicine and psychiatry. Annie Mithoefer is a nurse. They are a married couple and were co-therapists in this study. As mentioned earlier, they had many years of experience working together leading Holotropic Breathwork groups, which, through non-drug methods, produce powerful shifts in consciousness for participants in ways that are quite similar to psychedelic medicines, including that they can be quite intense and challenging at times and that they can be profoundly healing. This is all to say that the Mithoefers had very good backgrounds going into these experimental treatments with MDMA.

It's also important to note that Michael had done training in IFS before this study and was very skilled in it. I believe Annie does not approach PAP from an IFS frame and has not done training in IFS.

Nick is a military veteran of the second, 2003 US invasion of Iraq. Nick was in the US Marines and was assigned to be a gunner on an armored vehicle. On missions, he was positioned in a turret on the top of the vehicle with a powerful machine gun. A large part of his duties was defensive, to protect the other Marines and their vehicles from snipers, improvised explosive devices, and other attacks as they traveled on missions. He went through many missions during his tour and experienced frequent combat, often heavy. Most of his missions were in Iraqi cities.

Not surprisingly, he eventually developed severe PTSD. Back home in the United States, he was suffering horribly for years. He

---

[161] Ibid.

was often suicidal, unable to work, and the PTSD was impacting his marriage badly. Through the US Veteran's Administration healthcare system (VA), he had tried conventional treatments such as SSRI treatment and psychotherapy, but there was little to no improvement. He met criteria for severe, treatment resistant PTSD.

Before his participation in the MDMA study, he had tried working with psilocybin mushrooms intentionally, on his own, in hopes of getting relief from his PTSD. There was some important, but brief relief and some rich perspectives from those experiences. However, we might speculate that without an adequate container, that is, without ongoing helping relationships and a useful psychedelic framework, the benefits of his work with psilocybin mushrooms quickly petered out. But the experiences with the mushrooms did build some hope in him, "a little bit of excitement for life again," as he put it.[162]

That hope, that little bit of excitement for life, allowed him to push on further on a healing path. He researched on the internet for ways to get some much needed help and found news of the MAPS MDMA research. He found that one of the MAPS studies was recruiting participants not far from his home. He volunteered, met criteria, and was enrolled in the study.

Nick and the Mithoefers had three preparation sessions before the first medicine session. They went very well. From the videos and from Shroder's interviews with Nick and the Mithoefers, it was clear that the trust, safety, and connection established between Nick, Michael, and Annie was deep and simple. Nick had never worked with MDMA before and he had some trepidation, but he was trusting enough of the medicine. By the time of the first medicine session, he was very much a well-prepared person.

---

[162] Shroder, Tom. Acid Test: LSD, Ecstasy, and the Power to Heal. United States: Penguin Publishing Group, 2015.

For the case material here, I will switch between italics for describing the clinical situation and a regular font for discussing that situation.

First medicine session

Early in his first medicine session, Nick was having waves of anxiety. This is typical as MDMA starts to enter our system. MDMA is a form of methamphetamine, in some ways a strong stimulant. The Mithoefers had worked with Nick in the prep sessions on some breathing relaxation exercises to help with this initial tension. Nick seemed to find the relaxation exercises helpful and got through the initial "come up" tension without too much distress.

As we discussed in the Preparation Work chapter, relaxation breathing exercises for the initial, tense part of an MDMA session have their place, but they are different from the relational "being with, breathing with" practice that will be so important to Nick's medicine sessions and integration work.

Once getting through this initial tense side effect period, Nick began to have a vision. It was of traveling underground through a hole at the base of a tree trunk.

It seems possible that Nick had some co-creation of this vision of the underground hole. Nick had a meditation practice well before he came into the MDMA study. I'm not sure, but it sounds like his meditation practice might have been along the lines of Michael Harner's Core Shamanism work, of lower realms, upper realms, and a middle realm. In Harner's work, holes in the earth in visions are often seen as passageways into "lower realms."

I've also seen in my practice that during medicine sessions a very similar vision, of a hole in the earth that leads to a different realm, can come up spontaneously for people who have no exposure to Harner's work. So Nick's vision may have came up spontaneously. Or, if Nick co-created the hole in the tree and his journey into the lower realm, that would fit with Nick being central to his own healing: his choices, his agency as at least one cornerstone of his healing. This would also fit with Webster's salience hypothesis of psychedelics. To re-quote Webster, "... if in actuality, LSD causes only a measurable, definable amplification of a neurocognitive operation (as per the present essay) which the person then uses and builds upon voluntarily to enter the great range of psychedelic effects, his humanity is restored..."[163]

If Nick was co-creating this vision in some ways, that would not be to say that Nick was "making all this up." It was clear that he was in something with a reality, a "place" or a "landscape."

Maybe we could say Nick was being something of a *flaneur* in his journey.

Once underground, Nick met a sage figure who led him through underground passageways to a door, beckoning him to open it. Nick did. And there, chained to the wall, was a figure Nick expected to be a monster.

Then, I think I remember from the MAPS training videos, Nick turned towards this "monster," and at that exact moment, Nick became himself as a "sage."

I want to unpack this moment of the medicine session. I think it is important that it is a *moment*, not a process. If we take Nick turning into the sage as him being more there as Self, it's striking that it happens spontaneously *in relationship* with "the monster" -- in turning towards "the monster," in an act of some respect. We might see here the relationality of Self.

The relationality between Nick and the "monster" figure continues. When Nick sees this figure who he expected to be a

---
[163] Peter Webster, Kosmos: A theory of psychedelic experience, https://www.psychedelic-library.org/books/Kosmos+Cover.pdf.

monster, he finds that it is not exactly a monster chained to the
wall, but, as Shroder writes:

> *... a man dressed in Marine fatigues, hanging his head
> in sadness or despair. As [Nick] crept closer, the Marine
> looked up. His face, contorted with rage or pain, had
> glowing red eyes, like a demon's, and fangs protruding
> from his mouth. But what most horrified Nick was that
> the monster's face was his own. He wanted to turn
> away, to run, but the sage him refused to budge. Nick
> stood there forcing himself to look at the monster he
> had become. As he held that demonic gaze, something
> unexpected happened. His revulsion faded, then melted
> away, replaced by a swirl of other emotions; pity, regret.
> "I went up to him, and I took off the chains, and I
> remember saying something like 'If you want to rip me
> apart, I would understand, because I put you here. It was
> very wrong of me.' I remember the face melting, and us
> hugging each other—the sage me and the warrior me.
> It was just, like, this forgiving moment. I was inwardly
> forgiving myself. It was just so profound, like, 'Oh, my
> God.' It lifted me up to that point of ecstasy."*

Again, we might say that initially Nick, by turning towards the
supposed monster, was then in at least a critical mass of Self. And
as he then stood there as Self in relationship with the monster,
further unblending seems to have happened: Nick's revulsion
melted away. He then had compassion for what this part of him
had become, was going through, and had been through.

Importantly, he also had regret. Sometimes, part of healing
is us as Self needing to apologize to parts and to grieve ourselves
for what we've done to them, or haven't done for them. For not
going to them sooner. For catching a glimpse of them and hearing
their pleas and then turning away. For not trusting ourselves,

not knowing ourselves to be able to handle them, to be able to be with them, to listen to them, to love them, to help them. And then allowing protectors to take them back to the dungeon, out of sight, but maybe not out of earshot, and chain them back to the wall.

There is something else. Nick, as Self, even allows the possibility of his own destruction: "If you want to rip me apart, I would understand, because I put you here. It was very wrong of me." As both Richard Schwartz and Heinz Kohut, the founder of psychoanalytic Self psychology, have observed, loss of Self is the gravest psychological threat. Parts will choose suicide, biological death, over death of Self. Kohut called it disintegration anxiety.

Here, Nick, as Self, with utmost compassion, utmost courage, and utmost commitment, freely acts to allow even the ending of Self, exactly because of that compassion and commitment. That's *a lot* of compassion.

Nick steps closer to the monster, unchains him, and apologizes to him. The "monster" is then freed, and radically unburdens. Nick as Self and this part of him join into a powerful new relationship: they are together in forgiveness and love.

I want to underline that in the medicine session so far the Mithoefers have done very little, and this has been excellent technique. This has been Nick's journey. The Mithoefers only learned about this great healing vision after it happened, when Nick took off his eyeshades and headphones and enthusiastically told them.

Even with the Mithoefers doing very little, even with little to no guidance or active intervention from the therapists, this medicine session so far has been very IFS-y, eerily so.

We'll now look at a vignette from later in this medicine session when moral injury is manifesting, Nick confronting the moral injury of having killed people in the war.

Moral injury is usually considered a separate but very often co-occurring wounding with PTSD, at least as deep a psychospiritual wounding as that of PTSD. Moral injury can come from both what one did or what one did not do in an extreme situation. For example, of having killed or injured another, or of having failed to prevent someone from being killed or injured.

We could see moral injury as a form of loss of Self. Again, this is a grave psychological wound. This isn't loss of Self as in dissociation or depersonalization, but a loss of a sense of oneself as an effective, compassionate, courageous, connected being. Moral injury can have a sense that, having faltered, one's Self never was any good or never existed at all. Moral injury can then be experienced as a fundamental injury to one's soul. It can result in a sense of a deficiency, vileness, or loss of one's soul, of one's basic worth.

Moral injury has been particularly associated with suicide risk.[164]

In this vignette, the Mithoefers gently but clearly midwife some relationship, some companionship, with Nick and his moral injury.

Shroder brings us there:

> "I think that... I really think that I was punishing myself for... being... you know..." His eyes closed and his chest heaved; for the first time he seemed to be struggling to get words out. "... a..." A sob started in his throat, but he choked it off. "... a... killer."
>
> He sank deeper into the pillow, his eyes searching the ceiling as if something important were streaming in through the skylights. When he began to speak again, his voice was soft, shaken. "I would... I don't... you know whenever I shot people I didn't... I don't know, I didn't really feel anything. I didn't feel excited. I didn't feel bad. I just kind of felt numb, and that scared me. And when I got back here and think about those things, I

---

[164] Khan, A.J., Griffin, B.J. & Maguen, S. A Review of Research on Moral Injury and Suicide Risk. *Curr Treat Options Psych* **10**, 259–287 (2023).

don't know, I feel bad for doing those things and acting the way I did."

"Are you feeling some of that sadness now?" Michael asked.

Nick's eyes traced an arabesque on the ceiling. After a minute he said, "When I think about it now, the same thoughts come to my head that normally do, but now I'm not really bothered by them. I understand. Like, normally the feelings that rush up to me and make me all teary-eyed and emotional, now I think I understand why I cried and why I felt the way I did, and now the past is the past. Those things are always going to be with me, carved into my soul, scars on my soul. Whenever I thought about those scars, I got really emotional, I wanted them to go away, wished I never had them. Now I realize they're never going to go away, I'm always going to have them... It's like a splinter in the mind, but it's not going to come out. I've just got to file it down and smooth it out. Those things are just part of my life, part of my experience, and I should just not look at those scars in the mirror and get sad but just come to them and pat them down... I don't know how to describe it."

"If there's a splinter," Michael said, "it's important to get the splinter out, but there may be a scar; that is part of healing. It's still there, but it's healed. I don't know if that resonates."

"I still feel like there's something there that's... that's... kind of lurking around in the background..."

"Now might be a good time to go inside again with the music and just see what might be there," he suggested. "Does that feel right? Then come out and let us know."

Nick went back into Native American chants and wispy space music. The face behind the eye mask revealed nothing. Michael would later use the video of Nick's session to make the point to would-be therapists that in MDMA sessions it could often look as if nothing were happening when in fact worlds were being created or destroyed.

Ten minutes later Nick pulled off the eye mask. He'd visualized sitting around a campfire at night, he told them. "I had a powerful vision of something rustling around in the bushes," he said. He was there in his two incarnations, warrior and sage, but try as they might, they couldn't get the shadowy presence to reveal itself. "I don't know if it's bad, but I had this overwhelming feeling that I'm supposed to confront it... Makes me feel like I did when I was a kid. When you think there's something under your bed, part of you wants to look, and part of you doesn't want to see something scare the crap out of you, but if you don't look, you have to lie there wondering."

His moral injury manifests, of being "a killer." Not just as pictorial memories, but as emotions, fear, the numbness, the guilt, the ways of punishing himself.

Who knows why, but these medicines "go there." They find the exiles. The Mithoefers largely created the therapy protocols used in these studies and they trained and supervised many of the therapists who did the experimental treatment. Part of the study protocol was that if after two medicine sessions the participant hadn't brought up the "index traumas" of their PTSD in a medicine session, then the therapists, with tact and timing, would propose that the patient spend time with the index traumas in the next medicine session. The Mithoefers said that in all their own cases and all of their supervising, no therapists ever had to "bring up" the index traumas. They always manifested on their own in the medicine sessions.[165]

Going back to this vignette and unpacking it, after Nick started sharing with the Mithoefers some of his moral injury, Michael said to Nick, "Are you feeling some of that sadness now?" Maybe by this Michael was inviting a vulnerable exile into Self to part relationship.

It seems to me that then a protector blends with Nick, a very subtle, nuanced and skilled protector, who acknowledges and is resigned to the wounds and the feelings of the exile: they're there, they always will be there, but when they stick up and cause irritation, catch on things and get in the way, they can be pat down, filed down, and smoothed out. Until the next time they stick up, then repeat. The wounds will be managed.

We can see resignation as part of this protector's burden. Resignation is maybe a common burden of protectors. Resignation can look like a mature acceptance, it can maybe even look like Self to part relationship, so it can escape our "parts detector" as therapist. But resignation doesn't lead to healing. An exile "resigned to" stays stuck suffering with their burdens. Resignation can be a compromised form of exiling by a protector: "I can't get rid of this exile, so I won't fight that battle. I'll allow it to be there, but I'll do ongoing maintenance on it."

Michael presses on, maybe doing some implicit direct access with that protector: "If there's a splinter… it's important to get the splinter out." He maybe checks with the protector, "I don't know if that resonates."

Nick responds, perhaps more as Self, perhaps the protector is tentatively unblending some, letting the exile, the splinter, be seen by Self: "I still feel like there's something there that's… kind of lurking around in the background." Perhaps the protector is still scared of the exile, it is felt as "lurking around," but there is more openness to acknowledging whatever is lurking around out there.

---

[165] Michael and Annie Mithoefer, "MAPS training for MDMA assisted psychotherapy for treatment resistant PTSD class," 2021.

Michael then suggests a very simple intervention, we might see it as continuing to simply and gently offer to midwife some Self to part relationship: "Now might be a good time to go inside again with the music and just see what might be there." Michael also checks for consent about that, perhaps from the protector, from Self, and from the exile itself: "Does that feel right?" And Michael makes it clear this isn't an abandoning by Annie and him, they are fully with Nick and all his parts: "Then come out and let us know."

Nick then has the vision of sitting around the campfire, often a place of safety, warmth, and community at night. In that vision, there is "something rustling around in the bushes," at the periphery. That "something" feels to Nick again like maybe a monster, like the creatures that children fear to be under their bed: "...part of you doesn't want to see something scare the crap out of you, but if you don't look, you have to lie there wondering."

Exiles are often felt as monsters, as the most dangerous things. The things to be avoided, or hunted down and removed, or as we said, failing that, resigned to and managed.

Shroder doesn't write of this, but in the video Nick then spent quite a bit of time being very uncomfortable, not knowing how to proceed with this figure rustling in the bushes. Perhaps this was a continuing ambivalence of this protector: does it dare trust Self to see, to be with, the exile, the broken soul, the failed, defective soul that rises up every so often and needs to be skillfully smoothed out?

The Mithoefers again did something very subtle at this point. They simply suggested to Nick that he stay present with that unknowing and the emotions and experiences of that. They didn't set up any complicated dialogues. They certainly didn't try to problem solve the dilemma by siding with one side or the other, to confront or avoid.

"Be with, breathe with." Even with the indecision, even with the tension of not being able to decide what to do, with the pulls both ways: confront / avoid, confront / avoid, over and over and over. Be with, breathe with it all.

Nick took their advice to be present. This might have only gone on for a few minutes. To me, even at the safe remove of watching the video, it felt much, much longer; uncomfortably so.

The medicine session ended not long after, with that tension not being resolved, with Nick not confronting or escaping whatever was rustling in the bushes around the campfire in his vision. That thread would be followed up in the next medicine session.

Integration between first and second medicine sessions

In the interim, Nick did several integration sessions with the Mithoefers and lived his life, his marriage, and did a practice from one of the integration sessions, spending time in nature.

Shroder writes of this time:

> *Nick took the Mithoefers' advice to heart and took a drive into the country, to a place he knew where he could park the car and walk into the woods. As soon as he'd left the parking spot behind and could hear the wind sighing through the branches and see the leaves flashing silver in the sun, everything got clearer and all the insights he'd had during the MDMA session echoed in his mind. He was deep in thought when he heard the distinctive high-pitched cries of a hawk. He looked up and saw not one hawk but three circling on the currents directly above him. He looked away and the birds' cries grew more insistent, as if they were demanding his attention. When he looked up again, they went silent, sailing on the currents in lazy circles high above. Part of him wanted to believe that this avian trio was all about him and his journey back to health. The cynical adult in him scoffed at that narcissistic impulse. He*

kept watching, thinking the birds would drift off, go find another human to soar above. But they just kept circling above him. Suddenly he felt that same lurking, invisible presence he'd felt in his vision. Something about the hawks, but what?

Then he had a thought: there were three hawks, a trinity of sorts. He'd discovered two parts of himself, one of which he'd locked away in a dungeon. Maybe, it occurred to him, there was a third part, buried even deeper than that.

Nick's second medicine session

As Nick's second medicine session got underway, he struggled initially. He was expecting a clean continuation or repeat of the clarity of the first session. Instead, he initially just saw images of his difficult childhood, excluded from other kids, feeling profoundly different, partially from paranormal type experiences.

Often when the first medicine session was a great one, the second one can feel disappointing or awkward. Logically enough, we can go into the second medicine session expecting more of the same great stuff. But the second session often isn't a repeat. It's a moving on.

So at the beginning of this second medicine session, instead of epic healing adventures, Nick was stuck with images and feelings from difficult times of his childhood.

Annie counseled him, "Just be with it. Try not to move away. It's coming for you to see and feel it."

As I mentioned, Annie doesn't have training or an interest in IFS, but even so, we might read that she's offering Nick something like the possibility of witnessing these young parts of himself, helping them finally not be alone with what they felt and went through, and all they've been carrying through the years.

From this witnessing, Nick came to understand his childhood better and how his childhood experiences connected to parts of him that wanted to join the military, "a huge confidence builder." And how maybe the military could have been attractive as a way for a part of himself who felt great rage from his difficult childhood to be able to act on that rage, "part of me wanted to go over there and shoot someone." The Mithoefers stayed with him, befriending him and all parts of him.

Later in the session, as Nick continued to get to know his childhood and his child parts better, he told the Mithoefers:

> *"I had a vision of me now telling the young Nicholas, 'When you're older you'll have better friends than you have now, and people will like you,' but that young Nicholas wasn't getting it; it wasn't sinking in."*
>
> *"Sometimes that's what it takes with our young parts," Michael said, "to bring them into the present. Anything that young part wants to show us or you before he's ready to come to the present?"*

We could possibly say here that Michael was sharing with Nick and this part, in an implicit direct access, that retrieval and updating are real options, but that parts won't do that until they feel adequately witnessed, adequately seen and understood about what they went through. So that they never have to be alone with it again.

Michael asked, "Anything that young part wants to show us or you before he's ready to come to the present?"

Nick stared at the ceiling, slowly rubbing his thumb against his middle finger. When he spoke, his voice was vague, distant sounding.

"Just a lot of fear," he said. "Being alone in the world. I felt haunted when I was a kid; that's why I felt scared."

"Tell us more about that," Annie said.

Again, Annie probably wouldn't put it this way, but we might see this again as her offering witnessing to this part in implicit direct access, "Tell us more about that."

Nick then shared much with them about his childhood, but in the interest of brevity we won't explore that here.

I want to comment here on the simplicity and light touch we've seen throughout this clinical example so far. The Mithoefers seem to me like musicians playing a good note or chord of music here and there and then listening. Or like the singing of the hawks flying above Nick. Again, simplicity often seems to be the mark of masters.

I want to jump to later in this medicine session when Nick found who was rustling in the bushes outside the clearing. Again, we only learn of this experience after it's happened, when Nick "comes out" and shares it with the Mithoefers.

"I think I was depressed [initially in this second medicine session] because last time my inner self came to me so quickly and guided me and was able to provide the clarity I needed, and this time I wasn't getting it. I think I just expected that once the drug was in, I'd get the clarity again and be able to reconnect. I realized that I stumbled upon it the first time by blessing, and this time I needed to develop a route to connect with it so I wouldn't need the MDMA next time."

So he'd done what he'd always done when he prayed or meditated: just offered himself up, tried to let go of himself, and began to visualize the door in the base of the tree and falling down the rabbit hole into the subterranean world.

Suddenly he'd found himself as both the warrior and the sage aspects of himself around the campfire where the shadow lurked. "I caught a glimpse of that thing poking out of the darkness, shadowlike, and I got scared," he said. "But then I had a visualization of it coming out, and it wasn't a creature at all, it was little Nicholas, the true me, whoever we are inside. The best image my mind gives is me as a little boy, blond, green-eyed, a brilliance that outshone fire. And it felt like a completion of a trifecta, Little Nicholas in tune with my true self, at the top of the pyramid, branching down to the warrior me and sage me. I thought I was just being imaginative, but it felt so real and so right."

Feeling that release made him want to go deeper.

Perhaps the three hawks, the trifecta, were relevant here as additional Selves, as we discussed in the section above, "Multiple Selves in the room in medicine sessions." As discussed there, the hawks could possibly be seen as active healing agents themselves, as outside Selves. Or they could be seen as useful figures for Nick's psyche to project his own healing strengths onto, his own Self. Either way, maybe with those "other Selves" there, protectors were more willing to unblend, to allow the exile to be more available for healing.

Anyhow, it seemed to work. The deepest exile, his soul morally injured: a part of him seemingly turned into a creature capable of nothing but lurking around alone at the edges of community, peeking in at life, at the beautiful light, warmth, safety, and company of the fire. But then this part of Nick *somehow* emerges, spectacularly unburdened, to use an understatement. Understatements are all that we have here: A little boy with "a brilliance that outshone fire."

I think it's important to underline that as Self, Nick helps this deepest exile. Yes, the hawks may have been truly essential. Yes, the MDMA may have also been truly essential. But eventually, in this second medicine session, Nick realizes that he can't just wait around for something to help him. He gets busy as an agent, an agent in his own healing. As Shroder reports it, he then did "... what he'd always done when he prayed or meditated: just offered himself up, tried to let go of himself, and began to visualize the door in the base of the tree and falling down the rabbit hole into the subterranean world." Nick's agency here seems to have been decisive.

Again, this exiled part of Nick seems to go through *no* healing process. He just emerges fully healed. He was arguably witnessed at the end of the first medicine session. But here, this part seems to, all in an instant, be retrieved, completely unburden, and update into Self to part relationship.

This is astounding and beautiful and real. But as we will discuss in the Integration Work chapter, these sorts of seemingly instant and profound healings in medicine sessions can then be tricky for integration work: other parts don't get a chance to catch even a peripheral glimpse of the exile becoming healed, of them becoming themself as a Self again. So other parts can then need some very specific and patient integration work. Again, we will follow up on this in the Integration Work chapter.

Also very relevant to integration work is that Nick now knows that he can heal himself, without needing MDMA. That's not to say that MDMA can't continue helping him. Again, as he put it, "I think I just expected that once the drug was in, I'd get the clarity again and be able to reconnect. I realized that I stumbled upon it the first time by blessing, and this time I needed to develop a

route to connect with it so I wouldn't need the MDMA next time."
We might say that Nick has now seen that he himself, himself
as Self, is essential to any healing he will get. That is a powerful
healing. And again, we will follow up on this important thread
in the Integration Work chapter.

There's so much more that we could explore about Nick's medicine
sessions, but we've got to draw the line somewhere, so we'll draw
it here.

I want to say that these sessions were clearly not all about
IFS technique — or any kind of technique at all. In the session
videos, it's easy to see that even when it was hard, Michael and
Annie and Nick were simply three people happy to be together.
The trust of Michael and Annie for Nick and for all of his parts
couldn't have been clearer. And Nick's trust and safety with the
Mithoefers, the medicine, and their work together also couldn't
have been clearer.

Again, this is not really about technique. It is about relationship.
Self to part and Self to world relationships are not technique. I-Thou
relationships are not technique. Being together is not technique.

We will follow up with Nick and his healing path in the Integration
Work chapter.

Working with difficult patches in medicine sessions

Some parts of medicine sessions can be quite difficult for some
patients. There are indications that patients with difficulties in
relational attachment, quite possibly from interpersonal trauma
and deprivation in their past or their development, often have
harder medicine sessions.[166] It may be that they simply have
more to work through, more to heal. This can, of course, be truly
difficult at times.

---

[166] Stauffer CS, Anderson BT, Ortigo KM, Woolley J. Psilocybin-Assisted Group Therapy and
Attachment: Observed Reduction in Attachment Anxiety and Influences of Attachment Insecurity on
the Psilocybin Experience. ACS Pharmacol Transl Sci. 2020 Dec 9;4(2):526-532.

Besides typical clinical considerations of trauma or deprivation, it seems that medicine sessions can bring up and hopefully help our patients work through what we might call great existential / spiritual / religious / ontological realities, or whatever term. Many of these existential issues are not of the blissful variety. They can be some of the very hard things about just being human, about just being a being: of vulnerability, losses, losing, finitude, grieving. In medicine sessions, protectors can become far less active around such huge vulnerabilities, and then the medicine session can be not at all a spiritual walk in the park.

Medicine sessions can be very much the opposite of a spiritual bypass or any kind of bypass.

Whatever vulnerabilities come up, of personal traumas or of beingness, when it's a hard time for our patient in a medicine session, it can be hard for us as therapists.

Here's a vignette from a ketamine session that Robert Grant shared in a class:

Grant's patient had sought him out for help with terrible, long term, treatment resistant depression. In a ketamine session, the patient's depression manifested powerfully, directly putting the patient in agony. While excruciating, this was also a chance for some Self to part relationship with the depression.

Grant asked his patient to ask the depression what it wanted him to know. The patient was then silent for a good five minutes. Grant said those were about the longest five minutes of his life, worried that this extremely painful depression was just savaging his patient the whole time. Grant said he clearly had parts of him who wanted to help his patient, to save them from the presumed suffering. But Grant wasn't decisively blended with those parts. Even though he was struggling himself, he simply attended with his patient. He stayed there, showing up, even if silent.

We only need a critical mass of Self to be present.

Finally, his patient responded, with tearful joy and relief: "It wants me to know that I'm beautiful." The part that had been so painful for them as a highly attacking depression, somehow, in those five minutes seemed to unburden and take on a new role in the patient's life; as a great ally, a great friend, of reminding the patient of how beautiful they were.

These new roles, this new inner relationship, persisted over long term follow up.[167]

Notably, like in the Mithoefer's work above, Grant did not facilitate any explicit witnessing, retrieving, unburdening, naming and claiming qualities, and so on. Having facilitated some Self to part relationship – "What does it want you to know?" – his intervention was simply to stay in Self well enough, long enough. For five long minutes. His patient, their parts, and the medicine were cooking. If Grant's wonderful parts who wanted to save his patient had blended with him, Grant might have then tried to fix or distract his patient in some way: to lead relaxation breathing exercises or soothing visualizations; to get his patient to fight the depression; to try to argue or reassure his patient out of the depression; and so on. Had Grant not stayed in Self, this healing opportunity might have been lost.

If we do get blended with burdened parts of ourselves and "too much" try to fix, distract, or soothe our patient, I think we will likely get second chances. Our patient's exiles will likely try again to be seen and helped even if one healing opportunity is missed.

Bill Richards is famous for his maxim on difficult periods of a medicine session, "In and through!" This can be a sort of flight instructions, that when difficult things in a medicine session come up, to turn towards them, to be with them, and thereby to go through them.

Unfortunately, I think Richards' work has sometimes been taken out of its rich, clinical context and turned into something of a soundbite. Richards' work on difficult periods of medicine sessions is far more clinically complex than might then be

---

[167] Robert Grant, "Advanced KAP: IFS in ketamine assisted psychotherapy class," 2021.

supposed. Richards is not recommending a simplistic, muscular psychedelic kamikaze mission. His work is not a simple bashing through "resistance" that might come up. I think we will see soon in a clinical vignette from Richards' work that his "In and through" only makes sense within fully respectful relationality. And as we also saw in the Preparation Work chapter, his work is *foundationally* based on and only makes sense in the context of truly adequate relational preparatory work, of a patient having freely and realistically come to true and adequate trust and consent before the medicine session.

Let's turn to a first person report from Richards' work with a research participant in a high dose psilocybin session. This study was on psilocybin assisted psychotherapy for end-of-life anxiety. This participant had a history of cancer that was plaguing her emotionally.

Richards does not use IFS in his work and wouldn't use these terms, but I think we can say in this vignette that during a difficult juncture in the medicine session the participant comes to "In and through" only by her true consent; only as Self; and only in fully respectful relationship. The participant even negotiates her surrender directly with a seeming deity, her seeming Creator. That's a lot of Self there in that relationship! This is the opposite of any exiling of Self. She co-creates and leads herself to free surrender, as herself. From there, a truly profound healing happens.

> Early on the visuals came and dissolved so quickly I could not verbalize them in time... I had no doubt I was in the presence of the Infinite because I felt an overriding peacefulness that carried me through everything, even the very few seconds of "Yikes!" that showed up. I had a sense of losing my observer. I no longer witnessed the images. I was becoming them. This was not exactly creepy, but I did hesitate a minute, feeling my way slowly. There was a sense

of being engulfed. "Am I about to be possessed, is this okay?" I love this bit: I was unwilling to just hand over my body. I said, "If we do this I want my body returned to me in at least as good a shape as it is in now." The reply came, "Do you think I would disrespect my own handiwork?" I got the point and went with it.... My body lit up, all parts in succession. It was the brightest thing I have ever seen. I glowed brilliantly from within. My whole being fluttered. I felt I was being breathed through or played like an instrument. Stunningly beautiful. I got that every part of all of us is sacred. There is no speck in the cosmos which is apart from this breath. The point of it all is sheer pleasure. The world is a misery out of love, presenting us with constant opportunities to find our way home.... I am seeing myself in everybody, and everybody in myself.[168]

As discussed in the Overview of PAP chapter, unlike in some abusive relationships from so-called psychedelic helpers, Richards did not try to cajole, coerce, or force a "surrender" from this participant. She got there herself, as her Self. Crucially, I think we might say that she could do that so well in this medicine session because she was a well prepared person: she trusted Richards, she trusted the medicine, she trusted the setting, she trusted some sense of divinity, and she trusted herself. She was free in this situation, and as such, she could be a *flaneur*, we might say.

Relational alchemy and delos in difficult periods of a medicine session

At times in a medicine session, our patient might be being torn asunder, on impossible opposites, impossible paradoxes. Even in a sort of crucifixion: good/evil, saint/sinner, hope/terror, forward/

---

[168] Richards, William A., Sacred Knowledge: Psychedelics and Religious Experiences. United States: Columbia University Press, 2015.

backward, up/down, left/right. Of paradoxes impossible to name. Our patient unable to move, unable to choose, unable to stand still.

Standing still requires that there is something solid and unmoving to stand on.

Possibly, these very difficult times in medicine sessions "go there," to some of the horrible psychic experiences of trauma or deprivation, whether of personal history, or again, the vulnerabilities of being a being.

I'm reminded of Nick sitting by the fire in his vision, a creature rustling in the bushes outside the clearing, Nick utterly stuck. And stuck being stuck. Again, the Mithoefers counseled him to stay with all that, to stay with exactly the tension and uncertainty. We might say, they counseled him to stay with all of his parts, and with all of their feelings and thoughts, all their fears and needs and hopes.

Jung's work can be helpful here for understanding what parts might be going through in these impossible opposites. Jung, highly influenced by Hegel, wrote of "the tension of the opposites."[169] Hegel wrote of the irresolvable paradox of opposites, of thesis and antithesis: each is 100% true, and at the same time they are 100% incompatible with each other. A tense, irresolvable dead-end. Like Nick in his vision, stuck.

Jung counseled that if that tension is "held" long enough, something new emerges. He called this the "transcendent function," a third thing. Hegel's new synthesis: impossible to foresee, a third thing that shockingly resolves the opposites. Jung wrote that the transcendent function only happens *through* the tension of the opposites, not by soothing or avoiding the tension. Jung also wrote that the third thing doesn't obviate, deny, or destroy the opposites. It's not that kind of "transcendence." That could very much risk being a bypass of some kind. The opposites stay there, but something new emerges.[170]

---

[169] The Structure and Dynamics of the Psyche (Collected Works of C.G. Jung, Volume 8) by C. G. Jung (Author), Gerhard Adler (Translator), R. F.C. Hull (Translator)
[170] Ibid.

Here, our task as therapists is not to soothe or fix or problem solve the tension of the opposites, as badly as parts of us might want to do that. But instead, our role can be to help our patient stay with the tension of the opposites that they are dealing with, *but to not do it alone*: whatever flashes of their own Self they have access to at the time are there, and we are there with them.

This is a form of direct access. Again, an assumption here is that in our patient's worst traumas and deprivations they were pathologically alone. That pathological aloneness is exactly central to the etiology of some of what makes trauma so psychologically noxious and wounding. So our patients need something different in their healing: they need, in rightful ways, to not be alone. One thing they need is us as therapist to be present with them, as our Self, at least to a critical mass.

This can, of course, be quite hard for us as therapist: to be present with our patient as they are going through what might be literally hellish. So, just like our patient, at times we as therapist might just need to "be with and breathe with," or something like that. There might not be much more that we can do. And it can be crucial.

Here is a first person account from a patient in a medicine session. This vignette powerfully gets at the healing power, and the basic safety need, of the therapist staying present with their patient and all their parts during a very hard time in a medicine session. None other than Rick Doblin is the therapist here.

This person was working on horrible PTSD from a murderous rape. This was a high dose LSD session.

> The room seemed to fill up with people from my past who had hurt me, and with people who had tried to help me. My friend's eyes [Rick Doblin] seemed to be calling out to me, but then all of a sudden he changed and became transformed into the rapist. His toes and legs were those of the rapist

but I knew that the figure was my friend. It was horrifying to see him as the man who had caused me so much pain. The only reason I could deal with it was because my friend was so strong in being himself that even though his body seemed to be that of the rapist, the rapist could not take over his mind, and I could turn to him for support.[171]

At very difficult times of a high dose medicine session, our patient may be at what seems to be a breaking point of Self: beyond dialogue, in an impossibility of healing, an impossibility of anything. Just as they were, perhaps, at the center of the times of the traumas and deprivations, barely able to endure.

In the medicine session at times they are maybe being cooked in the *temenos*, the alchemical vas, the caldron. This is a near death experience. They are near total defeat, as again, they might have been in severe trauma or deprivation.

Here, we might say, we are at Good Friday. Christ has died. God killed by torture, fully in human body and mind, for no crime. Christ dies without even the solace of faith. In one of the Gospels, his last words are, "Father, why hast thou forsaken me?"

Good Friday is the only day of the Catholic calendar that there is no Mass available, no redemption available. As a Catholic, it hurts, I can tell you.

I love the old hippie cliché that goes, "Anyone who thinks psychedelics are a cheap shortcut hasn't worked with psychedelics."

Again, in addition to this being terribly difficult for our patient, this can of course be very difficult for us as therapists. Jung notes of his relational model, "The meeting of two personalities [in a treatment] is like the contact of two chemical substances: if there is any reaction, both are transformed.... You [therapist] can exert no influence if you are not susceptible to influence."[172] He even likens

---

[171] Unknown, Through the Gateway of the Heart : Accounts of Experiences with MDMA and other Empathogenic Substances, Adamson. Quoted in Acid Test, Shroder.

[172] Jung, C.G.. Modern Man in Search of a Soul. Taylor & Francis, 2014.

this to the real possibility of the therapist getting "infected" by the patient's illness, a common danger for healthcare providers.

So at times, both therapist and patient are there in the *temenos*, the cauldron, each in their own ways, in their own roles, but both are cooking. We as therapist are then not the alchemist, we are ourselves some of the *prima materia*, the raw materials of the alchemy. And we are also some of the *temenos*, the holding, even if we do not see a way forward. We must accompany our patient, and we must stay in our own bodies, stay Self. They need us with them, suffering with them to some extent. And they need us separate from them, a caring other who is present with them. A caretaking presence of some real friendship.

In historical traumas for our patients, not just the aloneness, but some of the worst of it might have been that rightful relational bonds were violently ripped asunder. The perverse aloneness of being with another as they are cruel.

Or the wrongful aloneness of deprivation, the literal absence of the important other or, even in the physical presence of the other, them not seeing us or not being with us, even as we are right before their eyes.

So in medicine sessions, these exiles might then not be alone. They might be witnessed and companioned by both our patient as Self — to whatever extent that is possible at the time — and by us as therapist as Self. And this happens psychically exactly in the places where these exiles are stuck, the places of trauma or deprivation, where they were previously wretchedly alone.

Psychedelics clearly heal in ways that are quite different than narcotics.

Something new always comes at daybreak, even if we cannot, by definition, know that in the true deepest dark of night. The medicines can take even that from us. Maybe they need to. Otherwise, it's not real: we and our parts wouldn't really have "gone there." Richard Tarnas, a great Western pioneer of both psychedelics and philosophy, has said of medicine sessions, "You have to deeply experience that everything's on the line."[173]

The Greek term *delos*, half of the term psychedelic, is amazingly instructive here. *Delos* can be translated as "a sudden revealing." The image of a *delos* could be of daybreak on the land or waters, with an emphasis on the sudden *breaking* of day.

The literal island of Delos in Ancient Greece had a thriving culture with a rich religious and commercial life. Of its genesis, it is said that Zeus had an affair with Leto, a titan, a lineage of immortals more ancient than the gods and goddesses themselves. Leto became pregnant with twins. Hera, Zeus' wife, one of the most powerful divinities, was enraged and divinely decreed that no place would hold Leto for the birth.

A horrible crisis, the impossibility of birth. What would come of mother and children? No way out or through, no relief. In despair and desperation, Zeus eventually broke down and implored his brother Poseidon, god of the waters, of earthquakes, and flowing and thundering horses, to create a new island, a place that hadn't existed at the time of Hera's decree, so that it could *possibly* accommodate Leto and her birthing. Poseidon did this right away, no time to waste, an instant revelation. A *delos*. The island of Delos.

Leto went right there and was able to deliver her and Zeus' children, the twins Artemis and Apollo.

It's very notable, I think, that even Zeus, the king of the gods, could not "solve" this alone. He needed a friend, he needed his brother. He reached out for help.

After the dark in medicine sessions, a daybreak, a *delos*, always seems to come. It might be the next moment. It might be minutes, hours. It might be days, weeks, or even years.

Years ago, a patient came into my practice complaining that he had used LSD recreationally 20 years earlier and that it was the worst experience of his life and that he had never felt totally

---

[173] Richard Tarnas, "Psychedelic Initiation in Postmodern Culture & the Contribution of Stanislav Grof" (Footnotes2Plato Podcast, December 10, 2021).

right since. He was very upset and worried about his health and well being. He seemed healthy to me and he had always been high functioning. He told me he could never shake some unnamable, deeply unsettling feeling or experience — or something — from the LSD experience and he was plagued by it.

He had eventually gone to his primary care physician to see if he had neurological damage. His doctor did a workup, gave him a clean bill of health, and referred him to me for therapy.

My patient and I were both at a loss. We just held this unknowing for the first few sessions. I stayed present with him, him with me. Inwardly, I trusted the medicine, unsure what else to do.

After a few weeks like this, he burst into my office at the beginning of his appointment time and excitedly announced to me that he had been grieving his father's death during the psychedelic experience, that he had never grieved before or since.

Over the next several weeks of the therapy, he was able to substantially work through grieving his father. He came to understand his father, their relationship, and himself much better. By the end, he was sweetly grateful for his psychedelic experience.

Leto became one of the prime divinities of birthing, of motherhood. She is honored and entreated in prayer and rituals, often, I imagine, in desperate times.

Her and Zeus' children, Artemis and Apollo, became arguably the most important of the new generation of the Olympians.

Many times, patients will report towards the end of their PAP that even if they went through hell in their medicine sessions with no seeming resolution, that they are now well improved. That they are "fine." They have no epic narrative for it, no healing story at all. It's just that the PTSD, depression, self-rejection, or end of life anxiety is not near the center of their experience anymore. They might say things like, "I'm okay. I have no idea why, but I'm okay."

Healing was impossible, but it went ahead and happened anyway.

CHAPTER SEVEN

INTEGRATION WORK

"Time is a circle."

— Dave Kiepert, Neenah High School jazz
band instructor

W e might say that in preparation work we planted a seed. Then in the medicine session, the seed sprouted and maybe flowered and bore fruit. It may have left behind tender shoots, further seeds, a stalk, and maybe a glorious memory. Now, in integration work, we could say we are helping our patient engage with and elaborate an ecosystem of health. That will be the main image here for integration work: engaging with and elaborating an ecosystem of health.

An axiom of this ecosystem sense of psychedelic integration is that if we do not make the benefits of a medicine session relational then they risk withering or stunting. A quick, simple, and beautiful example: let's say our patient has a vision during a medicine session of, "I'm good." This comes with a rare and simple relief, a calmness and a willingness to be present. That's — obviously — awesome. But now what? After the medicine session, if our patient just tries to hold on to that or intensify it in mainly some muscular or informational way, as something of an affirmation, a slogan, or as a "state" to hold on to or recreate, it probably won't endure long as a living thing. Because relationships are not just information or an experience.

As an entirely relational model of inner and outer relationships, IFS fits right in here. In this example, if our patient finds and gets into a living, ongoing relationship with the part of themselves who found themself as "good," who was healed, then our patient and that part can have each other, for the rest of their lives. A great friendship, a great inner family, can result.

For the protectors of such a part, if they can see that that part of our patient, the former exile, is now doing "good," then the protector or protectors can rethink their role. Maybe they now want to rest more, a lot more, trusting Self and the now healed part. Maybe the protector wants to shift into a quite novel role as a great helper. Or maybe the protector wants to stay in some level of a protective role, but with more nuance, and in some partnership and friendship with Self and the now healed part.

Through such relational integration of the healing there can be a living, new, complex, inner ecosystem of health and friendship. From there, our patient and their parts can interact with their outside relationships, enriching into an even more complex ecosystem of health.

Then, I think we can say that this IFS and psychedelic psychotherapy has gone very well.

So here in integration work we are stating and restating most strongly the central themes of this book: that psychedelics and IFS are always relational, are always about ecosystems. Following from this, we could say that everything we've been looking at in this book and doing in IFS PAP has been about integration. The integration in prep work: of Self and all parts of our patient preparing together in collaboration and possible consent for a medicine session. The integration in the medicine session: the same cast of characters and maybe new ones integrating into new relationships, perhaps as themselves, or as being seen and known, burdens and all, and now available for relationship and healing. And then here in integration the integration obviously gets the most explicit, simple, grounded, and ongoing.

By this, we could say that PAP is a circle. Circles famously have no beginning and no end. They're all integration.

In the quote opening this chapter, apparently the great high school music instructor Dave Kiepert would greet his students as they walked into the room for rehearsal by swinging his hand in a circle, snapping at the top in rhythm. When the students were settled in, he'd keep swinging his hand and say, "Time is a circle," and count them in on the snaps. "One and uh two and uh three and uh four and uh." And then on the one, they'd start playing together.

This chapter will be in roughly two sections. The first section will involve discussions of some big picture topics on psychedelic integration work and IFS. We will discuss some short-comings of common Western PAP integration work; the crucial topic of working with disappointments in medicine sessions; some differences in integration work in standard IFS versus in IFS PAP; and how integration work and medicine sessions are fully equal partners, including how medicine sessions can act as diagnostic aids and then pass on the actual healing to integration work.

This first section will be grounded in case material following and discussing some of Nick's crucial and powerful integration work.

The second section of this chapter will get into detailed discussions of some of the specific important relationships, inner and outer, of IFS PAP integration. As part of this, we will discuss some concrete suggestions for the first two integration sessions.

For case material in this second section, we will return to Claire and look at and discuss her first integration session in its entirety. That session will ground and illustrate many topics in this chapter.

We will end this chapter, and the clinical part of the book, by focusing on day to day integration practices that we might suggest to our patients. After all, by definition, our patient's day to day life is where the richest and most important integration can and needs to happen.

Integration as the Weak Link in the Chain of Western PAP

Integration work has poignantly often rightly been observed to be a weak spot for Western PAP. People might have had an astoundingly healing or powerful medicine session, but then the question quickly comes up, *"Now what?"* Often, satisfactory answers to that are sorely lacking. Of course, this can be a serious clinical issue for reasons of both efficacy and safety.

Luckily, IFS has epic contributions to make to excellent psychedelic integration work, which we will of course discuss throughout this chapter.

But before that, it can be important to have some understanding of why Western PAP has often been far too thin on integration. One way of thinking about this is that there have often been a few less than optimal assumptions brought into psychedelic integration by the Modern West: That we should be trying to integrate states of mind or experiences; that this whole PAP thing is an individual project; and that this is about a "mono mind."

None of these are relational, and therefore none of them will likely stand long.

Such assumptions about psychedelic integration can come from an unwitting and unfortunate carrying over to PAP of a simply Modernist worldview. By a Modernist worldview, I mean an essentially mechanistic, reductionistic, analytic, atomized take on things.[174] Such a worldview has great strengths, but integration, psychedelic or otherwise, usually isn't one of them!

As we discussed earlier, such a worldview brought into psychology can lead to a sense that who and what we each are is basically something like a standalone computer, fast and fancy, but maybe buggy or kind of broken. Psychology can then be seen as an effort to analyze such a faltering computer to better understand its small, constituent pieces, of either software or hardware, and then to put the computer back together maybe

---

[174] Tarnas, Richard. The Passion of the Western Mind: Understanding the Ideas that Have Shaped Our World View. United Kingdom: Pimlico, 2010.

with some new parts, of hardware, software, or data. This is a sense of psychotherapy and psychiatry as attempts to upgrade or repair the hardware ("the neurological networks") or the software ("the cognitive processes") of our minds.

This can unfortunately lead to little to no sense of relationality in our inner worlds, because in this view, our inner world consists of nothing like an inner family. It's just information being processed. We can also wind up with a shallow, thin, transactional sense of outer relationships: that our relationships are like one computer in a network of other computers. That our relationships are simply computers exchanging bits of information between each other, not beings being together.

In this Modern view, parts, our inner children, are unseen or are "seen through," invisible or neglected in plain sight as just information or states. And likewise, our very Self is unseen or seen through: by this view, in Martin Buber's terms, it's all "its," there are no Thous.

This will not do. We need to take care in the metaphors we think in as they can highly limit and color what we can see and what we can think. Psychology has long trafficked in metaphors of the current technology of its day. Steam engines were cutting edge technology during Freud's early career. In those days, he wrote of the psyche in metaphors of a hydraulic system with competing forces, thresholds, and release valves.[175] These days, we often read about the psyche in computer metaphors, or worse, as our minds as literally computers.

But such a computational, non-relational take is in fact not the "official" frame of Western psychology. Every intro to psychology or psychiatry class or textbook rightfully states the "biopsychosocial model" as the basic frame of our field. The biopsychosocial model can mean that rather than discreet networked computers, who and what we each are is a complex, relational integration of the "bio" – body and biology; "psycho" – psyche, mind or soul; and the

---

[175] Freud, Sigmund. The Psychopathology of Everyday Life: (1901). United Kingdom: Hogarth Press, 1973.

"social" – our world, our cultures, our external relationships, and our places in the world. The biopsychosocial model is a profound model of integration, and it is a basic assumption of this chapter (and of the whole book).

But in actual clinical practice, Western mental healthcare has struggled to adequately implement its own wise and rich integrative and relational model. In practice, we've particularly failed to integrate the "social." That is, we've generally failed or struggled to extend mental health beyond a sense of just solo, atomized individuals, and instead to include and embrace and implement community both in our sense of the etiology of psychopathology (the suffering of the soul) and in our sense of what healing and health are.

However, as we've seen, psychedelics are fully, profoundly, and unavoidably biopsychosocial: They are of body, they even have bodies themselves. They are of psyche, obviously. And they are relational, they are social, as we've seen over and over in this book so far and will see again and again in this chapter. Because of this, I have great hope that the reintroduction of psychedelics to Western mental healthcare can help Western mental healthcare finally realize its rich biopsychosocial model. And for some patients, optionally, to complexify this further to a relational, integrative biopsychosocialspiritual model.

Again, if we instead bring to psychedelic integration work a sense of computers as what we are, then the unwitting goal of integration work can then naturally come to be trying to integrate the new states, experiences, or insights from the medicine session into the mind as new code or wiring and thereby make the upgrade or fix permanent. This is a sense that that is what health is and what psychedelics can do for us.

To complicate this discussion, there is of course truth and importance to the neurologic and cognitive processing aspects of psychedelic practice. As we've seen repeatedly, psychedelics are ineffably interdisciplinary and supradisciplinary. No simplistic take on psychedelics will stand long.

But those of us who have tried to integrate from medicine sessions by trying to hold onto, recreate, or make permanent the states, experiences, or ideas from medicine sessions, however glorious and important, have probably found such integration to be inadequate in a lot of ways, no matter how strenuously or skillfully we might work at it. Been there, a lot.

So for this chapter, we will leave aside computer metaphors of psychology. Instead, the sense of psychedelic integration here is entirely about beings in relationships, inner and outer. Following from that, some of the most important clinical "technique" of integration work, as seen here, is suggested by some great clichés about relationships: Relationships, inner and outer, take work. They take time. They take showing up as ourselves, vulnerabilities and all. They take listening. They take honest response, at least with ourselves. That we are agents in our relationships. That healthy relationships are of giving and receiving. That, if they are healthy relationships, they are of two-way respect. And if they are of two-way respect that they can, if we so chose, be of some real trust in the other.

This relational take is a very grounded one on psychedelic integration. It could even seem like a disappointingly grounded take on psychedelic integration. I can hear a possible objection, "Isn't this pretty much what we've always had without psychedelics? Just us here in relationships. What about the epic psychedelic discoveries in seemingly other realms? What about the surprises of the profoundest?" Those are fully honored here. But they are seen as part of an ecosystem, as parts of the circle. The path of integration here will not be primarily about the bigness or the novelty of the experiences. The path of integration here will be primarily about the quality of the relationships.

After all, integration and relationship are just about the same thing.

WORKING WITH PATIENT DISAPPOINTMENTS

People often turn to psychedelics as a sort of desperate last hope. But psychedelics are not panaceas, and important disappointments often come with PAP practice. These disappointments especially show up in the integration phase.

No matter how great a medicine session, people often find after a medicine session that they are quickly back to the "same ole" of their suffering. And maybe even in some new distress if they have lost some hope in psychedelics as something of a permanent or complete cure. As we saw in the Preparation Work chapter, a common fear that parts have about doing a medicine session is a fear of losing some hope if psychedelics don't "work." These parts have real wisdom.

Crucially, IFS can help us work with disappointments in PAP as not failures of psychedelics, nor as failures of our patient or of us as therapist, but as some of the most important trailheads to healing. It's usually protectors who are most disappointed in PAP, and every protector is in relationship with an exile. The stronger or more pervasive the protector, the deeper the exile. So the sometimes profound disappointments in PAP can help our patients come to "see," be with, and get to know some of their strongest protectors and then their deepest exiles. And ultimately to help them.

For instance, in integration work, a patient feels defective, defeated, or bereft because they didn't get the profound healing or the profound experience from a medicine session that they think they needed. It can then be important to help our patient, if they are game, get into some Self to part relationship with this part of themselves who is feeling so bad. What did this part hope would happen for our patient? What are its fears for our patient now that that didn't happen? Are they protecting or protecting from anything or any part of our patient? Why?

If these inner dialogues go somewhere, then these parts, protector and exile, have now manifested much more clearly. Perhaps now some of the strongest and most pervasive protectors and deepest exiles can get the crucial healing they need. By this, I would say that the medicine session went excellently.

But that healing might actually happen in the integration work. This is a different sense of integration work than can be usual in Western PAP, where integration work is often thought of as simply looking backwards at the medicine session. Here, the view is that medicine sessions can actually hand off the healing to the integration work. This makes medicine sessions and integration work fully equal partners, not integration work simply in service of the medicine sessions.

A similar dynamic around disappointments can also eventually come up in integration work when our patient *did* have a profound healing or a profound experience in the medicine session. Maybe soon after such a session, protector parts, understandably enough, diligently try to take up that experience as a shield to ward off all vulnerability. But that probably won't work long. Life is hard. We'll likely be back to vulnerability and disappointments sooner or later. Then, to those protectors, the medicine session can seem to have ultimately failed. And then, once again, in IFS integration work, those protectors and any exiles they protect or protect from can now be far better known, and therefore available for relationship and ultimately healing.

Some of these parts might never have been revealed clearly enough without the "screen" of psychedelics onto which they could clearly cast some of their greatest hopes, their greatest needs and fears, and thereby become visible and available for concrete relationship and healing. So working with any disappointments in the medicine session or the PAP can be a "royal road" to some of the deepest healing.

Working with disappointments can also be a crucial safety issue because these disappointments can be about what a part or parts think is one of the last hopes for our patient. It might be dangerous if our patients go through any disappointments or frustrations like that too much alone.

Let's now get into some rich case material on integration work by following up with Nick in some of his integration work.

SOME OF NICK'S INTEGRATION JOURNEY

As we saw in the Medicine Session chapter, Nick had great healing in his medicine sessions with the Mithoefers, including no longer meeting criteria for PTSD. But, of course, his story doesn't end there.

As I think we will see, Nick's ongoing recovery was not simplistic. It was not a steady state of inner peace or bliss or ease. Far from it. It seems it was more about increased options for relationships, for Self to part and Self to Self relationships. Nick continued to suffer, but he had more options for relating to that suffering, both within himself and with the people in his life. More possibilities for intimacy.

After Nick's profound healings in his PAP, he began to rebuild his life. He could work. He started a new job.

On his third or fourth day at his new job, he started having a horrible flashback, seeing himself being shot in the warehouse where he worked, the warehouse aisles reminding him of the narrow streets of Iraqi cities. Tom Shroder brings us there again in the interviews he and Nick shared in *Acid Test*:

> "I started getting choked up and running faster to get to the bathroom. I remember before I finally got to the bathroom, tears were starting to come out of my eyes. By the time I slammed the door, I just went straight to the corner and curled down and

put my hand over my mouth so people wouldn't hear me screaming. Just screamed into my hand. Cried. Splashed some water on my face and stared in the mirror and told myself to pull my shit together. Went back out there. Walking back, I remember talking to the guys and saying, 'Oh, stomach problems.' ...

"My boss finally came to me and said, 'Is everything okay?' And I wanted to say to myself, 'Suck it up,' but that booming voice came into my head and said, 'Tell him!' So I said—I whispered it to him, 'cause all the other guys were standing behind him, and they were staring at me too—I was, like, 'I'm having panic attacks.'

The boss sent him home, and the next day he came back and admitted to everyone what had happened.

"If it happened again, I wanted them to know," Nick said.

As soon as he told them, he realized that his real problem had not been the daydream but that he had tried to suppress it rather than letting it come up, as he'd done in the MDMA sessions. "After that," he said, "I could have the same kind of rush of anxiety without manifesting it where I'm actually in a corner crying and screaming. Now I can meditate and just get back in touch with that inner healer. I can relive it, bring back that voice: 'Hey, you need to relax, this isn't something you should be worrying about.' Afterwards I'd feel this huge relief—like vapors just coming off my body."...

He says he became so mellow, and felt so comfortable talking about what he'd been through, that "guys at work, they'd say, 'You don't seem like you're a Marine,' and that's when I'd tell them about the therapy that I went through and stuff. I said, 'Hey, they gave me Ecstasy in these sessions, so it loosened me up and turned me into, I guess, a softie, you would say, so that's why I don't mind talking about these things, and I see the benefit in talking about it.' I learned how to keep the warrior without having to always have my shield up, my guard up, you know? Without having to have my head on a swivel, thinking something's always trying to kill me."[176]

This outcome, his flashback and panic attack post-treatment, might seem disappointing, a failure of treatment. But Nick clearly didn't feel that way. IFS might provide at least one sense of what's going on here.

We might see that in the medicine sessions, key exiles and protectors had been greatly healed, so now in his daily life they weren't so burdened and trying to blend with Nick. Nick could then be more present as Self and leading in his life situations. He could be much more there, unblended, in his external world and internal world even as his new boss and co-workers were all staring at him after the flashback and panic attack. A protective part of him still wanted him to navigate this situation by "sucking it up," by hiding his vulnerability and his difficulties from his boss, co-workers, and from himself. But there as Self more, he could then decide what he wanted to do or try.

What he decided to do probably completely shocked some of his protectors! As we saw, he told his boss the truth, that he was having panic attacks.

[176] Shroder, Tom. Acid Test: LSD, Ecstasy, and the Power to Heal. United States: Penguin Publishing Group, 2015.

The next day he went further and told all his co-workers simply and directly what was going on with him: "If it happened again, I wanted them to know."

Here again, harkening back to one of his medicine sessions, with the monster part of himself chained in a dungeon, we might see the possible relational nature of Self: that when Nick moved from seeing his boss and co-workers as things to be managed, to instead seeing them as full beings worthy of full relationship with, he then simultaneously became Self, and could then lead as Self.

And it wasn't just his outer relationships that became relationships of Self. Nick, as himself, didn't need to try to firefight away or manage away his anxiety. He could be with it and help it.

This was like what Nick had done so many times in the prep work with the Mithoefers and in the medicine sessions: stay with whatever's going on, inner or outer, whatever it is, and be with it and share his breath with it, be in relationship with it.

What had been unsayable, even to himself, had become sayable by Self, and in that saying became even a path to connection with his own vulnerability and with the people in his life.

I'd like to look at this vignette from another perspective, from something of a Zen perspective, as best I can. This is a bit idiosyncratic, but for me, Zen and psychedelics have always been something like two legs in walking. I hope that by bringing in this Zen perspective we might have yet another position to look at what was going on with Nick in his integration and thereby help us triangulate on it better.

The *Mumonkan*, a classic Zen book, is a collection of *koans*. We might think of *koans* as something like teaching jokes, as Barry Magid has so helpfully framed them. *The Mumonkan*, in its very title, is maybe something of a setup for a joke, a very serious one. It's often translated into English as *The Gateless Gate*.

What's *that*?

Mu is a famous *koan* from this book, the first one, "the great barrier" of Zen. For students meditating on *mu* in some traditional practices, the joke of *mu* often becomes a very dark one. For them, meditating with *mu* can become like they've been on a very long and tiring journey and night is falling. They know they will have no rest, no warmth, until home. But the great barrier of *mu* is blocking them at every turn. They can't get through it, around it, under it, or over it no matter what they do. The night darkens, the cold seeps in. Utterly trapped and stymied, it's a desperate situation and it's steadily getting worse.

In his life, Nick is slammed into a great barrier: PTSD, flashbacks, the panic wall. Impenetrable. Imprisoning him from his life, from his new job, from his wife, from his co-workers, crushing him into the impossibility of living, into suicidality —

But then Nick does an astonishing thing, maybe even astonishing to himself. Something that his preparation work, friendship, medicine sessions, and integration work with the Mithoefers showed him in therapy again and again, but now here he is in his real life, the real thing:

We might say, Nick turns towards the barrier and knocks on it.

Nick: "Knock knock."
Barrier: "Who's there?"
Nick: "Wait, what?!! Who's *there*??!"
Barrier: "Reality."
Nick: "Reality *who*??"
Barrier: "Reality you, me, them too."
Nick touches the barrier and connects through to togetherness.

Nick, leading as Self, turned the panic attacks, the flashbacks, and the PTSD into the very gates that swung open into deepened friendship and companionship, inner and outer.

It's very notable and terribly exciting that in the study that Nick was a part of, in addition to the 53% of the participants who no longer met criteria for PTSD at the end of the study period, on one year follow up an additional 7% of the participants no longer met criteria for PTSD.[177] That is, people tended to come to even more health after treatment stopped. That's some powerful, ongoing integration there: continued, ongoing healing post-treatment. And I want to underline that this study was working with people suffering from previously treatment resistant PTSD.

But, of course, psychedelics and PAP are not panaceas. By about two and half years after the study, serious stressors were weighing on Nick: his wife's very serious degenerative illness, witnessing a major car crash right outside their home, and the ongoing hits of what Freud called "normal human misery." Nick felt that further PAP treatment would be very helpful for him. But the psychedelics he had received as part of research were still not yet legal. The medical laws against psychedelics that were never based in science were still on the books. This is a sobering part of the story.

Nick knew that for his health he needed a return to the support and healing of PAP. I think it is terribly important to recognize that this need for further treatment is not a failure of treatment. Sure, who wouldn't want a "happily ever after" for their patients. But Nick had something more grounded: he knew what he needed in the continuing vulnerability of his life. He needed more support for a time.[178]

Psychedelics will not end our vulnerability or our patients' vulnerability. IFS will not end our vulnerability. The two combined will not end our vulnerability. Nothing will. Again, a crucial part of integration work as considered here will be helping our patients

[177] Mithoefer, Michael C et al. "3,4-methylenedioxymethamphetamine (MDMA)-assisted psychotherapy for post-traumatic stress disorder in military veterans, firefighters, and police officers: a randomised, double-blind, dose-response, phase 2 clinical trial." The Lancet. Psychiatry vol. 5,6 (2018): 486-497.
[178] Shroder, Tom. Acid Test: LSD, Ecstasy, and the Power to Heal. United States: Penguin Publishing Group, 2015.

integrate with their ongoing vulnerability and not being alone with that.

Even though Nick knew this, he was badly thwarted from getting further psychedelic assisted psychotherapy. The very government that had sent him to a deceitful "war of choice" which wounded him greatly psychologically was now blocking him from readily available healing. As a clinician, as a citizen, and as a human being, I smolder at this. I expect more from my government. We can maybe be heartened that the governments of Australia, Canada, and Switzerland have approved psychedelic assisted psychotherapy, and it seems that, later rather than sooner, the US FDA will follow suit.

Very notably, such crucial regulatory changes have happened in no small part directly through Nick's own great contributions, through his commitment to share the story of his healing path so powerfully.

We will end our discussion of Nick's healing journey here. If you happen to read this, Nick, my deep thanks. Like I said, you've helped this work tremendously, including in my own ongoing healing journey.

Let's now turn to further topics in integration work.

Some differences in psychedelic IFS integration versus standard IFS integration

Everything in this integration work chapter is standard IFS. But, as we'll see, at times in psychedelic integration work things need to be shuffled differently and can need different emphasis than in integration of healing in standard IFS therapy. So, we'll now look at some differences between integration in PAP and integration in standard IFS.

Because the healing in medicine sessions can be so direct, so seemingly instantaneous, so intense, so "strange," or even just so simple, one important difference is that in psychedelic integration we might need to check carefully that all the healing "steps" of standard IFS therapy have happened.

With an exile, this could mean checking that they've been fully witnessed, fully updated, retrieved, or any of the "steps." And if some of the IFS steps of a healing process didn't seem to have happened fully enough in the medicine session, then we can help our patient and an exile do those steps in the integration work.

For protectors, after a healing in a medicine session they can sometimes wind up having *zero* knowledge that the exile they've been protecting and protecting from is now healed and doing well. This can of course be a major problem for integration.

Differences like these can start to show that psychedelics don't just "do IFS." Psychedelics and IFS clearly have great overlap, but we can start to see that they each also have their own strengths — all the better for them to have a truly great partnership in very rich healing.

In Claire's first integration session (later in this chapter), we will see a very clear instance of needing to shuffle standard IFS integration work differently. But again, we'll also see that it's all IFS work.

INTEGRATION WORK AND MEDICINE SESSIONS AS FULLY EQUAL PARTNERS

As we've discussed, in a lot of Western PAP, integration work can be seen as primarily in service of the healing of the medicine session. That is, there can be a view that integration work is simply retrospective, that it is trying to take the healing from the medicine session and integrate it into our patient's life.

But as we've also discussed, the view here of integration work is that it is fully primary healing work. We can start to see that this can make medicine sessions and integration work fully equal partners, each with some sometimes differing and complementary strengths for healing and health.

We clearly saw this in Nick's integration work: Nick's integration work was active, primary healing work. And it was some of the most crucial healing work because it was exactly in his day to day life. And of course, these crucial healings of integration work might really not have been possible without the help and healing of medicine sessions.

Again, medicine sessions and integration work as fully equal partners.

Medicine sessions acting primarily as diagnostic aids; hyperblending

Building on this great partnership of medicine sessions and integration work, an assumption here is that sometimes medicine sessions seem to act primarily as a diagnostic aid, and then hand off the actual healing to the integration work.

We might see this in a major way in what we've been calling "hyperblending" in medicine sessions. As we saw in the Medicine Session chapter, hyperblending can be when a burdened part (exile or protector) blends *intensely* with our patient. With *psychedelic* intensity. This can be almost completely overwhelming for Self, with seemingly no path for unblending.

The part who was blending in the medicine session may or may not eventually get any healing in the medicine session. If not, this can seem like a huge failure of a medicine session, even a disastrous one. All pain, no gain. And if not worked with well in integration, it can in fact be disastrous or just very painful and disorienting for our patient (and for us as therapist).

But hyperblending in a medicine session can be very important in integration work. Like in working with any disappointments our patient might have about the medicine session, through hyperblending a part can become far better known and can then be available for relationship and healing. This is because some of the deepest exiles and most pervasive protectors seem to only be able to be known, to manifest, through the intensity of hyperblending.

Hyperblending in a medicine session can help us, both patient and therapist, far better understand what's going on. This gets to the etymological meaning of diagnosing, "to better know through and through" (in Greek, *gnosis* means knowing, *dia* means through).

A couple of examples: perhaps during hyperblending in a medicine session an exile with OCD burdens breaks through its protectors fully for the first time in years. That can be truly harrowing for our patient, not only to have to face such an exile, but to face them with the force of psychedelic hyperblending. But if worked with well, perhaps primarily in integration work, this can ultimately be key to opening crucial healing chances for this part. Having finally manifested, they now have a real path for healing and relationship.

Or, a seeming protector might hyperblend with our patient during a medicine session and block just about *anything* from happening. Maybe someone even sleeps through a whole high dose medicine session. Then in integration work, it may be that this very strong, very broad protector might be known with some real clarity and relationship for the first time.

Importantly, hyperblending brings us back to what is sometimes called HPPD, or Hallucinogen Persisting Perception Disorder. We started discussing this in the Preparation Work chapter in the context of something like HPPD as one of the most common fears parts have about doing a medicine session, of "going crazy" forever.

Again, HPPD can be when some psychological turmoil from a medicine session can go on for days or weeks or months after the medicine session. HPPD is rare, but real and important. IFS might help us understand HPPD as perhaps when a part who was hyperblended with someone in a medicine session then stays blended with them to some extent after the medicine session.

Again, this seems to particularly happen with extremely high doses of medicines, like into overdose territory; when little to no preparation work has been done before the medicine session; or when the medicine session is done too much alone, that is, without adequate relational support, even if in a crowd.

A few people have been referred to me for difficulties like this after psychedelic sessions. IFS integration work around hyperblending can be very helpful in these situations. If we can help our patient be in some Self to part relationship with what is coming up in the HPPD, not only can this very much help resolve the HPPD, but it can lead to some very important healing as that part, and any parts it interacts with, are seen and understood and ultimately helped.

We saw this in the example of my patient who seemed to have been thrown into grieving his father's death during a recreational psychedelic experience. He had been plagued by that feeling for 20 years, until we could do some integration work on it. Once he could overtly grieve, that turned into a rich healing path and the blending subsided.

HPPD is rare while hyperblending in medicine sessions is fairly common. Hyperblending almost always only lasts for a portion of the medicine session and does not lead to anything like what's being called HPPD.

And again, hyperblending might be one of the "royal roads" to healing in integration work.

AN OVERVIEW OF SOME OF THE MAIN RELATIONSHIPS OF INTEGRATION WORK

Let's start looking at some of the main relationships of IFS PAP integration work. These relationships will inform the rest of the chapter, including some detailed suggestions for the first two integration sessions.

As part of these topics and relationships, later we will also look at Claire's first integration session.

The topics and relationships we will look at are:

- Establishing ongoing Self to part relationship with a former exile who got healing in the medicine session
- Checking about external constraints and working with those, if need be
- Helping protectors integrate into the more healed psyche of our patient, especially in light of any healed exiles
- Helping our patient integrate Self
- Helping our patient do integration and healing right in their daily life

Once again, this is all standard IFS. It's just brought into relationship with the psychedelic ecosystem.

Let's look at how we might start working with these relationships in roughly the first two integration sessions.

GETTING THE BALL ROLLING; SOME SUGGESTIONS FOR THE FIRST INTEGRATION SESSION

Timing the first integration session

If at all reasonably possible, it can be important to do the first integration session the day after the medicine session. The internal family might have been through a lot and could really need some company! Even for a very positive, joyful, and clearly healing medicine session, doing the first integration session the next day can be very important. A big healing in a medicine session is of course wonderful, but as we'll see, there can then be a lot that needs fairly immediate integrating to keep it vital, healthy, and alive.

Prioritizing working with protectors early in integration is particularly important after a very positive, very impactful medicine session. Protectors who have not been integrated into the healing can get quite concerned about any big healing and might want to exile the healing. Or they simply don't know the healing happened so they keep doing their old burdened jobs. And, protectors need their own healing, we definitely don't want to forget about them.

It's also important to do the first integration session soon for potential safety considerations. This is true even for a very positive, very smooth medicine session. We'll particularly see this with "external constraints," which we might briefly define here as when healing can cause shifts in our patient that people in their world might want to block or thwart, or even hurt or attack our patient for. An example of external constraints is our patient feeling freer and more assertive in a relationship that has some controlling or even abusive dynamics. In such a relationship, the other might attack our patient in some way for their healing, attack their agency and health. Similarly, for some patients, given racist, sexist, classist, anti-queer, and other oppressive problems in cultures, healing and health in our patient following a great medicine session can be attacked, subtly or not, putting our patient and their healing in danger. It can be very important that any external constraints are at least noticed and named right in the first integration session and worked with as best possible. We don't want healing to put our patient at risk.

We'll discuss external constraints in its own section further on in this chapter.

As we've discussed, there can also be disappointments coming out of a medicine session. These can be crucial to bring into integration work early on because any disappointments can be quite painful for our patient, and they can lead to safety concerns. This is especially true for people who have been seeing PAP as a sort of "last hope" for themselves. And, as we discussed, disappointments about a medicine session can be some of the most important trailheads to healing.

In general, there can be a lot of vulnerability coming out of a medicine session. Newly healed exiles might be seeing the light of day for the first time in many years. Healed exiles, even when retrieved, unburdened, and in Self to part relationship, can still be some of the most sensitive and vulnerable parts of ourselves. That is often one of their great gifts to our whole, complex self. But they need to not be alone.

For these reasons, in my practice, if possible I like to schedule medicine sessions on a Thursday and schedule the first integration session for that Friday. This timing can also have a big advantage in that it can give patients the weekend for integration activities with their parts, as we'll discuss further on in this chapter.

Possible priorities in the first integration session

Again, if it's been a really positive, really wonderful medicine session, I think it can be important to prioritize working with protectors in the first integration session. This is partially for the protectors themselves. Protectors carry heavy burdens. Integration work can be the prime healing opportunity for protectors.

And if protectors aren't well integrated with the new healing, they might want to protect from it, essentially to try to exile even a healed former exile. But if given a chance for integration, protectors can change or moderate their roles and possibly come into teamwork with this now healed former exile and with our patient as Self. Healed protectors can be wonderful ongoing members of the internal ecosystem, of the internal family.

Or, if it's been a seemingly lackluster, maybe disappointing medicine session, it might sound counterintuitive, but I think it can then be important to prioritize working with any *possible* exile who got healing in the medicine session. The rationale here is that *if* there was some healing that happened in the medicine session, then it could wither if it is not seen and integrated. Essentially, without integration work, a young, healed part might be left unseen and alone. That will likely not go well.

I personally come to this work with an assumption that *something* good will come from a medicine session. I don't hold that assumption with a strenuous grip. I'm willing to be wrong. But I think it's a helpful assumption to bring to the first integration session even if nothing much seemed to have happened in the medicine session. If we're wrong and it seems no healing came from the medicine session, then we've wasted a bit of integration time looking for it. But if we're right, then we might be able to help a vulnerable, healed exile come into relationship and thrive.

So in the first integration session we might start to roughly make a choice, in collaboration with our patient, to either prioritize working with protectors or working with a possible exile who got healing. We'll see how some of this prioritization played out in Claire's first integration session.

Regardless of whatever particular prioritization, it's important that in the first integration session we at least spend some time and hear from any relevant parts: any protectors, any exiles who got healing in the medicine session, and any exiles who may have been seen and found in the medicine session, but have not gotten healing yet. As usual, if necessary because of time or energy, we can also let parts know that we would like to spend more time with them in the next integration session, if they would like.

A parts detector is very helpful in all of this, so let's return to that.

PARTS DETECTOR IN INTEGRATION WORK

I seem to like to start the first integration session with just debriefing the medicine session. Just chatting about it. I often learn a lot. Sometimes I have something relevant to add to the conversation. After all, it was my patient's medicine session, not mine. I can't pretend to be the expert on it.

But I think it's also important as we're discussing the medicine session that, to some extent, we as therapist have our "parts detector" on. As we discussed earlier, a parts detector is a felt sense or a surmise that therapists can get that there might be a part present: that our patient is talking about a part, or relating with a part, or that our patient is currently blended with a part and talking as that part. This can all be in the absence of any explicit language or image of anything like parts.

For instance, as our patient debriefs the medicine session, they mention that their body feels lighter and more relaxed, their chest is more open, and they're breathing more fully than usual. Our parts detector might go "*ding, ding*" in us a bit. A part that got some healing? Our patient has more room to be there as Self?

Or maybe our patient talks about some disappointment in the medicine session, that it didn't get at what they hoped it would have. *Ding ding*? Is that maybe a protector speaking? An exile who still needs healing?

For most of us, developing a good parts detector is probably best done by having been through this kind of therapy ourselves. This is one reason why being a real patient, really presenting our suffering, in IFS therapy and in IFS PAP is central to doing this work as a therapist. We might then learn firsthand about the shifts in our own bodies, emotions, hearts, relationships, thoughts, imaginations, minds, beliefs, and behaviors, and what that might all mean for us.

Then we might have a much better sense of what might be going on with our patients. We might get an experiential sense and better notice how parts might show up and get active or relax more. We might get a better sense in medicine sessions and in integration work of what might be a part getting healing, what might be a protector blending, of what our patient being unblended, being Self, might look like and act like.

This gets back to training in PAP as at least substantially an apprenticeship model. That can be the best way to develop a parts detector.

AN EXAMPLE INTEGRATION SESSION: CLAIRE'S FIRST INTEGRATION SESSION

Before we get into more topics about possible integration work, I think it might be helpful at this point to look at an example integration session. So let's return to Claire's work, who we met in the Preparation Work chapter, and some of her integration work.

We will look at a nearly full, annotated transcript of Claire's first integration session after her first medicine session. This is also fictionalized and amalgamated to address more topics.

I first want to situate the session and discuss an overview of it and then we'll get to the actual transcript.

Claire's first medicine session, with ketamine, had been the day before. It had been fine for her, but nothing mind blowing or clearly of great healing benefit. So, as discussed above, in this session I chose to prioritize working with any possible exile who might have got healing in the medicine session. Again, I tend to go into integration work with an assumption that *something* good happened in the medicine session.

This session centers strongly on some "parts detecting." In this instance, Claire and I did very much find a young exile who got healing in the medicine session, but this young, healed part was only very briefly visible in the medicine session.

I then helped Claire get into Self to part relationship with this young former exile who seemed to get healing in the medicine session, when she showed up totally unburdened. Because the healing in the medicine session was so briefly visible and didn't make a big impact on Claire or her whole, complex psyche, I chose to spend a good bit of time with them together just in simple Self to part relationship. This was to hopefully deepen their connection and give them a chance to establish some real intimacy.

Eventually, we shifted to working with integrating protectors. Then, a very interesting thing happened: the protector still saw a burdened exile. Maybe this was another exile, or the part who had showed up healed in the medicine session was not fully healed. It ultimately seemed to be the second option, that the exile still had more healing to do. Maybe there were levels to the burdening of this young former exile? So I chose to go through all the healing steps of IFS to make sure they had happened for this part.

We then did explicit integration with protectors, helping any protectors get to know and see this now healed former exile, and then shift their roles, if they wanted to.

Finally, we helped Claire as Self and this wonderful young part of her start integrating together in her daily life.

This is a lot for one session. I want to point out that often a first integration session might not be this complete. Claire had a very easy and natural access as Self to her parts. We might wonder if the ketamine session the day before had something to do with that, but I actually doubt that in this case. She had the same easy access as Self to her parts in our preparation work, before she had ever worked with psychedelics in her life. I wonder if this is partially because she had been through so much previous treatment, psychotherapeutic and medical, with some benefit but not enough, so she had already gotten to know a lot of her parts decently. And, possibly, her protector parts had come to the conclusion that what they were doing wasn't working great and they were willing to allow her to show up as Self in our PAP treatment.

This might argue in favor of one of the things that Raquel Bennett stated that we discussed in the Medicine Session chapter, that ketamine sessions can seem to help consolidate previous therapy. Maybe that happened here. But very notably, if so, this only became clear in the integration work. The ketamine session alone would likely have been of much more limited benefit, a happy memory and maybe of some biochemical benefit, but not something of really ongoing and integrated health for Claire and her whole inner family.

We had done the ketamine session the day before in my office. She worked with ketamine delivered sublingually at a dose of 200 mg. It seems that the bioavailability had been quite high. (There can be a wide variation in how much ketamine actually gets into one's system from sublingual delivery; that is a major downside of sublingual ketamine sessions.)

She had been calmly quiet and still throughout the medicine session. And she had not been very capable or interested in being verbal even in the "sunset" period or after the session. So we had just done a basic check in after the medicine session, quietly listened to some "landing" music together, and had a little walk around the neighborhood, partially as a safety check.

During the sunset period she did tell me that the session had been quite strong, almost overwhelming at times; that the music was very helpful for her, quite powerful, and it had often seemed to match or guide or structure the session; and that she was feeling safe and fine, but rather woozy.

So we hadn't done anything like explicit therapy during the medicine session or in the sunset period. My interventions had been very much of companioning. And I still didn't know much at all about what went on for her in the medicine session.

I myself had found the medicine session quite satisfying. Mostly, I had simply been present and trusted Claire, all her parts, and the medicine. Parts of me had gotten active and wanted me to "*do something*" because this was her first psychedelic experience and she was just lying there quietly with a very neutral expression on her face and not moving much. Those parts had wanted me to make sure she was okay, that she wasn't having a horrible experience. Again, that sense of a part speaking to me in italics is a tell for me that a burdened part of me is trying to blend with me. During the session, I had been able to take some time to acknowledge those parts, ask for their wisdom, and ask them to let me lead in the session. That is, to ask them to unblend from me. I think they pretty much had. A couple of times, as Self well enough, I had simply asked her how she was doing. She had responded, "Fine, thanks," and gone back "inside." That seemed to be where she knew she needed to be, so I just trusted that and accepted that.

Let's get to the transcript. Again, this will be long.

My comments are enclosed in brackets.

Transcript of Claire's first integration session

Therapist: So I was thinking today we could kind of just debrief, chat, about the ketamine session yesterday and see about working it into some of the psychotherapy or just, you know, see where this goes. So how does that sound?

[-- Proposing a contract for the session, a pretty informal and relaxed contract.]

Patient: Uh, good, yeah.

Therapist: Okay. Yeah, so what was your experience like?

Patient: I mean. It's so hard to answer. It was definitely like, fun. You know, in the moment, with the ketamine, I definitely felt lighter. Yeah, it was just kind of fun. I'm not sure what that means in terms of my depression, but it was fun in a way that's hard to describe.

[-- My "parts detector" went *ding ding* at hearing about the "fun," but I still had little sense of what the session was like for her, especially given how she had said at the end of the session that it was very strong.]

Therapist: Okay. Um, what's up with your mood? What was your mood like last night? Today?

[-- I wanted to check on any seeming biochemical antidepressant effect of the ketamine.]

Patient: Now, I mean. Now the same. Depressed? Not really any different than before. You know, yesterday, during, I definitely felt lighter. And then I just kind of came home and, I don't know, I was tired. I don't know how to really describe my mood when I got home.

[-- It seemed like there wasn't a strong antidepressant effect.]

Therapist: Okay, all right. So maybe it sounds like it was maybe disappointing in some ways? Not what you maybe would have really liked or hoped would be the outcome?

[-- I was guessing that this might all be disappointing to her in some ways, just some fun, but no noticeable improvement in mood, which was her main goal in this PAP. I wanted to name something like that, to put that possibility on the table so that parts could talk freely about any disappointments and not have to exile any disappointments. I wanted to get this on the table partially out of respect and honesty, and partially because, as discussed previously, disappointments in PAP can be some of the best trailheads to some really crucial healing.]

Patient: Well, I mean — You know, I came into it with, you know, pretty open eyes that it wasn't going to be like a game changer, like the way I hear about maybe mushrooms being more of a game changer. It felt safe doing it with you. But not disappointed because I feel like we can keep going, hopefully. I guess it met my expectations that it wasn't going to be a game changer.

[-- It doesn't sound like she had big disappointments, partially because she didn't have big hopes. She actually sounds reassured, and parts seem relieved that nothing bad happened, that she felt safe with me, and she and her parts are interested in pressing on with PAP.]

Therapist: Yeah, yeah, okay.

Patient: It wasn't bad. Like there's no negatives. Like I didn't experience any side effects or, you know, anything that made me worry about my body or anything like that.

Therapist: Yeah.

Patient: So that to me is a positive.

[-- Again, it was a relief for some of her parts that nothing bad happened medically or psychologically, which had been a couple of her fears that we had discussed in the preparation work and that she had discussed with her psychiatrist. I was happy to hear about all this and that she was feeling good about the outcomes of the session.]

Therapist: Okay, so all right. One frame that I think can be just kind of useful to bring to this and that I actually, you know, I personally subscribe to it, is that something good's going to come from it. And you know, even if we just bring that frame to it, then maybe we find something good. So I'm curious about, you know, feeling lighter, and having fun. Would you like to spend some time with that?

[-- I want to press on with working with this session, not just make it a "safety check" for future sessions. Part of my respect for the medicines and any parts who got help is pressing on to get in relationship with any good that is there. Plus, as I said to her, if nothing else, such a frame makes it more likely to find something good. Again, the "fun" and the "lightness" had my parts detector going and I want to check if that was from a part or parts, and if that's the case, help her get in relationship with them.]

Patient: Sure, yeah.

Therapist: All right, tell you what, if you're game, can you find any of that now in your body? You can kind of maybe invite it. It might be subtle, in your emotions or your body or your mind or images in some way.

[-- Asking her to check if there is a part or parts with the fun and lightness. Find it, if it's there or if it's willing to be there now.]

Patient: Yeah, it's there, yeah.

[-- Seems to be a part or parts.]

Therapist: All right, great. So just notice however it's there, again, maybe in your body, your emotions, thoughts, who knows what. And as it's here with you now, like we did in the preparation work, just be with it, maybe share your breath with it.

[-- Fleshing out a bit and maybe getting into some Self to part relationship with it.]

Patient: Right. [pause]

Therapist: And how are you feeling towards it as you notice it right now?

[-- Checking for Self to part relationship.]

Patient: I mean, honestly, the word that comes to mind is bemused. Like, just definitely kind of tickled about it. Does that sound normal, I don't know?

[-- No "C words" there, but C words are just a mnemonic device to remember some of the qualities of a Self to part relationship. This sounds to me like a warm connection and a relationship of respect. I'm thinking she's in a Self to part relationship.]

Therapist: Sure, sure. So it sounds to me like you're kind of enjoying its presence.

Patient: Yes, definitely.

Therapist: Yeah, all right, great. Can you maybe let it know that you, it sounds like you like it. You enjoy its company. You're having fun.

[-- Asking her to deepen the Self to part relationship, making it "face to face," so to speak, in the moment. This will also help check if she is in a Self to part relationship because it won't work if she isn't.]

Patient: Like, how do I let it know that?

[-- She is still new to IFS work so she can use some guidance and she asks for it.]

Therapist: Like, I don't know, sort of in your thoughts or like you were talking to someone you just met, or talking to one of your kids, or a friend.

[-- I provide some guidance. I want to make it open ended and relational, not a mechanical technique.]

Patient: Mmm, okay.

Therapist: All right. How does it seem to respond to that from you? Just notice it. Just see if there's any kind of reaction.

Patient: I mean, it definitely likes to be noticed.

[-- They seem to be in a good Self to part relationship.]

Therapist: All right, great, great. Do you feel open to getting to know it better? This fun, this lightness in you?

[-- Seeing if she wants to deepen the Self to part relationship.]

Patient: Yeah, yeah.

Therapist: All right, so maybe, just ask it if there's anything it wants to share with you about itself, and then just wait and see if there's any kind of response.

[-- This can deepen the Self to part intimacy and connection. It can also start to be some witnessing.]

Patient: To you, out loud?

Therapist: Oh, it doesn't have to be. It's just most important that this is, you know, that this is between you and your own psychology, your own complex self. You can tell me, absolutely. But if that gets cumbersome, if that gets in the way or you don't want to tell me for any reason, you don't have to, no.

[-- Again, providing some guidance and in this case emphasizing and prioritizing the relationship of Self to part. Also, not letting any concerns about me be a rate limiting step in the intimacy with this part, that if there are things the part or she does not want to share with me, that that doesn't block the part from sharing with her.]

Patient: Good.

Therapist: Yeah, so does it share anything with you?

Patient: Uh, yeah, it does. Yeah. Do you want me to tell you?

Therapist: Sure, I am curious.

[-- I just answered honestly, I was curious.]

Patient: It said — she said, "I'm still here."

Therapist: What's that like for you? Does that ring any bells?

[-- That is so beautiful and important, but I don't know exactly what that means, and I want her and this part to deepen their intimacy if possible.]

Patient: Well, I mean, just the background on what I'm experiencing. And I did yesterday a little bit. Now that I'm thinking about it, it's funny to be talking about. It was just like that lightness, really what I saw was just this little kid on a swing, just like, going for it. Pumping. Just having a ball. Yeah.

[-- They're really there together now. Wonderful.]

Therapist: Is that you as a little girl?

[-- I'm curious, and if this is her as a little girl, that would be very important for their intimacy, for their relationship going forward.]

Patient: I am guessing so.

Therapist: Oh, okay, yeah, great. What's that like for you hearing that? I mean, "I'm still here."

Patient: Yeah, like, I, I was so fun as a kid. I had so much fun, you know, like, when I wasn't at home, just out and about. I don't know, I just keep seeing the swing. So that's on the playground. Just, just like — Yeah, I was fun, and I had fun.

[-- This is like a witnessing, a witnessing of this part as unburdened, as herself. This is also deepening the Self to part relationship.]

Therapist: Wow. And she's — she's still here. She's right here, huh?

[-- I was just kind of full to the brim with the beauty and happiness of them meeting. "Wow" was about all I could say!]

Patient: I guess.

Therapist: Wow.

Patient: Well, yeah. But it's, you know, it's confusing because, I mean, yesterday it was just brief. It was just brief. I guess that's how it's supposed to be.

Therapist: Yeah. How are you feeling towards her? Just notice her. She's there. She's so fun.

[-- I think she was right. Somehow, what was right during the ketamine session the previous day was for her to just catch a brief glimpse of this unburdened little girl part of her. This highlights how crucial good integration work is. Without integration work like this, that glimpse would have been just a brief flash of gold that might then be almost totally lost.]

Patient: She's awesome.

Therapist: Wow. Yeah.

Patient: I admire her. Yeah, she's like — weightless. Like all the crap, all the buildup, all the stuff is just not on her. She is — you know, me before fucking life got in the way, I guess.

[-- She's finding a foundational part of herself, and that part of herself is awesome. She's seeing the burdens and muck that accumulated on or in that part of herself and how they are not of the primary nature of that part of herself.]

Therapist: Can you just let her know how awesome you think she is. How much you appreciate her, how great you think she is. Really let her know. Show her your heart for her.

[-- Asking her to deepen the Self to part relationship and asking her to "mirror" this awesome little girl in her awesomeness. Like in child development, we often find ourselves, see ourselves most clearly, in the eye and the heart of a loving other: like their eyes and heart are mirrors reflecting who we are.]

Patient: Yeah, um. [pauses]

Therapist: And how are you two doing?

Patient: I mean, good, I think. You know, we were always good. Just, you know, you don't get to see it very much.

Therapist: Do you want to maybe ask her? Like why? Why had she been so hidden? Have there been any moves in you that had to hide her?

[-- I want to start integrating with any protectors.]

Patient: That's a good question. I just assumed she got hidden. But you're saying maybe part of me needed to hide her?

Therapist: Yeah, I'm wondering.

Patient: I mean, yeah, I would say as I got older. You know that kind of — I'm not really reckless, but that "out there," fun, cackling kid was not very well tolerated by my mother as I got bigger and, my mom was super strict and kind of punishing. So that makes sense.

[-- We start to see why a protector or protectors had to get into a protective, exiling role.]

Therapist: Uh, so what's the fear? What would have happened if this little girl, just so fun, so free, was just there in your family as you got older, with your mom, maybe especially. What's the fear?

[-- This question about the fears of protectors usually shows the vulnerabilities that had to be exiled; they point to exiled parts. But I was asking here for integration, to maybe help Self understand the protector and its burdens better, so they could hopefully come into more Self to part relationship.]

Patient: I mean, like withdrawal. My mom was cold. And if things were kind of like chaotic or out of control or, you know, she got colder.

Therapist: Um, so you would have lost connection with your mom.

Patient: Yeah.

Therapist: Yeah, and what might that have been like for you?

[-- Really trying to get to what this protector was afraid of.]

Patient: I mean, as a kid. Terrifying. Yeah, yeah. Because as cold and bitchy as she could be, she's still my mom, and she's still, you know, she's a good mom. I think she did the best she could, but she was definitely severe at times.

[-- The protector has been pretty well understood and validated by Self.]

Therapist: Yeah, um, can you find that one who was afraid of losing connection with your mom? Your mom withdrawing from you.

[-- I pressed on, checking about any exile even though we started the dialogue with what seems like an unburdened exile. Like we discussed previously, the healings from medicine sessions can be immediate and powerful, but then in the integration work, doing the IFS healing steps can make that healing more thorough and more integrated. Again, medicine sessions and integration work often best work together as fully primary healing work.]

Patient: Mhm, all right.

Therapist: How do you notice them right now?

Patient: How do I do what?

Therapist: How do you notice them right now. How are they here with you right now?

Patient: Just like a shriveled up — Little grey, kid. Just kind of pathetic.

[-- I don't know if this is another exile or that same little girl part of her. Sometimes I think of burdens on parts as having "overtones" like in music; one note contains multiple notes, each ascending tone fainter, but there. So we're maybe seeing another octave of the burdening and exiling that wasn't touched by the medicine session. Regardless of whether this is the same part or another part, it's clearly a part of her who needs help, so we press on.]

Therapist: Stay with them. Just notice them. And how are you feeling towards them right now?

[-- Checking for Self to part relationship.]

Patient: I feel sorry for her, she's like a raisin.

Therapist: Do you want to help her?

Patient: Yeah.

Therapist: Can you let her know that? That you're with her? How does she respond to you?

[-- Deepening Self to part relationship and also a simple "do over" or corrective emotional experience of this part not being alone.]

Patient: I mean, well, I mean, she's just looking for some, like, attention. Mhm.

Therapist: Do you want to give her attention? Are you giving her attention right now?

Patient: I guess so, yeah.

Therapist: Can you really go and be with her. Give her your full attention. How does she respond? How is she responding to getting that from you?

[-- Deepening Self to part relationship.]

Patient: I mean, pretty easily. She's definitely easy to connect with.

Therapist: So, yeah, you really like her. She's really easy to connect with. Yeah. Let her know that.

Patient: Mhm, um.

Therapist: Can you ask her, what's it been like for her to be shunted away and, you know, it sounds to me like she's been alone for a long time.

[-- Offer the possibility of doing some witnessing.]

Patient: That's what I was going to say. Yeah, like lonely.

Therapist: Can you let her know she doesn't have to be alone now. She doesn't have to be alone anymore. She's got you.

[-- Deepening Self to part relationship.]

Patient: Mhm.

Therapist: She doesn't have to be alone. Can you ask her to share with you, let you know, what's it been like for her alone, so that she doesn't have to be alone with any of those feelings, any of those experiences when you were a kid or over the years?

Patient: Buried. Yeah, it's been scary. You know, makes it harder to do things. It's harder to want to go to the swing.

[-- Witnessing. "Buried." "... harder to do things." "... harder to want to go to the swing." We can hear the depression as burdens.]

Therapist: Sure, yeah. Ask her, does she think you really get it? What it's been like for her? Or is there anything more so she doesn't have to be alone with any of it?

[-- Checking for more witnessing that the part needs.]

Patient: That's all.

Therapist: All right, ask her if she would like to get out of there and come be with you?

Patient: She said yes.

Therapist: All right, so just take her out of there. She can come and be with you. She doesn't ever have to go back and live there. She doesn't have to be stuck there anymore.

[-- Retrieving her.]

Patient: All right.

Therapist: So is she there with you now?

Patient: Yeah, she's there.

Therapist: All right, great. And ask her to just look at herself and her body, her thoughts, her emotions, any kind of feelings. Beliefs. Roles. And is there stuff in her or on her that is not her primary nature? Is there stuff that she maybe got twisted into or got mucked on her?

[-- Ask the part to find the burdens that have accumulated.]

Patient: For sure.

Therapist: Yeah, so ask her to just find all that. All that's not her true nature. Not just who she is. That's from the outside. It's just from all those old circumstances, all those old times. And, if she'd like, she can get rid of that stuff. She doesn't need to keep anything that's not her primary nature. Would she like to get rid of that stuff? Some of it or all of it?

[-- Offer the option to unburden.]

Patient: For sure, she would.

Therapist: Okay, so ask her to maybe pick something in nature to give it over to, sort of compost it. It will know what to do with it.

[-- Ask the part to pick something to give the burdens over to.]

Patient: It's so funny that you said compost. I just keep thinking of her as a little raisin.

Therapist: Mm.

Patient: Dried, shriveled up, desiccated raisin, yeah.

Therapist: Yeah, so what would she like to give all that over to, that dryness? That shriveledness? It sounds like that's not true about who she is.

Patient: Yeah, it's like that compost word that you said.

Therapist: So would she like to give it over to the earth?

Patient: Yeah, yeah.

Therapist: Okay, so ask her to just find all that about herself. All that stuff that's not true about who she really is and just give it over to the earth. Let her know she can take her time. Just let us know when it's all out. When it's all done.

[-- Ask the part to unburden.]

Patient: She's ready now. Me as the grown up version feels like, this feels good now, but how will it be sustained? I can't imagine that that raisin is not going to come back.

[-- She's naturally going to the next step in integration, establishing ongoing Self to part relationship between her and this healed little one.]

Therapist: Yeah, good question. I really think, it doesn't need to come back. I think it can be sustained, I think basically through your friendship with her...

Patient: Mhm, mm.

Therapist: ... your relationship with her. It doesn't have to come back at all.

[-- Providing some guidance to her question.]

Patient: So I'll be interested to see if that's the case. I hope so, yeah, you're right.

Therapist: Just check with her, ask her. Is it all out?

[-- Returning to unburdening to make sure it's complete.]

Patient: [pauses] Yeah, I think so. She thinks so, yeah.

Therapist: Great, great. Can you ask her to just thank the earth for helping?

[-- Thanking for the help.]

Patient: Um, yeah.

Therapist: And then ask her to just look at herself. Who is she? Without all that. What are qualities about herself. Can she name them?

Patient: She's fun. She's curious.

[-- Name and claim or call in qualities.]

Therapist: Yeah, great. Ask her to really claim those things about herself. "Yeah, this is me. This is true about me. This is who I am."

[-- Really claim them.]

Patient: [pauses]

Therapist: All right, great. Is she maybe the same part of yourself that you saw a bit in the ketamine session that you enjoyed so much?

Patient: Yeah.

[-- I wanted to double check. It seems this was the same part.]

Therapist: Great. Can you ask maybe that move in yourself, that part of yourself that got into that job of having to kind of lock her away to keep connection with your mom?

Patient: Mhm.

Therapist: Can you ask that part to come in and see her and see that she's doing well, and she's got you and she's not stuck in those places anymore?

Patient: Yeah, that makes sense.

[-- Helping the protector integrate into the healing and get their own healing.]

Therapist: Yeah, so just ask that move, that protective move in you, would it like to maybe take on a new role in your life now?

Patient: Yeah, I mean, theoretically. I mean, how do you find that role?

Therapist: Just ask it, ask what it would like to do if it didn't have to do that old job that it was doing for so many years and was so crucial to your well being. It could just rest, could retire or could do something that fits its own nature more. Integrate into, you know, your life in a new way.

Patient: I like the idea of retiring. That's a good word. Mm.

Therapist: Ask it. Would it like to do that? It's really important that it chooses.

[-- Clarifying and advocating for the protector that it really needs to choose their new role, otherwise it could just be a new burden on the protector.]

Patient: Mhm. Yes, it would.

Therapist: All right. So can you really thank it? It's worked so hard, so diligently.

[-- Deepening Self to part relationship.]

Patient: Yeah, that's crazy to think about. Thanking it for doing something that made me feel like shit. But I guess what you're saying is it had a place.

Therapist: Sounds like it. Yeah, it sounds like it was a huge job. That it was protecting you from losing connection with your mom?

Patient: Yeah, yeah.

Therapist: Let it know, it can retire now. It can rest. Does it want to do that?

Patient: Totally.

Therapist: Yeah, so let it go ahead and do that.

Patient: [pauses]

[-- Protector assumes their new role.]

Therapist: All right, now, can you ask this little girl, is there something she might want to do with you in the next day or two? Something that's not too difficult to do. That doesn't involve a lot of travel or anything. Just something special she'd like to do with you. She could just ask you for some special time together.

Patient: [pauses] Sounds crazy. She just wants to read.

Therapist: Yeah, do you get that?

Patient: I mean, I do, in a way. I mean, I don't do that anymore.

Therapist: So the two of you maybe take some nice time and read together?

Patient: After I can get my kids to bed. Yeah.

Therapist: Yeah, does that seem doable? Because it's important that we try and find something that's doable, it's most important just that you spend time together, it doesn't have to be a big elaborate thing. So is it doable for you to get some time to read maybe tonight, maybe tomorrow night?

Patient: Yeah, I can make that work. I think so. I think I'll ask my husband.

Therapist: Yeah, great, I was going to ask about that. Can you ask her how she might want to do that? Is there maybe a place in your house she might want to read together with you. You know, anything to make it really nice, really special for you two to be together?

Patient: Yeah, I mean, the nook at the top of our stairs comes to mind.

Therapist: All right. Anything in particular she might want to read with you?

Patient: Yeah, that's a good question. I mean, yes, she wants to read these old books that we used to read a lot when I was a kid, over and over and over again. And, yeah, I think even as a grown up, I guess I could be down to doing that. It's not my typical fare, but then my typical fare right now is I never have time to read.

Therapist: Great, great. So do you feel like you can, you know, really commit to her that you'll do this together? Tonight, tomorrow night?

Patient: Yeah, that's easy. I can totally commit to that.

Therapist: All right, great. Let her know. Great.

Patient: All right.

Therapist: It's really important, it's like, you know, making a commitment to a child. It could be ten minutes. It's more like the quality time kind of thing, but it's really important to follow through.

Patient: No, that's a great idea.

Therapist: Great. And we were talking about your sort of ongoing friendship, relationship with her. I think it might be good to have some way of making that concrete, like it could be maybe you do a drawing of her or hum a tune that reminds you of her, of being with her. Or it could be going to your nook. Maybe that becomes a special spot that, when you pass by the nook, you just check in with her. Or you sit there for a bit. Spending time with her is something that can go on for the rest of your life. You don't have to nail it down right now, but I think it'd be important that it becomes something concrete in your life.

Patient: I think the last thing you said is probably the most realistic knowing me, just with the nook.

Therapist: Okay, cool, cool. You can also go there in your imagination together. And she can suggest it too. She can maybe bring the nook up in your mind and you can meet her there for a moment.

Patient: Yeah.

Therapist: How does she like that?

Patient: She likes it a lot, she's happy.

Therapist: All right, that's wonderful. So just do that the next night or two.

Patient: Well, then. Question: this is a little off topic, but I'm really curious, because, you know, I had this agreement to try it once. And I feel like it went well. Should I do it again? When do I do it?

Therapist: Right. I mean everyone's working this stuff out on the fly, honestly. You know, I'm not a medical person. I can't talk about like glutamate receptors or God knows what. There is an idea of doing like six ketamine sessions over like maybe a four to six week period. That doesn't mean that's the only way to do it, but it's something that's been researched and found to be safe and effective.

Patient: Yeah, okay.

Therapist: But yeah, my interest in this stuff is mostly psychological. And it seems like you got a lot out of this psychologically. From a psychological point of view, I think you could, you just could ride with this, and it could become part of the therapy we could do together. For the medical angle, I think you could talk with your psychiatrist about her recommendation. Do you have a sense of what you want to do next in terms of ketamine?

Patient: I mean, I guess I don't feel like I need to rush into it like, tomorrow, but I would be curious about trying this again.

Therapist: Yeah, all right, great. What about maybe we try and do another session in about a week?

Patient: Yeah.

Therapist: Sounds good.

That's it for this example integration session.

We'll now continue with more topics of IFS PAP integration work, many of which came up in the example integration session.

We'll first turn to integration work with protectors, partially because that wasn't the main option I chose as the priority in this integration session with Claire.

INTEGRATING PROTECTORS INTO THE HEALING THAT HAS HAPPENED

Without a thoroughly relational systems psychology like IFS, it would be easy to assume that once healing happens in a medicine session then any sort of old protective moves will just go away on their own because they're no longer needed. It sure doesn't seem to work that way! In fact, just like in standard IFS, most ongoing integration work in PAP is with protectors. This often seems to mean slowly and repeatedly helping protectors have opportunities, in relationship with Self and with now-healed exiles, to choose new roles and new relationships in the inner family.

Having ways of understanding, helping, and respecting protectors after a great medicine session is very important. Without some understanding of protectors and working with them, a lot of integration falls off the rails and gets stuck. As we've discussed, if we don't do integration work with protectors, our patient can continue to suffer in some of the same old ways. It's like the protectors don't know the healing happened. They're still living psychologically in the old scenes of trauma or deprivation, still carrying their old burdens of extreme protecting. They often just keep doing their same jobs with no diminishment in intensity. They may very much believe they are protecting an exile who has in fact left those old scenes and is doing well.

This can happen in all healing work. But again, psychedelic healing can be unique in some ways that can leave protectors particularly unintegrated, even profoundly unintegrated.

As we just saw in Claire's integration session, sometimes the healings of an exile in a medicine session just *happen* — with *no* seeming process leading up to them. This is a big disadvantage for integrating protectors. In standard IFS, even when protectors have unblended and maybe "gone into the next room" during a healing process of an exile, they still often seem to have some real sense of the healing process of the exile. Protectors often "look through the keyhole" at the exile's healing process, as Kay Gardner, an IFS trainer, put it. This can be a great help for those protectors in integrating into the healing that has happened, because they're already somewhat up to speed on the healing. But again, in healings in medicine sessions, sometimes protectors get no sense or intimation of any healing, so they've done no natural integration with the now healed and safe exile.

It's not only seemingly instantaneous healings in medicine sessions that don't allow protectors much chance at natural integration. Even if there is a clear and even dramatic healing process going on for an exile in a medicine session, protectors can somehow just be so calm at the time that they don't particularly note the healing of the exile. They're maybe just "going with it," like hippy cliché. *Nothing* is much of a blip on their radar in the medicine session.

Or sometimes the healing of an exile in a medicine session is so weird, or so embedded in an intense cacophony, that the healing doesn't register to protectors. Sturgill Wilson sings of healing in medicine sessions, "Where reptile aliens made of light / Cut you open and pull out all your pain."[179] Such a healing can seem to protectors like just one of many, many weird things going on in the medicine session, when in fact it might have been an epic, profound healing.

So again, sometimes after a healing in a medicine session, protectors seem to have no awareness that an exile was healed. Then, of course, in our patient's day to day life when things seem

[179] Simpson, Sturgill. "Turtles All the Way Down." Track 2 on Metamodern Sounds in Country Music. High Top Mountain, 2014.

dangerous to the protector, based in their old burdens from the traumas and deprivations, the protector will still try to blend with our patient and try to have our patient do their old protective strategies.

And this isn't just behavioral. In our patient's emotional life it can be similar. At times even after a profound healing in a medicine session, it can *feel* like no healing has happened at all. This can be because protectors know the burdens of their former exiles so well that they often carry those burdens in a secondary way, by proxy. So when protectors who are unintegrated into the healing blend with our patient, they can pretty much bring the old emotional and psychological burdens back. Then our patient can be flooded with much of the same shame, fears of vulnerability, or whatever else that the exile used to carry.

This all can be, of course, quite disheartening and difficult for our patients, and for us as therapists.

And there are even more reasons that integration with protectors is so crucial. Sometimes, even if protectors are quite aware of a healing in a medicine session, after a great healing they can have big concerns about massive shifts in identity, social roles, or the whole worldview of our patient. "Who the hell am I now? My old ways just don't fit the data much anymore. Grumpy 'realist' was always my 'brand.' Warmth and connection?? What do I do with *that* in my life? What will people think? How disruptive will this be?"

Even positive changes can be legitimately daunting and even scary.

This can also get into external constraints, which we will discuss in detail soon.

And far from lastly, the protective jobs and intentions of protectors are their own burdens, their own secondary "stuff" that keeps them away from being themselves. Protectors very much need their own healing. Integration work can be their time to shine.

So for all these reasons, sometimes by the second integration session our patient can be in some real distress about protectors in their daily life. They might report something like, "I've seen the light [maybe literally]. I've been with my little self as they were gloriously healed. So why aren't I living that? Why do I keep doing the same patterns in my life? The same distancing and lashing out, the same giving in, the same feeling awful about myself at times?!" Our patient is perhaps halfway in a metamorphosis of healing.

Because of all this, by the second integration session, it's pretty common that protectors can be very important "target parts" to work with, to help integrate. By the second integration session, a protector might have come up in our patient's daily life, fully in an old extreme role, and blended with our patient, getting our patient to do its old job. Again, this can be bewildering and demoralizing to our patient. And this can be a great healing opportunity. Because that protector manifested right in a daily life situation for our patient, this can be an opportunity to help make the integration work *very* specific and *very* integrated in our patient's daily life. So these can be excellent trailheads for some very specific and grounded integration work.

Finding a specific protector to start with

So in the second integration session (or the tenth or the fiftieth), if it seems to us that we might be hearing from or about a protector in our patient's distress, we can of course listen to our patient about what happened in their life and have compassion for what they went through and any confusion and frustration that they have about it. And then, if it seems fitting, we can offer the option of working with that, to spend time with and hopefully help any parts involved.

If our patient does want to do some of that "IFS stuff" with what happened, we might ask them to find or invite the part or parts of themself involved. Be with them, focus on them, flesh them out, check on Self to part relationships, and so on.

This could of course go in many directions. But in psychedelic integration work, it can be wise to eventually check with protectors about some of their healing steps. We're checking that these steps happened, and if not, we can help fill them in. This is very much like what Claire and I did with the formerly exiled part of her who got healing, but here we are doing it with a protector.

When it seems some good Self to part relationship is happening between our patient and the relevant protector, we could ask our patient to ask the protector:

- If the protector saw or can now see the healed part (the former exile) as healed, as themselves, even peripherally or briefly
- If the protector sees that the former exile is no longer living in the old scenes where they were burdened
- If the protector sees that the former exile now has a close and direct relationship with our patient as Self
- If the protector sees our patient (Self)
- If the protector sees our patient as "updated," as their own age or life stage, as living in the present versus back when the exile got burdened

If all this is going well — that is, if the protector realizes they have seen the former exile as healed and safe and also sees our patient as updated as Self — then we're well along in that protector integrating into the healing, into new relationships of health and togetherness.

But if the protector doesn't see some of this, then we can offer to help fill in what is missing for the protector.

One way of doing this is to *ask* the former exile if they are willing to show up and be with our patient and this protector now. It is crucial that we also ask the former exile if they are willing to show up and be with the protector. Sometimes former exiles can have fear, hurt, or anger at their former protectors.

It is also crucial to ask the protector if they are willing to be with the former exile and our patient. Sometimes protectors can have a lot of guilt about what they did to a part in exiling it. Protectors' jobs often weren't pretty.

I think it's important that we make the invitation clear, that we are inviting these parts to be with each other *and with our patient*; that is, with Self. That can be reassuring to these parts. If they have some real trust in Self, then they will rightfully be more likely to feel safe enough to show up in such a three-way dialogue.

If the former exile or the protector is not willing to show up with each other, we might ask them to help us understand that better. Ultimately, we must respect their wishes and needs. They need to be in free consent for any work like this. We can proceed well enough with this integration work with the protector if they caught even the slightest glimpse or intimation that their former exile is doing okay now and is with Self. If the protector has no sense of that at all and we can't respectfully set up a three-way dialogue, then the integration work might just need to go slower. But it's important that we keep coming back to it in future sessions. I've found that when an exile is truly healed, given time and experience, protectors do come to realize that something is different in our patient's day to day life. Protectors can then reach enough earned, realistic trust in the healing and in our patient as Self to start doing some direct integration work.

If the former exile and the protector are willing to show up in a three-way situation, we can ask our patient to ask the protector to see the former exile as they are now, with no burdens in them or on them, as their primary nature with all their great qualities, as they are as a Self. This can be a big integration for a protector.

Or it could be that even if the protector is willing to show up, the protector might not be able to see the former exile or to see our patient as Self. If so, we can ask if there is another part who is blocking that protector from seeing the former exile or our patient. That would likely be another protector, and then we could help our patient get to know that protector and eventually ask it to unblend. Or, if it isn't willing to unblend, then that protector becomes the target part and we go from there, getting to know their fears, and so on.

Assuming we do eventually get to a situation where the protector sees the former exile as healed, as no longer stuck in the old traumatic or depriving situations, and as with our patient as Self, we can ask our patient to ask the protector:

- If they now might want to choose a new role or modify their old role
- If the protector, in the situations where they might have usually tried to blend with our patient and lead, would consider letting our patient be present in those situations, offering their advice or opinion to our patient, and then letting our patient lead
- If the protector might be willing to even experiment with a new role, or with our patient leading more in the coming week (or whatever timeframe). Again, protectors often seem to really like a time-limited "experiment" period.

I've found that the healings of exiles that happen in medicine sessions last. But then in therapy a lot of the ongoing daily life integration work is with protectors. This again very strongly underlines that psychedelics are best not a standalone practice, that some sort of relational, ongoing healing path and work are essential to good psychedelic practice. Like therapy.

Having discussed doing some integration work with protectors, let's now turn to the related subject of external constraints, which can be when protectors are quite right about potential dangers leading from healing.

EXTERNAL CONSTRAINTS ON HEALING IN INTEGRATION WORK

To again define external constraints as we will use it here, external constraints can mean that given some realities of the world, even very positive healing and health can be legitimately dangerous or worrisome. Again, external constraints can be very important in integration work because of real safety concerns and because they could lead to the exiling of healing.

Abusive relationships of one kind or another are situations where external constraints can come up. In abusive relationships, dynamics of illegitimate power, vulnerability, sadism, and sociopathy or psychopathy can be operative, subtly or not subtly. These could be personal relationships, for instance in a marriage, family, romantic relationship, or with a friend, co-worker, or a boss. And there can be larger scale relationships with abusive dynamics, like social issues of racism, sexism, classism, and anti-queer hatred.

Here are some examples of a range of external constraints:

Our patient might have legitimate concerns that by being much less depressed after a medicine session that now people in their life will pile unrealistically high expectations on them about career or school.

A Black patient might find in a medicine session that they are a strong leader, but protectors might be very concerned that if they act on that, then racist people, who don't want there to be Black leaders, might attack.

Protectors of a patient who is in a romantic relationship where there is a dynamic of their partner demeaning them might be concerned that if our patient brings into their life their strength and wisdom, or other qualities that they found about themself in the medicine session, then their partner might attack them, even subtly, but still destructively, trying to exile the health found in the medicine session.

Or a patient in a medicine session who finds their sexual orientation, gender identity, or gender expression to be different than how they've understood it before can have real concerns about aggression or discrimination if they act on these realizations or "come out" along those lines.

As we've mentioned before, if concerns about dangerous ramifications of healing come up in integration work (or elsewhere), they should become a top priority for that session.

Concerns about external constraints might particularly come up in the first integration session when we start dialoguing with protectors, or our patient as Self might simply bring up those concerns directly.

Working with some external constraints can be particularly tricky when we as therapist haven't lived in the societal role of our patient. For example, a white therapist trying to help a Black patient navigate racism is usually a difficult setup. But having said that, it's also important that therapists from social roles of relatively high privilege and safety don't just get overwhelmed and freeze in the face of difficulties their patient might be facing.

Once again, in these situations and in general, a great strength of IFS is that our patient in Self to part relationships can usually lead the best. So a crucial thing we can often best offer is to help facilitate some Self to parts relationship and dialogue around an external constraint. We can help initiate and midwife dialogues between our patient as Self, any healed parts, any protectors, and any vulnerable parts, burdened or not, who might want a voice in such a dialogue around an external constraint.

Again, in such Self to parts relationships is likely where the most wisdom and health is available.

But as part of such dialogues, we as therapist might eventually want to offer some direct access; that is, we as therapist joining in the dialogue. Part of this is because we are not leaving our patient just alone to deal with the situation. We as therapist offering to come in in direct access can also be important if we think or feel that our patient is not being realistic about the dangers at hand. We might ask our patient something like, "Is it okay with you and these parts of you if I jump in here and offer something?" We can also do direct access if our patient explicitly asks us to. They might simply ask, "What do you think about this?" Our role then, in my opinion, is to be one voice of many, not to be the "final answer" or the "smartest person in the room." Ultimately, our patient as Self has to decide.

A good outcome of working on an external constraint is that our patient and their parts truly think and feel that they have a way or ways to be safe enough in any potentially difficult situations, while also being able to honor and integrate the healing of the medicine session.

With very fraught external constraints, we might want to offer our patient at least the option to check in with us in between sessions and reiterate how we are reachable for any crisis that might come up.

And of course, it will be important to circle back to these concerns and issues in the next integration session.

INTEGRATING WITH A NOW HEALED FORMER EXILE

I think it's clear, but to state it: it's not enough for an exile to just get healing in a medicine session. It's usually not enough to simply celebrate and wonder with our patient at a powerful healing from a medicine session. The risk could be to leave a healed part by the side of the road as we happily move along. We're right back to an ecosystem model of integration and to IFS as a thoroughly relational systems model.

For this discussion of integrating with a healed exile, we'll assume that our patient has found a formerly exiled part of themself who got healing in the medicine session. This might have been very obvious in the medicine session, such as Nick finding a part of himself as a child with "a brilliance that outshone fire." Or, as we've discussed and have seen in Claire's work, through our "parts detecting" we might start to get a sense that there was an exile who was healed in the medicine session. Or healing may have happened not in the literal medicine session itself, but that night in a dream, in a seeming synchronicity a few days later, in a conversation with a friend or family member, in some time in nature, or in meditation or prayer. Somehow, the healing showed up.

We can then offer our patient IFS integration work: helping that healed part integrate with our patient's wider psyche and helping our patient's complex psyche integrate with that former exile, and from there into the world.

Checking on IFS healing steps

Just like we discussed with protectors, because psychedelics don't just "do" IFS, in integration work with exiles it can be wise to check if all the main healing "steps" of IFS have happened for any exile who got healing in a medicine session. And if any of these steps haven't happened or haven't happened fully, we can then offer to help fill them in.

As we saw in Claire's integration session, we might wind up doing a full IFS healing with an exile. In post-medicine session healing, this will probably go a good bit quicker and smoother than in standard IFS.

Here are some ways we can check on the healing steps of a former exile. After establishing some Self to part relationship, we can ask our patient to ask the former exile:

- If the now healed little one can "see" Self
  - This can check if the Self to part relationship is a two-way relationship, which is very important for full healing and for integration. If the part cannot "see" or notice our patient as Self, then we might ask our patient to just offer to the part that they turn towards our patient and notice them and be together. If the part still can't see or notice Self directly, we can start to wonder if there is a protector

blocking the part from seeing Self out of some fear. We can ask our patient to check on that. We could offer, "Could you check if there is a protector or another part blocking that young part from seeing you?" If so, we can help our patient get to know that protector, Self to part, eventually asking them if they will give enough room to let the now healed exile see our patient as Self.

- How old the now healed exile thinks Self is
  - This can check if the part is updated. If the part does not see our patient as their current age or developmental stage, then we might wonder if the part is still psychologically stuck in the old situations, the old "time bubble" of when our patient was younger and in the situations of trauma or deprivation. If so, that part might need more witnessing, updating, retrieval, and so on.
- Where the part sees themself as being right now
  - This can also check if the part is retrieved or if they are still living in and stuck in the old situations.
- If the part feels they've really been seen and understood by Self about what things were like for them in the trauma or deprivations, and about what things have been like for them all these years.
  - This can check if real, full, and adequate witnessing has happened.
- If the part notices any burdens in, on, or around themself, anything not of their primary nature, anything that is from outside themself. They might have beliefs, emotions, feelings, bodily sensations, "muck" or "dark clouds" in, on, or around their body, or just anything that seems to them from the outside.
  - This checks if they are still burdened in some way.

- What qualities do they see as true about themself? Who do they see that they are, as themself?
    - This is checking if they see themself as their primary nature.

Again, if any of these weren't done or weren't fully done, we can now offer to help do them, and that can probably happen pretty quickly at this point.

Agreeing on spending time together, Self and part, in our patient's daily life

If we're pretty sure that a former exile has really been witnessed, has had the "do overs" or corrective emotional experiences that they needed, and has been retrieved, unburdened, and found themself as a Self, then it's very important to help our patient and this part form an ongoing relationship. This is key to what integration means here: an ongoing relationship.

So in the first integration session, even if briefly, it is crucial that we help facilitate some plans for ongoing Self to part relationship between our patient and this now healed part. We can do this by our patient asking the part if they would like to do a special activity or have special time together with our patient as Self. Then Self would optimally lead to have that happen that day or the next.

This now healed part asking to do something special with our patient is very much like a child getting to ask a parent to do something special together and then the parent follows through on that. This can strongly and directly deepen their relationship and their togetherness. And crucially, this happens directly in our patient's daily life, in their "real world," so this can be very specific and strong integration.

We saw this in Claire's integration session with her little, healed exile asking to read together. They decided to do this together in a nook in her house. That nook became a special spot where they can meet, either literally or in imagination.

This sort of thing can become something of a natural or spontaneous ritual for Self and this part being together. This could go on for years, and really, for the rest of their life.

Let's assume that this part does request some special time together or a special activity with our patient. It's important that we then check with our patient that what this part wants to do is in fact doable for our patient. We want this to be a set up for success. If it seems to our patient too iffy that they can pull it off or if it might be too logistically difficult, or anything like that, then our patient can explain that to the now healed part and ask them about something simpler that they can do together.

It doesn't really matter *what* they do together. It's most important that it's just a special time together.

For instance, maybe instead of a hike in a place that might require a bunch of travel time, weather contingencies, and so on, our patient and a part might come to an agreement to spend some time together in their yard, or a special place in a park, or on a trail near home. They could also do the "bigger" hike later in the week, if possible.

If our patient has been able to keep an open or light schedule for the days following the medicine session, doing this kind of integration time together can then be much more doable and more enjoyable.

An added benefit to logistically simple activities is that they might be much easier to do with some regularity. Again, this can result in regular, natural, and enjoyable times together, like Claire and her young part regularly reading together in their nook or just sitting there together for a moment.

Once the part has made what our patient thinks is truly a doable request, it's important that we ask our patient if they are really willing to follow through with that. We can tell our patient that this is very much like making a commitment to a child who is in a very sensitive state, who has been through a lot and has been far too alone for years and this might be their first foray, free and loved and in rightful company, into the world. It's a big deal, even if the activity is simple.

If our patient is truly up for it, they can tell the part that they agree to do the activity or time together.

Then it's our patient's role to make the special time or activity together happen. The special time doesn't have to go "perfectly." That's not a necessary ingredient for this being a healing, integrating time together. Regardless of the "content" of the experience, just trying to do the activity together and being together strengthens, deepens, and develops the relationship between our patient and this part.

When I was a kid, my dad used to take my sister and me fishing a good bit. We rarely caught fish. A lot of the time we got lost driving on backroads and never got to the stream. I really didn't care. My dad would get frustrated. But the main thing to me was that we were spending time together and *trying* to do something special together. Those times together were more than good enough for me.

The special time together might also inform further integration work or healing work. Perhaps a now healed part asked our patient to spend time together at the beach, and our patient and the part found they unexpectedly formed a particular relationship with a tree there.

Additional healing for other exiles and protectors can even come during these activities, in Self to part relationship, and maybe with help from that tree.

Doing some art about or with a now healed part

In addition to planning some special time together, we might recommend to our patient that they think about doing some kind of art that reminds them of this now healed exile. It could be a simple drawing, a little melody, a line of lyrics, or a more complete work of art. Of course, this isn't about the "product" of the art. Crucially, it can be a way of having something quite concrete that reminds our patient of this part and can become a focal point to regularly connect with, honor, and spend some time with the part.

Debriefing the special time together in the second integration session

It's then important in the second integration session that we follow up with our patient about the special time together with the now healed exile.

Good things can come from such a debriefing. In one of the examples just now, of our patient and a now healed part spending time together at the beach and having a very nice experience there with a particular tree, our patient and that part might only realize the significance of that tree in the debriefing. Our patient and that part might then see that going to that tree is a special thing for them. We might float the possibility that they can go to that tree regularly. We could also suggest to our patient that they and this part could meet there together in imagination.

Meeting in a special place in imagination is an especially easy way to have some Self to part time available right in our patient's daily life, and it is fully effective emotionally, relationally, and psychologically.

Doing this special time for about four weeks

We can offer to help our patient structure time together with this now healed exile over the next four weeks or so. Optimally, this time together would be daily or near daily. Four weeks can be an adequate amount of time to really make this relationship a priority. After that, the relationship can be less intensely structured. It can be more of the natural ebbs and flows of that relationship.

To help structure this, we could suggest to our patient that they could tie spending time with this now healed part to an already existing routine. For example, maybe when our patient goes outside for the first time in the morning they could spend a little time together with this part, maybe for just a few moments or a few breaths together, or longer. Or when our patient brushes their teeth; after work; as part of a period of meditation, prayer, or journaling; in nature together; or as part of a bedtime routine.

This doesn't have to be an onerous "homework assignment." It can just be a brief hang, like we might do in our daily life with family members or friends.

It can be helpful for us as therapist to check in for maybe the first four sessions after the medicine session around these daily life ways of being together. That can help our patient prioritize and organize the times together.

We can also offer some time in sessions for our patient to be with this part.

Again, after about four weeks of regular, fairly structured times together, our patient and this part might choose to continue this same routine of daily or near daily time together, or our patient and this part might find their own patterns and rhythms that work for them.

This can then be a lifelong, living, dynamic relationship. That is obviously excellent integration.

If our patient did not follow through on the special time with the now healed exile

As we debrief the special time together in the second integration session, our patient might say that they totally forgot about the special time together or that something got in the way. Stuff happens.

It's possible that a protector blocked our patient from spending time with that part for some reason. We could just ask our patient to ask or check if there is a protector who blocked them from doing the activity.

If the special time together was in a public place, maybe they find a part who was concerned that social anxiety might have come up for our patient if they had done the special activity. That's an important trailhead and that part could become important to focus on for some time and possibly for some healing, if our patient and that part are up for it.

Shame or punitiveness might come up in our patient around forgetting to spend time with the now healed exile. That could of course be from an important burdened part of our patient. That could also be an important trailhead and could eventually become the focus of important healing work.

Of course, working with this failure to spend time with the now healed exile optimally wouldn't be punitive from us as therapist. If it is, or even if we're just feeling that way, that would likely be from a burdened part of us who has blended with us to some extent. "How do I feel towards my patient and their parts?" We could then work on our own unblending, and then, more as Self, we could get back to our patient and their parts.

And we'd then have found an important trailhead for ourselves in our own healing. In our own therapy or consultation, or however we heal ourselves, we could offer that part some time in Self to part relationship and a chance for healing.

In any of these outcomes, it would be very important, if possible, that by the end of the second integration session our patient and their now healed exile spend time together right in the session. It would be very important that our patient does that as Self, so it would be important to check on Self to part relationship: "How do you feel towards this young, healed part of yourself?" And to help our patient unblend if need be.

If there was a protector who had blocked the special time together, while our patient and this now healed exile are together in the session, our patient might then explain to the now healed exile about the protector and the fears of the protector. If it's true, our patient might explain that they were able to help that protector to some extent and that our patient as Self is going to be leading more in these kinds of situations, and that the protector welcomes that.

Our patient might also ask this now healed part if they want to share what it was like for them when our patient didn't do the activity with them.

Eventually, our patient could ask for a second chance to do the special activity, but if it might make it more doable, maybe doing it in a simpler way, like in imagination. If the part would like that, they can do the special time together in imagination right there in the session.

It's important eventually in the session that our patient and this part come up with a doable, realistic way to be together in the coming week.

In the next integration session, it would then be important for us to check in again on how the special time together went.

IN THE ROOM RELATIONAL WORK AS PART OF INTEGRATION

A lot manifests in a medicine session, both for patient and therapist. This can and will affect the relationship between therapist and patient. So in integration work, it can be good to have a chance to acknowledge what came up in the medicine session and how it might have impacted the relationship.

This can be about "positive" things or "negative" things. It might sound odd, but often, it is most important for our patient to have the chance to share positive things about the relationship. This can be important healing work. Many patients carry burdens from lack of connection with important people in their lives and the inability of those people to talk about the relationship directly. So our patient being able to express to us gratitude, warmth, admiration, humor, and feelings of friendship, and then us accepting those, can be quite healing for some parts of some of our patients. This could be a sort of "do over" or corrective emotional experience.

And of course, we can do all this and maintain the therapeutic "frame," the rightful roles of therapist and patient. That frame is not there just because of "uptight" rigidity or as a bogus "cover your ass" liability protection. The frame is really there for the safety of all involved and for efficacy. It makes therapy better.

Or, after a medicine session our patient might have something like what Brené Brown calls a "vulnerability hangover." We can get quite vulnerable in medicine sessions! Maybe in the intensity of the medicine session our patient shared things they've never said fully to anyone, like of doing eating disorder behaviors or of having bullied someone in their childhood. Or our patient did things in the medicine session that they rarely or never have done in front of anyone. Maybe they danced, cried, or asked for help. Maybe they were assertive towards the therapist, even just saying no to something minor. Maybe they were disappointed and shared that, or hid that. All of these can lead to feelings of vulnerability in integration work. A vulnerability hangover.

So with all this, an important relational question as part of integration work could be something like, "Would you like to see if you or any parts of you have any reactions to me or to things that happened between us in the medicine session? This could be hurts, warm feelings, embarrassments, confusions, whatever."

This could lead to direct healing, as we discussed, and it could lead to awareness of very important parts and trailheads for our patient.

This could also lead to us hearing from our patient that we did some sort of misstep during the medicine session that hurt them or was hard for them. That could be hard for us as therapists to hear. We of course want to be helpful people, and we can have parts who get into extreme roles around that.

Personally, if my patient shares something that I did or didn't do that was hard for them, I tend to start with an assumption that they are right, even if I don't get it at first. I might need to work to understand their hurt from their point of view. If in the first place I understood the potential hurtfulness of what I did or didn't do, I would have been far less likely to do it! So I might need to ask them some questions to help me understand their hurt or anger better.

Once we understand their hurt or anger, I think we can apologize, simply and briefly. We could also offer, if they are ready then, or perhaps later, to let them and their parts know that we are willing to hear what this was like for them.

We also might eventually offer to share some brief self-disclosure of what was going on for us and our parts, if our patient thinks that might be helpful for them or their parts. And to probably keep it brief, to not make it about us. I personally like that take on self-disclosure that therapist self-disclosure is helpful to the extent that it is helpful for their patient.

This sort of relational work of admitting our mistakes can be a powerful healing for some parts of some of our patients, once again, a sort of do over. It might be a very rare experience for them that an important person in their life was able to acknowledge hurting them and apologize for that and hear them about the whole thing.

Like medicine sessions themselves, this relational work can be quite an intense way of working. And it can lead to some of the most important healing for our patient.

One more time, I'd like to bring up the excellent chapter where Richard Schwartz spelled out IFS as a fully relational psychotherapy. It can help us get deeper into nuances of this relational way of working. The chapter is, "The Therapist-Client Relationships," in *Internal Family Systems Therapy: New Dimensions*.

There are also many schools of relational psychoanalytic therapy that have great contributions to make to this kind of "in the room" relational work.

And, as we saw in the Medicine Session chapter, Jung's work was a pioneering and undersung radically relational model, especially as seen in his writings on alchemy and transference.

"Trusting the Medicine" in the Integration Phase; the Medicine Session Lasts for About Two Weeks?

I tend to offer my patients a frame that they might want to wait for about two weeks until they form a final conclusion or judgment about the medicine session.[180] As has come up before, maybe our patient has an important dream the night after the medicine session. Or our patient has a seemingly important synchronicity of some sort in the days after the medicine session. Personally, I think those healings fully "count."

This sense of the medicine session lasting for about two weeks fits with what we briefly discussed at the end of the Preparation Work chapter, of our patient "planting the seed" of their intention, ask, or prayer for the medicine session and then not overly futzing with it for about two weeks. That can give the intention time to be protected and nurtured so it can root and sprout before working with it too much.

This "two week" medicine session can also be a way of trusting the medicine.

Spiritual Bypassing in Integration Work

It might seem counterintuitive, but after a glorious, healing medicine session, protector parts might take something from the medicine session, maybe an experience of reverence, peace, joy, or safety, and make that into their new protective burden. That protector might then try to apply that, in an extreme role, as a way of trying to help protect and exile any vulnerability in our patient.

John Welwood, an American psychologist and Buddhist meditator, coined the term spiritual bypassing and did some very clear work it the mid-1980's in the context of Western Buddhist meditation practice. His work applies equally well to psychedelic practice.

---

[180] Rainer Scheurenbrand, private communication, 2015

Some examples of new or intensified spiritual-bypassing protective burdens could be, "I'm going to make Self and all parts blissed out forever / kind forever / reverent forever / strong forever / joyous forever / quiet forever / peaceful forever / loving forever. That way, everything will be as good as it was in the medicine session forever!" These can become very powerful protective burdens, sometimes all the more powerful because those protectors are riding the incredible energy of a big medicine session.

This can all sound like healing, and it is based in healing! But again, it gets into extreme roles and that can lead to problems, like any extreme role can, such as exiling vulnerable parts or getting into polarities of protectors.

Spiritual-bypassing burdens could be taken on by a manager to try to implement a *permanent* new state, so that any suffering of parts is exiled. Spiritual-bypassing burdens could also be taken on by firefighter parts to use spiritual bypassing as an emergency measure to try to "put out the fire" of any suffering of parts.

Either way, suffering of parts will arise in life eventually, of course. We are just vulnerable beings living in an often hard world. So spiritual-bypassing protectors tend to have very fraught jobs.

IFS obviously has crucial and powerful contributions to make to working with spiritual bypassing. Besides the understanding of spiritual bypassing that we just discussed, it can be important to note that spiritual bypassing can often be talked about in a disdainful way and as something to be strenuously avoided or corrected. That doesn't tend to help much. IFS can offer a way out of that, a way of not trying to exile or shame a protector for doing spiritual bypassing. We might start to see how spiritual bypassing is just a part doing its best to try to help out. And again, the stronger the protector, the deeper the need and the deeper the vulnerability of the exile. So working with such big, spiritual-level protector burdens can help lead to some of the most crucial healing.

I'm reminded again of Robert Falconer's great line, "Protectors aren't blocking the therapy, protectors are the therapy."

This can be tricky work for us as therapists. When our patient is doing spiritual bypassing, they are probably doing it out of great need and great hope. And it may be working for them in some substantial ways, maybe distracting or looking beyond some real suffering they have. Again, our lives can be very hard and a very powerful medicine session can seem to offer a way out of that.

Tact and timing and us being Self enough can matter here a lot. We don't have to have a big agenda to confront or undo spiritual bypassing. So maybe for a while, we mostly hold these seeming parts of our patient in our hearts and in our respect: the protector or protectors who think they've found a way out of suffering, and the exile or exiles who are vulnerable. And we could trust that this process will go somewhere good.

Maybe, if we're doing it enough as Self, we eventually float the idea to our patient that possibly a part of them is using an experience from the medicine session as a protective move.

Oftentimes, this will come up naturally. A part doing spiritual bypassing might find the next medicine session pretty frustrating. That protector may expect the same great experience from the new medicine session and they hope to use that to recharge or deepen their protective path. But, as the great cliché goes, every medicine session is different.

We saw some of this dynamic in the beginning of Nick's second medicine session where he was initially frustrated and "depressed" that the second medicine session wasn't like the first.

So it might be in integration work after a second medicine session that working on spiritual bypassing naturally comes up, maybe via a part's frustrations or disappointments about the second medicine session.

Working with spiritual bypassing can dovetail very well with the crucial topic we discussed early in this chapter on how disappointments about PAP can be powerful trailheads to some of the most important healing. Again, the more powerful or pervasive the protector, the more vulnerable the exile. And therefore, the deeper, and more needed, the healing that's available.

DAILY LIFE, IN SITU, INTEGRATION PRACTICES: ONGOING RELATIONSHIPS WITH PARTS

So many patients know they need ways in their daily life to work with their mental health. Mental health, of course, can't just be about therapy sessions or psychedelic sessions.

IFS opens up some really useful, simple, and doable daily life practices that we can recommend to our patients. These are all basically integration practices.

These are also mostly unblending exercises. These are exercises, dialogues, practices, or relationships for our patient to be more there as Self in their daily life, more leading as Self, and more in relationships as Self.

And very importantly, because these daily life practices often involve parts directly relevant to the medicine session, these daily life practices can be quite directly and naturally related to the healings of the medicine session. This is important and a great strength because a lot of general PAP integration suggestions can be very good things, but they are often fairly generic and not directly related to the healings of the medicine sessions. For example, integration suggestions such as doing a meditation practice, spending time in nature, less time on screens, eating healthy foods, journaling, and so on. These can all be truly important practices, and I do most of them myself daily. But they can also be very broad, general practices of health, not directly grounded in and related to the specific healing of a medicine session. Because they are so broad, they can be blunted in their effectiveness as integration and can leave important parts too alone.

Let me unpack this more. If we go with the assumption that the healings in medicine sessions are about relationships, then we can look at this through an analogy. For this analogy, let's step outside of psychedelic practice and into general practice. Let's say our patient in therapy is in a new, very positive relationship. It could be with a new friend, romantic partner, colleague, whoever. If we then suggest to our patient simply that they journal, spend time in nature, exercise, do a meditation practice, and so on, then those suggestions are so broad that they might not be directly connected to that new, positive relationship.

So the goal with the daily life integration practices here is that they are focused on and relevant to the relationships of the medicine session, often of parts. And again, because our patient can do these relational practices right in their daily life — exactly with the situations, themes, relationships, and triggers of their daily life — these daily life practices are highly integrated and grounded integration work.

I like to suggest a few possibilities for daily life practices or daily life inner dialogues. Then my patient will have several options and will likely make one or two of them regular or "as needed" options in their daily life.

These aren't really step by step procedures. They have structure to them, and that's important because it makes them more readily doable in our patient's daily life. But these are really just about relationships. That is always the spirit of these practices.

Let's look at some suggestions of such daily life practices.

Special time with now healed exiles and protectors

One of the most important daily life integration practices or relationships is one that we just discussed extensively above, of our patient spending special time with now healed exiles and protectors.

Healed and healthy parts of ourselves need our companionship and friendship. This is important in good times and in bad. It can be important to underline with our patients that even healed, unburdened parts suffer. Because a part is hurting doesn't necessarily mean they are still burdened. Sometimes life is just hard.

These can be lifelong relationships, however those relationships might play out and be co-created between Self and parts.

Being with, breathing with

We're back to another standby: Being with and breathing with. As we saw in the case material of Nick's integration, something like this was a crucial and even decisive integration practice for Nick. And it's a very simple and grounded one.

With this practice, we can suggest to our patient that if things get hard in their daily life — or if they get good! — that they can take a moment and be with that, in whatever ways it is there. Maybe be with the situation, with their feelings, with parts as they are showing up in their body, with their thoughts, imagination, stuff that's unnamable, whatever. And breathe with or share their breath with all that. Maybe just half a breath, or a few breaths or longer.

Again, this isn't a "fix it" job. This isn't a relaxation exercise. It's not trying to make everything all better — or to make anything even a little better. It's really just relationships in the moment. And being together in relationship can lead to good things.

When I do this myself, I often just spontaneously get the image of my breath as like a pot of warm tea, and I imaginally offer a cup of tea to whatever or whoever I'm being with, in my inner world or outer world. I fill my own cup as well, and we sip our tea together. There is no intent at making things better. It's just a cup of tea together.

But again, good things can come from sharing a cup of tea together. Even if it's just sharing a cup of tea together.

Another image for this practice can be a parent being with their upset child. Maybe the child is too upset to talk right then. Maybe at school that day their best friend sneered at them at recess and yelled, "I hate you!" and ran off and played with a new friend.

Maybe the best the parent can do then is sit with their child, maybe on the edge of the bed while their child is sobbing under the covers. Be with. Just be with. No intent to problem solve, to make things better, to cheer up, to look at things from another perspective. Just be with and breathe with.

Again, good things can come from this. Even if it's just that child and parent not being alone in that hard moment.

"Let me be here as well"; "How about I lead here?"

Here we start to get into some exercises that are more overtly about our patient trying to do some unblending in their daily life.

We might suggest to our patient that if something intense comes up for them in their daily life, like our patient is triggered by a difficult situation, that they can take a moment or so and notice whatever is coming up for them, whether it's just a bunch of feelings and reactions or more clearly parts, and turn towards all that, however it's showing up, and say to it all, "Would you please let me be here as well?" And then, "How about I lead here?" Or however our patient might want to put it.

Maybe then a part or parts seem to agree to that to *some* extent. Then our patient can be there in the challenging situation more as Self.

Maybe then our patient sees things they didn't notice before, data, interpretations, or understandings about what is going on. Maybe they see options to lead themself in that situation in a way that they hadn't before.

With this practice, it can be important to remind our patient that they can't force parts to unblend. Burdened parts are just too dedicated. We can mostly just ask them and go from there. Maybe it doesn't go great. Or maybe we wind up 5% more unblended. We're then 5% more there as Self. That can make a very important difference.

It's also important to note that this practice isn't about trying get anything to going away or calm down. It's just our patient asking whatever is going on in them for some room to be there *as well*.

What happens from there — who knows? Our patient doesn't have to know what's going to happen. Self leadership, like any leadership, isn't necessarily about having all the answers. It's often more about helping foster a team who then works together and has each other. It's often not like a Hollywood caricature of leadership where a solo action hero or scripted CEO single handedly saves the day, with perfect little quips strung along the way. Hopes for such leadership are often the hopes of protector parts, the hope that an extreme role will prevent suffering.

Parts are used to being advised and managed by other parts, and by parts of other people. Sometimes Self just saying, "I don't know either" to a part who is having a hard time and is at a loss is something that that part has needed for a long time.

And in that togetherness and not knowing, at least maybe a hole isn't dug deeper by the extreme actions of a burdened protector. That can be an important win.

Once again, even if nothing improves much in the actual situation from some increased Self leadership, at least the team has each other, win, lose, or draw. That might be "all" our patient gets from this exercise. And that can be enough, even the decisive thing, for health.

Or perhaps a part of our patient or them as Self does *eventually* see some novel ways forward, that are worth at least a try. Maybe that new way goes very well. A very important and new fork in the road has been taken.

Again, I think we saw something very much like this in Nick's integration work.

"That's me"; "I am" [181]

Here's another unblending exercise in daily life.

In or after an upsetting time, our patient can turn towards whatever is up and say, "That's me." That is, claiming what's there — parts, emotions, body, and so on — as us, as ours.

Parts rightly can like to be claimed, to be acknowledged and held in way that is a very intimate relationship: identification. "That's me."

After that, our patient might then say to themselves, "I am here." Or even simpler, "I am." We might think of this "I am" as an acknowledging of Self, and therefore Self might be more present. But our patient doesn't have to exactly know what that "means." They can just say it to themselves, "I am."

Maybe our patient finds they are then there somewhat more as Self, less blended with their parts. And then some more Self leadership and some Self to part relationship might be possible from there.

Again, this isn't trying to "make" more Self or pump up more Self or push out anything to get to more Self. Those moves would be from a burdened part. This is just claiming Self and claiming all one's various parts: "That's me."

Protectors in daily life integration practice

This exercise is pretty much a variation on the other exercises here, but it is focused specifically on protectors in daily life situations. As we've discussed, so much of psychedelic integration and standard IFS integration is with protectors. And again, if our patient can work with their protectors right in the real life situations where they get scared and active, then that can be very specific and therefore powerful integration for those protectors.

For this daily life exercise, it's important that our patient gets a sense that a protector is active for them, wanting to blend with them, or has blended with them. That awareness, by definition,

---

[181] This is adapted into IFS from the work of Barry Magid and Jose Stevens.

can be very hard to get precisely because when a protector has blended with us, they then don't seem like "a protector," they seem like us perceiving the truth!

So this way of working on integration might often not work in "real time." Personally, I can only occasionally do this practice in real time, but it's a good option to have.

Again, one thing that can help quite a bit is helping our patient get a sense of their "tells" that they are blended with a burdened protector. One simple "tell" is that our patient will have a powerful urge or impulse or thought to "*do something!*" Again, that sense of *italics*. The impulse, urge, or thoughts could be to lash out, avoid, or comply in some way or another. Roughly, fight, flight, freeze, fawn, or submit.

Not that those protector driven urges are necessarily wrong. We all need protectors. But if it's a still-burdened protector wanting to protect in an extreme way, then that can lead to difficulty for our patient. So again, this isn't about getting rid of or simply correcting the protector, however burdened they are. It is to complexify the situation, for Self to be more present with that protector.

So when our patient notices that they might be blended with a burdened protector to some extent or another, they might turn towards the protector, however they're noticing it in the moment, and say something like, "Hey, let's try something different. Let me be here."

If the protector does unblend, then the protector might see that Self can lead well enough, or at least better than the protector can! The protector might then decide they'd like to rethink their role in our patient's life. This could lead to that protector unburdening, getting their own relief and healing.

Integrating Self

Not all health or healing in medicine sessions is just about parts. Some of the health and growth that comes from medicine sessions is very directly about Self. So I'd like to discuss integrating Self.

Integrating Self is harder to talk about than integrating parts. Heck, even the phrase "integrating Self" kind of makes no sense. Again, it's like talking about making water wetter.

As has often been observed in an IFS take on psychedelics, somehow *a lot* of unblending can happen in medicine sessions. Burdened parts can, for a time or forever, be released from their burdens. The inner family can then settle down *profoundly* during the medicine session. Then, our patient might be there very richly as Self. That can be a very freeing sense in a medicine session, that I am me and everyone and everything is themselves.

Our patient might notice, on reflection, that they didn't go through any kind of process to be themself. They didn't need to improve; they didn't need to have anything fixed; they didn't need to develop; they didn't need to learn anything or achieve anything to be themself. They are simply there as themself. It's really not that we *become* our Selves, it's that we *are* our Selves.

So our patient might say in a medicine session or in the first integration session something like, "I'm me!"

In terms of helping our patient integrate Self, I love and sometimes recommend another simple practice recommended by Jose Stevens, of saying "Hello." Of turning towards whatever or whoever and saying hello.

Our patient could do this, maybe inwardly, as they walk down the street and see people, "Hello." Or to a tree. To the earth. In their daily life to their partner, a colleague, their boss, a friend, their child. A simple, inward or outward "Hello."

This is a practice that is based in the sense that Self is radically relational, and therefore of relationships as a fundamental way of integrating Self. We might see that when we relate to another as a Self – "Hello" – then we are there as Self well enough.

Martin Buber's work might help us understand this better. When we relate to another as a Thou, not as an it, then we are the I of an I-Thou relationship, an I of our whole being, which is different than the I of an I-it relationship.

We're back to that great cliché about psychotherapy, "It's all about relationships."

External relationships in integration work

In ending this chapter, and the clinical part of this book, I'd like to highlight one final perspective on integration. I want to come back to and underline the idea that IFS is of course not just an internal model. It is also about relationships in and with the outer world. That is, with others. As we saw in Nick's integration work, integration of healing naturally gets into external relationships. Nick's integration richly shows us the integration not just of Self and parts, but also the integration of external relationships: of co-workers, bosses, spouses, friends, medicines, therapists, woods, and birds.

Again, the "point" or goal of healing as seen here isn't to be a standalone, self-sufficient island of health. Yes, the inner relationships and the health of the inner family are crucial. But integration is also into the world.

The "point" can be instead that we will all always be vulnerable, and we will all always live in the world. A world, as Kasey Musgraves sings, of "… all kinds of magic / It's hard to believe."

But also, it's often a very hard world in many ways.

So, maybe much of the point can be to not go through the magic and vulnerabilities of this world alone. As Musgraves and her co-writers continue, "And then there is you."[182] We don't go it alone, inside and out.

---

[182] Tashian, Daniel, Kacey Musgraves, and Ian Fitchuk. "Oh, What a World." Track 4 on Golden Hour. MCA Nashville, 2018.

Participating in an ecosystem of health, inner and outer, that enriches and complexifies, season by season.

Maybe that's what we can hope for in integration of health and healing.

In the previous three clinical chapters, we've discussed that psychedelics can be profoundly healing, but that if they are to be safe and of the greatest effectiveness they must be paired with some sort of adequate relational practice, a sort of culture of psychedelia of one scale or another. And I think we have seen that IFS therapy is an excellent relational, small, and portable culture of psychedelia. The purpose of this book has been to at least start spelling out this great two-way partnership of psychedelics and IFS.

I think we've also seen that all PAP is about relationships. Preparation work, medicine sessions, and integration can all be seen as at base about ongoing, living relationships.

In this third part of the book, I'd like to try to extend these themes of ongoing relationship into some big picture views.

The next chapter, the Conclusion chapter, will bring this relational sense into some possible paradigm views on Western PAP.

In the Epilogue, I will get into some of my personal considerations and hopes on where Western psychedelia has been and where it might go.

I offer these concluding considerations in the spirit of dialogue, of looking for good questions more than looking for answers. We're dealing with psychedelics here — we might get more questions than answers! And good questions might be mostly what we need now.

Chapter Eight

Conclusion: Towards an Ecology of Paradigms Rather Than a Battle of Paradigms

This chapter will attempt to explore some paradigm considerations for the field of Western mental healthcare now that psychedelics are once again part of the "official" culture of the West, one of the Great Books of the West, we might say.

It has become a both commonplace and shocking observation that psychedelics are pushing a paradigm shift on Western mental healthcare and even Western culture. To expand on the discussion of paradigm transitions that we started in the Introduction and Overview chapter, here is more from Thomas Kuhn: "Normal science, the activity in which most scientists inevitably spend almost all their time, is predicated on the assumption that the scientific community knows what the world is like."[183] It has also become a commonplace and shocking observation to many that in light of psychedelics we no longer know what the world is like, including what psychological healing is like. Even the word "psychological" can begin to ring awkward. We, in our field and even culturally, are in a paradigm turmoil.

Returning to Kuhn as quoted in the Introduction and Overview chapter, "When the transition is complete, the profession will have changed its view of the field, its methods, and its goals." This is big stuff. A paradigm transition is no walk in the park and can feel fraught.

I don't think we know yet where this is all going for our field. But I would like to be so bold as to offer some discussion of at least the process we are in. And who knows, to a large extent maybe not knowing and a richer process *is* what this paradigm shift is?

---

[183] Kuhn, T. S. (1962). The Structure of Scientific Revolutions. University of Chicago Press.

I'd like to suggest here that what the West is going through with psychedelics is not just a normal Kuhnian paradigm shift, but it is — or it could be, with our participation — something of a paradigm shift on paradigm shifts. That is, this doesn't have to be a traditional paradigm shift of a new paradigm battling the old one, slaying it, and standing victorious and alone, at least for a while. Or of the old paradigm defeating an upstart paradigm and continuing its grand rule alone, for a while.

I would like to argue that any such sole victor model of paradigms will not stand long with psychedelics, and that it would not serve us well for good Western PAP. What I am proposing in this chapter is that we as practitioners now find ourselves in an ecosystem of paradigms, and it is on us to get good at living there.

To flesh this out and support it, I will draw on sources to explore roughly three levels of an ecosystem of paradigms. First, we will look at Andrew Weil's work on "integrative medicine," a term he coined, as an existing clinical model that already draws on an ecosystem sense of paradigms. Then to provide a deeper philosophical grounding for an ecosystem model of paradigms we will explore Richard Tarnas' work on what he termed a "participatory worldview." And finally, attempting to ground an ecosystem model of paradigms even further and broader, into possibly a radically relational ecosystem model of all that is, we will draw on "case material" from Homer Simpson (yes, *that* Homer Simpson!) and on the work of Eihei Dogen, a thirteenth century Japanese Zen teacher, widely considered one of the greatest Zen teachers.

IFS will be central here. IFS has great contributions to make to living in and working in an ecosystem of paradigms. Ecosystems are (obviously!) systems, and they are entirely relational. That is exactly the stuff of IFS.

A CLINICAL MODEL OF AN ECOSYSTEM OF PARADIGMS: ANDREW WEIL'S INTEGRATIVE MEDICINE

Andrew Weil is a physician who has pioneered a coherent model of integrative medicine which seeks to draw on and integrate a rich and diverse ecosystem of paradigms. As such, Weil's integrative medicine provides an existing and well articulated ecosystem model of paradigms that is highly compatible with and useful for Western psychedelic healthcare practice.

The simplest take on Weil's integrative medicine is that it seeks to judiciously and critically integrate the already existing paradigms of "alternative" and "conventional" healthcare, drawing on the strengths of each and avoiding the pitfalls of each to best help our patients.

Weil's integrative medicine also famously seeks to integrate and draw on approaches to body, mind, spirit, and community for health. We could roughly think of "body" as biomedical approaches broadly. This could include nutrition, exercise, sleep, pharmaceuticals, and surgery, as well as body as meaning, as part of what it is for us to be the beings that we are. We could think of "mind" as psychology. "Spirit" as — well, that's harder to define, but we could quickly say that spirit here can include "spark of life," meaning, ethics, spirituality, religion, divinity, divinities, the numinous, "higher powers," and an agnostic "something larger but unknown." "Community" can include relationships of different scales, including one to one relationships, families, societies, cultures, and our relationships with the biosphere in which we all live.

Notably in terms of "community," Weil's integrative medicine explicitly integrates the practitioner and patient relationship. The stated first principle of Weil's integrative medicine is, "Patient and practitioner are partners in the healing process."[184] This creates or emphasizes a key clinical, relational ecology in healthcare, of patient and practitioner.

---

[184] "What Is Integrative Medicine?" (AWCIMagazine, April 4, 2024).

Community in Weil's model also makes health and suffering not just issues of solitary individuals. Health and etiology of suffering are seen as fully embedded in community.

Integrative medicine is fast becoming mainstream. I have been fortunate enough to study with Weil at the University of Arizona. In a class, Weil once said that someday the term "integrative medicine" will disappear and it will simply be called "medicine."[185] At the time, in 2015, that seemed to my classmates and me like an exciting and distant possibility. I have since been shocked at how quickly it is happening or has already happened. Weil's model could be restated as a mature form of a biopsychosocialspiritual model. Such a model seems pretty mainstream these days.

As I think we've seen, psychedelics fit right in with such a complex, interrelated biopsychosocialspiritual model. As I said previously, I have a hunch and a hope that as psychedelics enter the mainstream of Western healthcare that they will help speed up, enrich, and deepen such an integrative model.

Weil's work also seeks to critically and relationally integrate different epistemologies in healthcare, different "ways of knowing," each with strengths and weaknesses. The idea here is that different epistemologies brought into dialogue with each other can help create better outcomes for our patients.

Weil includes the Modern, reductionistic, materialist healthcare epistemology, which has a strong emphasis on standardized, single compound medicines and on single variable randomized control trials. The epistemology of a randomized control trial has strengths and limitations, like any epistemology. RCT's can shine light on some things, but not others. Randomized control trials are an epistemology that can be a great aid to clinical practice, but they are not a "pure" or sole "way of knowing" to inform clinical practice. Nor are they bogus or useless. They are one paradigm to get into relationship with.

---

[185] Andrew Weil, "IHLP class," 2015

Weil's model also integrates traditional healing traditions, with their own epistemologies of thousands of years of diverse and rich clinical, cultural, and familial practice and experience. These traditions often involve plants, food, and cultural and religious practices.

Integrative medicine also integrates the epistemology that is the experience and clinical judgment of practitioners and the experience and wisdom of our patients. Weil notes that "experience" and "experiment" share the same etymological root.[186]

Interestingly, Weil's model not only fits very well with psychedelic practice, but Weil has a long history in psychedelic practice.[187]

A PHILOSOPHICAL MODEL OF AN ECOSYSTEM OF PARADIGMS: RICHARD TARNAS' "PARTICIPATORY WORLDVIEW"

I'd like to broaden a view on an ecosystem model of paradigms by turning to the philosophical and cultural studies work of Richard Tarnas. Tarnas is the author of the masterful book *The Passion of the Western Mind: Understanding the Ideas that Have Shaped Our World View*. He is a professor emeritus of psychology and cultural studies at the California Institute for Integral Studies, he was a long time faculty member at the Esalen Institute, and he was a professor at Pacifica Graduate Institute.

In the Epilogue of *The Passion of the Western Mind*, Tarnas states his view that the contemporary West, in this post-Post-Modern period, is currently most alive in a "participatory worldview."[188] By way of introducing this, Tarnas quotes Robert Bellah, a sociologist of religions:

> We may be seeing the beginnings of the reintegration of our culture…. If so, it will not be

---

[186] Ibid.

[187] Weil, Andrew. The Natural Mind: An Investigation of Drugs and the Higher Consciousness. United States: Houghton Mifflin, 1998.

[188] Tarnas, Richard. The Passion of the Western Mind: Understanding the Ideas that Have Shaped Our World View. United Kingdom: Pimlico, 2010.

on the basis of any new orthodoxy, either religious or scientific. Such a new integration will be based on the rejection of all univocal understandings of reality, of all identifications of one conception of reality with reality itself. It will recognize the multiplicity of the human spirit, and the necessity to translate constantly between different scientific and imaginative vocabularies. It will recognize the human proclivity to fall comfortably into some single literal interpretation of the world and therefore the necessity to be continuously open to rebirth in a new heaven and a new earth. [189]

By this, in a participatory worldview we are participating with different paradigms, different "scientific and imaginative vocabularies." And not only that, by Tarnas' use of the word "participatory" we are *agents* in this ecosystem of different scientific and imaginative vocabularies. As agents, as participants, we are in active, two way relationships with each other and with different paradigms.

With Tarnas' participatory worldview, we are squarely in multiplicity and relationality. Psychedelics fit right in here. Psychedelics, I'll go ahead and assert, complexify! Any one reified thing, any "univocal understanding," will not stand long with psychedelics (or with life). I was talking with a colleague once and they commented, "I think psychedelics have a queer bias." I loved that. Then something struck me and I responded, "I think reality has a queer bias and psychedelics help us see that." They loved that too. Maybe once again we see that psychedelics turn up the volume to 11 and show us what's already there: multiplicity, queerness, that we're not in Kansas anymore, and that Kansas never was in "Kansas."

---

[189] Quoted in, Tarnas, Richard. The Passion of the Western Mind: Understanding the Ideas that Have Shaped Our World View. United Kingdom: Pimlico, 2010.

And again, we are all agents here. What Tarnas is arguing for in a participatory worldview is hermeneutic, dialogical, relational. This is very much like Hans Gadamer's work on interpreting a "text," where a text can be anything we wish to understand. In hermeneutics and in Tarnas' participatory worldview, there *is* a text there — this isn't a "create your own reality." But our understanding of the "text" is always relational. We are always participants in our relationships and dialogues with the text and with other "readers" of the text.

Along these lines, to then think we can ever get to an "immaculate perception"[190] of the "text," free of our participation and relationships, is impossible. And it would obviate us as Selves and those of our community as Selves. Any univocal take on a "text" will be a failure of relationality.

Intersubjectivity theory can also help us deepen into Tarnas' participatory worldview. In an intersubjective worldview, we are both co-created by the ecosystems we live in and we co-create those ecosystems. So, we live in particular "ecosystems," of our field, our world, our communities, our relationships, and our paradigms, and those shape us. But we are also agents, so we make choices and those choices impact the world and change the conditions, the ecosystems, we live in. Then those conditions further co-create us. And on and on and on.

IFS is again extremely relevant and helpful here: in an intersubjective view, we are Selves in yet another complex system.

Like in Weil's integrative medicine, the participatory ecosystem of paradigms we might be co-creating around and with the help of psychedelics could be inhabited by established paradigms, such as conventional Western mental healthcare, as well as currently exiled paradigms and novel ones. Just in this book we have at least touched on so many paradigms, so many fields. Psychology, research methodologies, different schools of psychotherapy,

---

190 Nietzsche, Friedrich. Thus Spoke Zarathustra. United Kingdom: Penguin Books Limited, 1974.

different religious traditions, ecology, cultural studies, history, cross cultural dialogues, philosophy, history of science, etymology, morality, archeology, botany, neurology, computer science, ontology, chemistry, biology, medicine, economics, business theory, systems theory, music, art, education, politics, comedy, patent law, criminal law, anthropology, sociology, human rights. And we've just scratched the surface. Psychedelics will not be held by any one paradigm.

Once again, IFS can help greatly here. Just as "there are no bad parts," we could say "there are no bad paradigms." But just as there are burdened parts that can make things hard for us, that are "stuck in time" and are in extreme roles, we could say that paradigms can get into extreme roles as well. For instance, extreme "alternative" paradigms and extreme "conventional" paradigms, to name one polarity. And just as the healing of parts only happens in relationship, in relationships of Self, it will be the same with paradigm healing, if it is to be. When parts are healthy, they participate in richer relationships. So it can be with healthy paradigms.

This all gets back to the idea that good Western PAP is going to take a village. And IFS can help us understand some of the good ways of village life: relationships of Self to Self, of I and Thou, of respectful dialogue and of being together.

It is again notable that Tarnas' work on a participatory worldview is not only highly compatible with psychedelic practice, but Tarnas himself is a seasoned psychedelicist.[191]

AN ONTOLOGICAL MODEL OF AN ECOSYSTEM OF PARADIGMS: HOMER SIMPSON AND EIHEI DOGEN

I'd like to look at grounding this ecosystem of paradigms into deeper, maybe even bottomless foundations.

---

[191] Tarnas, Richard. "LSD Psychotherapy, Psychoanalysis, and Spiritual Transformation." PhD diss., Saybrook Institute, 1976.

Perhaps we're in an ecosystem of paradigms because we're simply completely in an ecosystem. By this, ecosystems are our home, maybe our only home.

I'd like to explore this ontological ecosystem worldview by looking at one of my favorite works of Western psychedelic art, "The Simpsons Movie."

Here is a scene from what we might call a session of Homer's PAP:

> A shaman serves Homer a fiery psychedelic brew. He drinks it, screams, and then asks, "More, please."
>
> She then leads Homer in a sort of call and response singing or chanting.
>
> Homer: [interrupting the singing] How long are we doing this?
>
> Shaman: Until you have an epiphany.
>
> Homer: Okay.
>
> They keep singing.
>
> Homer: What's an epiphany?
>
> Shaman: Sudden realization of great truth.
>
> Homer: Okay.
>
> They continue singing. Homer then has a vision of traveling to an underground realm, encircled by trees in a clearing.
>
> Shaman's voice from above: Unless you have an epiphany, you will spend the remainder of your days alone.
>
> Homer: [desperate] Epiphany, epiphany, epiphany! Bananas are an excellent source of potassium?

Americans will never embrace soccer? More than two shakes and it's playing with yourself?

The trees disapprove and dismember Homer. He watches this happen, watches himself come apart and start to melt.

Homer: Hey, what are you doing? Oh, do whatever you want to me. I don't care about myself anymore.

Shaman's voice from above: Because...?

Homer: [excited] Because other people are just as important as me — Without them, I'm nothing! In order to save myself I have to save Springfield! That's it! Isn't it?

There is a cacophony of applause, from the trees and from the shaman above, as Homer joyfully returns to the shaman's home.

Homer: That was the most incredible experience of my life! And now to find my family, save my town, and drop 10 pounds! [192]

We might say that Homer goes from *ego*, Latin for I, from a supposedly reified, solo sense of a self to *eco*, Greek for home, to a sense of his only being as the completely relational being-at-home-in-the-world, to riff on Heidegger.[193] Once again, we can see the possibility of the completely relational nature of Self, Self as only existing in relationship, of even Self *as* relationality.

Well, at least Homer is Self to a critical mass. His literal third thought after "the most incredible experience of [his] life" is to lose 10 pounds! He is Homer, after all. Maybe we all are. I know I am.

By this, by Homer's epiphany, which he freely and fully co-creates, we could say that psychedelics seem to often expand

---

[192] Silverman, David, dir. The Simpsons Movie. 20th Century Fox, 2007.
[193] Heidegger, Martin. Being and Time. United Kingdom: SCM Press, 1962.

and complexify a sense of a separate and somewhat embattled self, a self that sees itself as somehow separate from the world. (Where else would it be?) From an isolated monad, to a self at home in the world.

This isn't a simplistic "losing the self." It is instead an utterly relational self. This isn't the "oneness" of a blender or a smoothie. This is the oneness of a salad.

By this, within this home, this ecosystem we live in, it's then relationships all the way down. To all sides. Up. All the way forward. All the way back. Right here.

We're back to Tarnas' term "participatory." It completely implies selves and it completely implies relationship. It is an exquisite term.

Let's press on with Dogen. Dogen maybe expresses this ecosystem, relational sense of self and home most thoroughly and with the best poetry, here seen in his *Mountains and Rivers Sutra*:

> Mountains do not lack the qualities of mountains. Therefore they always abide in ease and always walk. You should examine in detail this quality of the mountains' walking.
>
> Mountains' walking is just like human walking. Accordingly, do not doubt mountains' walking even though it does not look the same as human walking...
>
> If you doubt mountains' walking, you do not know your own walking; it is not that you do not walk, but that you do not know or understand your own walking.[194]

[194] Quoted in Stambaugh, Joan. Impermanence is Buddha-nature: Dōgen's understanding of temporality. United States: University of Hawaii Press, 1990.

Maybe what Dogen is trying to help us see is that even walking — and by extension, everything — is completely relational, completely participatory: if you walk in the mountains, that walking is co-created by the mountains and you. The mountains help create your walking, and you and your walking help create the mountains as they are. They wouldn't be the same without you, you wouldn't be the same without them.

This gets even richer. There is, maybe, also a thoroughly participatory sense of time in Dogen as well. "[Mountains] *always* abide in ease and *always* walk [emphasis mine]." Those who have walked in mountains will always abide there, in the deep ease of night falling at camp on a rock outcrop surrounded by a deep snowfield. And the mountains will always have our company, they will always have us on that rock outcrop. All of the past is present now by its participation. And by our participation, we in the present will always be participants in all that is to come. This is not determinism, at least not a strong determinism. This is relationship. We are not bound by the past, but we are completely in relationship with it. And we cannot calculate or dictate what the future will be, but we will, in this moment, and this moment, and this moment, always be part of it. We will always be co-creators of all the future.[195]

Again, ecosystem, relationship, and participation as maybe all there is, our only home.

By this, we all matter — or, **Matter**, as psychedelics might put it, nice and loud. We matter as Selves, and we matter as partners in relationships. At the same time, we are all vulnerable. Life is good and life is often hard. What do we do with this, that we all *matter* and that we're all terribly vulnerable? I think that can maybe only be a point of relationship and a point of dialogue with each other.

---

[195] I am indebted to Barry Magid's discussion of Stambaugh's book Impermanence Is Buddha-Nature: Dōgen's Understanding of Temporality, amongst many other things.

EPILOGUE

We are in a time of deep cultural crisis. Rabid capitalism is winning a terrible defeat. Adam Smith warned about this possibility when he studied capitalism in its nascent stages, just 250 years ago. As he saw it, the newly budding Modern capitalism, with its invisible hand of the market and what he called, "the vile maxim of the masters, all for us, none for anybody else,"[196] could, if not adequately restrained, buy out and cripple governments, democracy, and civil society.[197] [198] In its frenzied grab, it has already bent the very throats of love, community, and the biosphere itself.

By sleight of hand, some of our Selfhood has been stolen from us and replaced with brand. [199] [200] The very *temenos*, the sacred sanctuary of friendship, was recast, against the evidence of our very eyes, as a commercial port.

But despite more Reagan-esque propaganda, virulent capitalism, with its particular strains of the profound public health diseases of racism, classism, sexisms, isolation, and biosphere destruction, is not a fact of physics. Capitalism is a historically recent set of human decisions, of even simple legal decisions. Different decisions can be made. Hope is far from lost.[201] [202]

We're also in a Western renewal of psychedelics and of wider cultures of psychedelia, of souls manifesting, and it is spreading rapidly. Terence McKenna, the great psychedelic philosopher and comedian, once said in a talk of the West's cultural crisis, "In a way, it's the poets who have failed us. Because they have

[196] Smith, Adam. The Wealth of Nations. United Kingdom: Random House Publishing Group, 2000.

[197] Samuels, Warren J.., Perry, William H.. Erasing the Invisible Hand: Essays on an Elusive and Misused Concept in Economics. Warren J. Samuels. United Kingdom: Cambridge University Press, 2014.

[198] Elliott, Larry. "The Invisible Hand's Crippling, Deadening Grip on Economics." The Guardian. October 7, 2011.

[199] Lanier, Jaron. Ten Arguments for Deleting Your Social Media Accounts Right Now. United Kingdom: Henry Holt and Company, 2018.

[200] Fromm, Erich. The Sane Society. United Kingdom: Rinehart, 1955.

[201] Arendt, Hannah. The origins of totalitarianism. Saint Lucia: Harcourt Brace Jovanovich, 1973.

[202] Reich, Robert B., Saving Capitalism: For the Many, Not the Few. United States: Knopf Doubleday Publishing Group, 2015.

not provided a song or sung a vision that we could all move in concert to."[203]

As we've seen, psychedelics seem to help manifest I-Thou relationships, Selves. Like all real teaching, this can't be a reprogramming. That would obviate Self. Instead, we are agents in what we learn, we have co-creation and responsibility in what we learn.

If we choose, maybe in a renewed psychedelic West we can sing songs of I-Thou, songs of Self to Self. A note or two, any note or two, from I to Thou, will do. The simplicity of these songs can be part of their power. We can look to the birds and the insects. They've been singing far longer than we have.

Let's return to and expand on our history of Western psychedelia from Chapter 3. Psychedelics have been exiled in the West for the last 1,600 years, with untold, understudied, but in all likelihood profound implications for Western society, Western minds, Western hearts, and Western souls. Brian Muraresku, in his crucial book, *The Immortality Key*, tells the story best. In 364 CE, the early Christian Roman emperor Valentinian moved to end the likely psychedelic Eleusinian Mysteries and related ceremonies. Praetextatus, a high initiate of the Mysteries, facing the threat of the ending of the 2,000-year lineage of the Mysteries, pleaded with Valentinian with a dire warning: ending the Mysteries "would make the life of the Greeks unlivable."[204]

The Greek word there for "unlivable" is very important. It is of great interest to Muraresku, as it was to Carl Kerenyi, a classicist, interdisciplinary scholar of mythology, and a close collaborator of Jung's. Muraresku, himself a skilled classicist, writes, "The Greek word for 'unlivable' is *abiotos* (ἀβίοτος)—literally, the absence or opposite of 'life' (*bios*). It's a rare, evocative word."[205] He notes

---

[203] McKenna, Terence. "Opening the Doors of Creativity." https://www.asktmk.com/talks/Opening+the+Doors+of+Creativity.

[204] Muraresku, Brian C.. The Immortality Key: The Secret History of the Religion with No Name. United States: St. Martin's Publishing Group, 2020.

[205] ibid.

that "Kerenyi concludes that the word was consciously chosen to inform later generations that the Mysteries 'were connected not only with Athenian and Greek existence but with human existence in general.'"[206]

Emperor Valentinian maybe got it and he did relent. But in 392 CE, one of his successors, Theodosius I, outlawed the Eleusinian Mysteries and similar ceremonies. This ended the line of "official" psychedelics in the West. One of the living roots and foundations of Western culture was destroyed. This was a fateful day. Again, the impacts of this are far understudied.

And notably, with Theodosius I's decree, not just psychedelics were exiled from the West, but women were also removed from the center of the religious and spiritual life of the West. The best documented of the Ancient and Classical likely psychedelic Western rituals were either entirely led by women, like the Dionysian festivals, or were co-led by women and men of equal religious respect, such as the Eleusinian Mysteries.

The central vision of the Eleusinian Mysteries was the kidnapping, descent to near death, and eventual return to life of a goddess, of Persephone. And of the near heart stopping grief of her mother, Demeter, the goddess of fertility.

Demeter, desperately searching the world for her daughter, unable to go on, unable to bless the land with her fertility, dropping her sacred scythe to the ground. The people and the land starving.

Finally, all but broken, she sat down. A kind company of people approached her. They offered her a healing drink, a *kykeon*, a special mixture of water, barley, and mint. Then — *somehow*, a *delos*: finding her daughter, the return of her daughter. Mother and child reunited. Connection, life, fertility renewed. Suffering and death conquered.

This happened each year in the Eleusinian rituals, over and over and over for maybe 2,000 years. The would be initiates were served the likely psychedelic *kykeon*, perhaps expertly prepared

---

[206] Ibid. Original quote from Kerényi, Karl. Eleusis: Archetypal Image of Mother and Daughter. United States: Princeton University Press, 1991.

for them by female priests from the special grain fields and ergot on the outskirts of Eleusis.[207][208]

There is also evidence that women may have led at least some of the literally underground early Christian churches, in the burial catacombs under Rome. Regular, possibly in some instances psychedelic Christian ceremonies. Highly illegal, to the point of death. Not because of the possible psychedelics — that was fine at the time. But because Christianity was deeply illegal in its early days. Groups of people putting their very lives on the line to pray together. Perhaps reliving the Last Supper. The sacred wine, the sacred bread, eaten and drank together. Possibly visiting the dead, visiting death itself, and returning to life. Over and over and over. [209][210][211]

There's nothing quite like experiences of defeat, of near death, and return to life, to connection and friendship, to get one's priorities in order.

But in 392 CE, with psychedelics and female priesthood exiled, Western culture entered a new epoch, one that came to often be called "the Dark Ages."

There is much here to be witnessed.

My personal sense is that Praetextatus' warning was staggeringly correct. Western life has become for many "unlivable," a half-born life, a somapsyche dry life, one of facing a stone wall with no retreat possible. Perhaps Praetextatus' term *abiotos* means something very much like Buber's I-it relationships. The I of I-it

[207] Webster, Peter & Ruck, Carl & Perrine, Daniel. (2000). Mixing the Kykeon. ELEUSIS: Journal of Psychoactive Plants and Compounds. New Series 4.

[208] Carl P. Ruck, Peter Webster - The Mythology and Chemistry of the Eleusinian Mysteries, presented at LSD - Problem Child and Wonder Drug International Symposium on the Occasion of the 100th Birthday of Albert Hofmann, 13 January 2006, Basel, Switzerland. Video available at https://www.youtube.com/watch?v=uwfkJkvbR-I

[209] Muraresku, Brian C., The Immortality Key: The Secret History of the Religion with No Name. United States: St. Martin's Publishing Group, 2020.

[210] Macy, Gary. The Hidden History of Women's Ordination: Female Clergy in the Medieval West. United Kingdom: OUP USA, 2012.

[211] Muraresku, Brian C., The Immortality Key: The Secret History of the Religion with No Name. United States: St. Martin's Publishing Group, 2020.

relationships is a devitalized I, a ghostly I who lives in a world of its, a devitalized world of just stuff, a "disenchanted" world, as Richard Tarnas puts it.[212]

Maybe at some point, after much witnessing and companioning, Western psychedelia will consent to be retrieved, to unburden, and to claim — well, that's the magic of real relationships of Self: to hear what the other says for themself, of themself. That would require us to be sensitive enough to hear. And to be ourselves well enough in response, in relationship.

[212] Tarnas, Richard. Cosmos and Psyche: Intimations of a New World View. New York: Penguin, 2006.

Curt Kearney is a psychotherapist practicing in Evanston, Illinois. For information on his practice, classes, events, and retreats, please visit www.curtkearney.com.

WORKS CITED

Aitken, Robert. The Gateless Gate. San Francisco: North Point Press, 1991.

Alcoholics Anonymous. 1984. Pass It On: The Story of Bill Wilson and How the A.A. Message Reached the World. Alcoholics Anonymous World Services.

Anderson, Brian. "CIIS Class." Class lecture, 2021.

Angermayer, Christian. "An Open Letter to Tim Ferriss about the Value of Patents in the Psychedelic World." LinkedIn, March 9, 2021. https://www.linkedin.com/pulse/open-letter-tim-ferriss-value-patents-psychedelic-angermayer/.

Arendt, Hannah. 1973. The Origins of Totalitarianism. Saint Lucia: Harcourt Brace Jovanovich.

Aridjis, Chloe. "On María Sabina, One of Mexico's Greatest Poets." British Council, March 30, 2015. https://www.britishcouncil.org/voices-magazine/maria-sabina-one-of-mexicos-greatest-poets.

"Aristotle's Biology." Stanford Encyclopedia of Philosophy, February 15, 2006. https://plato.stanford.edu/entries/aristotle-biology/.

Baker, MaryEllen. "Therapy with Native clients class." Class lecture, American Indian Center of Chicago, 2014.

Barlow, John Perry. "Stopping the Information Railroad." Electronic Frontier Foundation, January 17, 1994. https://w2.eff.org/Misc/Publications/John_Perry_Barlow/HTML/Stopping_the_Information_Railroad_jpb.html.

Bateman, A., and P. Fonagy. 2010. "Mentalization Based Treatment for Borderline Personality Disorder." World Psychiatry 9 (1): 11–15.

Baum, Dan. "Legalize It All." Harper's Magazine, April 2016.

Beecher, Henry K. "Ethics and Clinical Research." New England Journal of Medicine 274, no. 24 (June 16, 1966): 1354–60.

Bennett, Raquel. "Ketamine assisted psychotherapy class." Class lecture, 2021.

Beyer, Stephen. 2009. Singing to the Plants: A Guide to Mestizo Shamanism in the Upper Amazon. Albuquerque: UNM Press.

———. "Hallucinogens in Siberia." Singing to the Plants, February 18, 2008. https://singingtotheplants.com/2008/02/hallucinogens-in-siberia/.

Blake, William. The Marriage of Heaven and Hell. Quoted in Aldous Huxley, The Doors of Perception. 1st Perennial Library. New York: Harper, 1970.

"The Brakes Put on Ecstasy Research." Alberto Gayo. Interviu, April 28, 2003. Translation from Spanish by Marcela O'talora.

Buber, Martin. 1970. I and Thou. India: Free Press.

Burns, Kimberly. "The State of Psychedelics in Canada in 2023." lexpert.ca, May 24, 2023. https://www.lexpert.ca/thought-leadership/the-state-of-psychedelics-in-canada-in2023-/.

Busby, Mattha. "MDMA Trials under Review in Canada over Alleged Abuse of Study Participants." The Guardian, June 20, 2022. https://www.theguardian.com/society/2022/jun/20/mdma-trials-under-review-in-canada-over-alleged-abuse-of-study-participants.

Campbell, Joseph, et al. "Ritual and Rapture: From Dionysus to The Grateful Dead." YouTube video, 1:24:38. November 1, 1986. https://www.youtube.com/watch?v=bPAH5JnPjAY.

Cicero, Marcus Tullius. 2017. On the Commonwealth: And, On the Laws. Edited by James E. G. Zetzel. Second edition, Cambridge Texts in the History of Political Thought. Cambridge: Cambridge University Press. https://doi.org/9781316498934/10.1017.

Clancy, Maira Evelyn. "Creating Greater Safety in Psychedelic-Assisted Therapy Spaces." MA thesis, San Francisco State University, 2023.

Cleary, Thomas F. and J. C. Cleary, trans. 1992. The Blue Cliff Record. Boulder: Shambhala Publications. Case 89.

Cohen, S. 1960. "Lysergic Acid Diethylamide: Side Effect and Complications." Journal of Nervous and Mental Disease 130: 30–40.

Cover Story. "Power Trip." Cover Story, November 10, 2021. Podcast.

Crowley, Mike, and Ann Shulgin. 2019. Secret Drugs of Buddhism: Psychedelic Sacraments and the Origins of the Vajrayana. Second edition. Santa Fe: Synergetic Press.

Dikanska, Claire-Marie. "Is Psychedelic Therapy about to Go Mainstream?" swissinfo.ch, July 8, 2024. https://www.swissinfo.ch/eng/science-tech/is-psychedelic-therapy-about-to-go-mainstream-/48672328.

Eccles, Mari. "Dutch Panel Recommends MDMA for Post-Traumatic Stress Disorder." politico.eu, June 6, 2024. https://www.politico.eu/article/dutch-panel-recommends-mdma-for-post-traumatic-stress-disorder/.

Eichler, H.-G., F. Pignatti, B. Schwarzer-Daum, A. Hidalgo-Simon, I. Eichler, P. Arlett, A. Humphreys, S. Vamvakas, N. Brun, and G. Rasi. 2021. "Randomized Controlled Trials Versus Real World Evidence: Neither Magic Nor Myth." Clinical Pharmacology & Therapeutics 109 (5): 1212–18.

"Eleusinian Mysteries." Wikipedia. 2025. https://en.wikipedia.org/wiki/Eleusinian_Mysteries.

Elliott, Larry. "The Invisible Hand's Crippling, Deadening Grip on Economics." The Guardian, October 7, 2011.

Evans J, Robinson OC, Argyri EK, Suseelan S, Murphy-Beiner A, McAlpine R, et al. 2023. "Extended Difficulties Following the Use of Psychedelic Drugs: A Mixed Methods Study." PLoS ONE 18 (10): e0292464.

Falconer, Robert. "IFS and psychedelics class." Class lecture, 2021.

Ferris, Tim, and Richard Schwartz. "Richard Schwartz — IFS, Psychedelic Experiences without Drugs, and Finding Inner Peace for Our Many Parts (#492)." Podcast, January 14, 2021.

Fetty, Nick. "The Origin of the Term 'Psychedelic.'" The New York Academy of Sciences, April 4, 2024. https://nyaspubs.onlineibrary.wiley.com/doi/10.1111/nyas.15095.

Freud, Sigmund. 1973. The Psychopathology of Everyday Life: (1901). United Kingdom: Hogarth Press.

Freud, Sigmund, and James Strachey. 2010. The Interpretation of Dreams. New York: Basic Books.

Fromm, Erich. 1955. The Sane Society. United Kingdom: Rinehart.

Gabbard, Glen O. 2017. "Sexual Boundary Violations in Psychoanalysis: A 30-Year Retrospective." Psychoanalytic Psychology 34 (2): 151–56.

Gabbard, Glen O., and Drew Westen. 2003. "Rethinking Therapeutic Action." The International Journal of Psychoanalysis 84 (4): 823–41.

Gasser, P. 1995. "Die Psycholytische Psychotherapie in der Schweiz (1988-1993). Eine katamnestische Erhebung." In Yearbook of Cross-Cultural Medicine and Psychotherapy 1995, 143–62.

Gershman SJ, Balbi PE, Gallistel CR, Gunawardena J. 2021. "Reconsidering the Evidence for Learning in Single Cells." Elife 10: e61907.

Gonzales v. O Centro Espírita Beneficente União do Vegetal, 546 U.S. 418 (2006).

Goodwin, Guy M., Rosalind Watts, Emma V. V Ohu, Matthew M. W Davies, Stephen Williams, Timothy Erritzoe, Charlotte Stockdale, et al. 2022. "Single-Dose Psilocybin for a Treatment-Resistant Episode of Major Depression." The New England Journal of Medicine 387 (18): 1637–48.

Graeber, David. "There Never Was a West." 2007. https://theanarchistlibrary.org/library/david-graeber-there-never-was-a-west.

Grant, Robert. "Advanced KAP: IFS in ketamine assisted psychotherapy class." Class lecture, 2021.

———. "Level 1 IFS class for psychedelic practitioners." Class lecture, 2023.

Guerra-Doce, E., C. Rihuete-Herrada, R. Micó, L. Sànchez-Romero, J. J. Jiménez, Y. V. Homs, and X. Bartrolí. 2023. "Direct Evidence of the Use of Multiple Drugs in Bronze Age Menorca (Western Mediterranean) from Human Hair Analysis." Scientific Reports 13 (1): 4782.

Haikazian, Sipan, David C.J. Chen-Li, Danica E. Johnson, Farhan Fancy, Anastasia Levinta, M. Ishrat Husain, Rodrigo B. Mansur, Roger S. McIntyre, and Joshua D. Rosenblat. 2023. "Psilocybin-Assisted Therapy for Depression: A Systematic Review and Meta-Analysis." Psychiatry Research 329.

Hall, Will. "Psychedelic Therapy Abuse: My Experience with Aharon Grossbard, Francoise Bourzat... and Their Lawyers." Medium.com, September 18, 2021. https://willhall.net/09/2021/psychedelic-therapy-abuse-my-experience-with-aharon-grossbard-francoise-bourzat-and-their-lawyers/.

Hardy, Rich. "The Problem at the Heart of Modern Psychedelic Clinical Research." New Atlas, June 13, 2021. https://newatlas.com/psychedelics/psychedelic-clinical-research-blinding-placebo-bias/.

Hartogsohn, I. 2017. "Constructing Drug Effects: A History of Set and Setting." Drug Science, Policy and Law 3.

Hartogsohn, Ido. "The Meaning-Enhancing Properties of Psychedelics and Their Mediator Role in Psychedelic Therapy, Spirituality, and Creativity." Frontiers in Neuroscience, March 5, 2018.

Heidegger, Martin. 1962. Being and Time. United Kingdom: SCM Press.

Hendricks, Peter S., Grant Jones, C. Brandon Ogburn, Adam T. Snider, and Roland R. Griffiths. 2015. "Classic Psychedelic Use Is Associated with Reduced Psychological Distress and Suicidality in the United States Adult Population." Journal of Psychopharmacology 29 (3): 280–88.

Hendricks, Peter S., C. Brandon Ogburn, Adam T. Snider, and Roland R. Griffiths. 2018. "The Relationships of Classic Psychedelic Use with Criminal Behavior in the United States Adult Population." Journal of Psychopharmacology 32 (1): 37–48.

Hill, Amelia. "LSD Could Help Alcoholics Stop Drinking, AA Founder Believed." The Guardian, August 23, 2012. https://www.theguardian.com/science/2012/aug/23/lsd-alcoholism-bill-wilson-aa.

Hillman, James. 2017. The Soul's Code: In Search of Character and Calling. Ballantine Books trade paperback edition. New York: Ballantine Books.

Hodes, Dave. "Pending Patents: Can Any Company Own Psilocybin?" Green Market Report, January 13, 2022. https://www.greenmarketreport.com/pending-patents-can-any-company-own-psilocybin/.

Hood, R. W. 1975. "The Construction and Preliminary Validation of a Measure of Reported Mystical Experience." Journal for the Scientific Study of Religion 14 (1): 29–41.

Hu, Jane C. "5 Questions for Manoj Doss." The Microdose, November 22, 2021.

———. "India, Hinduism, and Psychedelics: 5 Questions for Scholar Swayam Bagaria." The Microdose, December 16, 2024. https://themicrodose.substack.com/p/india-hinduism-and-psychedelics5-.

Huxley, Aldous. 1970. The Doors of Perception. 1st Perennial Library. New York: Harper.

———. 2012. The Perennial Philosophy: An Interpretation of the Great Mystics, East and West. United Kingdom: HarperCollins.

James, Henry. 1909. Italian Hours. United Kingdom: William Heinemann.

Jiang, Kevin. "Unexpected Depths." Harvard Medical School, December 5, 2019. https://hms.harvard.edu/news/unexpected-depths.

Johnson, Robert A. 2009. Inner Work: Using Dreams and Active Imagination for Personal Growth. United States: HarperCollins.

Jones, Grant, Peter S. Hendricks, C. Brandon Ogburn, Adam T. Snider, Kelly E. Dunn, and Roland R. Griffiths. 2022. "Associations between Classic Psychedelics and Opioid Use Disorder in a Nationally-Representative U.S. Adult Sample." Scientific Reports 12 (1): 4099.

Jung, C. G. 2014. Modern Man in Search of a Soul. Taylor & Francis.

———. 2024. The Collected Works of C.G. Jung. Edited by Herbert Read, Michael Fordham, and Gerhard Adler. Translated by R. F. C. Hull. New Jersey: Princeton University Press.

———. The Structure and Dynamics of the Psyche (Collected Works of C.G. Jung, Volume 8). Gerhard Adler (Translator), R. F.C. Hull (Translator).

Kangaslampi, S. 2023. "Association between Mystical-Type Experiences under Psychedelics and Improvements in Well-Being or Mental Health – A Comprehensive Review of the Evidence." Journal of Psychedelic Studies 7 (1): 18–28.

Khan, A.J., B.J. Griffin, and S. Maguen. 2023. "A Review of Research on Moral Injury and Suicide Risk." Current Treatment Options in Psychiatry 10: 259–87.

Kimmerer, Robin Wall. 2013. Braiding Sweetgrass: Indigenous Wisdom, Scientific Knowledge and the Teachings of Plants. New York: Milkweed Editions.

King, Martin Luther, Jr. 2018. Letter from Birmingham Jail. Penguin Modern. London, England: Penguin Classics.

Ko, Kwonmok, Emma I. Kopra, Anthony J. Cleare, and James J. Rucker. 2023. "Psychedelic Therapy for Depressive Symptoms: A Systematic Review and Meta-Analysis." Journal of Affective Disorders 322: 194–204.

KOSMOS: A Theory of Psychedelic Experience. Available at https://www.psychedelic-library.org/.

Kotkin, J. 2020. The Coming of Neo-Feudalism: A Warning to the Global Middle Class. United Kingdom: Encounter Books.

Kreutzmann, Bill, Jerry Garcia, and Robert Hunter. 1975. "Franklin's Tower." Ice Nine Publishing Co, September 1, 1975. Music score.

Kuhn, Thomas S. 1962. The Structure of Scientific Revolutions. University of Chicago Press.

Küng, Hans. 2001. The Catholic Church: A Short History. Translated by John Bowden. Modern Library ed. New York: Modern Library.

Lambert, A. 1909. "The Obliteration of the Craving for Narcotics." Journal of the American Medical Association 53 (13): 985–89.

Laing, R. D. 1967. The Politics of Experience. New York: Pantheon Books.

Lanier, Jaron. 2018. Ten Arguments for Deleting Your Social Media Accounts Right Now. United Kingdom: Henry Holt and Company.

Leary T, Litwin G, Metzner R. 1963. "Reactions to Psilocybin Administered in a Supportive Environment." Journal of Nervous and Mental Disease 137: 561–73.

Leger RF, Unterwald EM. 2022. "Assessing the Effects of Methodological Differences on Outcomes in the Use of Psychedelics in the Treatment of Anxiety and Depressive Disorders: A Systematic Review and Meta-Analysis." Journal of Psychopharmacology 36 (1): 20–30.

Letcher, Andy. 2008. Shroom: A Cultural History of the Magic Mushroom. 1st Harper Perennial ed. New York: HarperCollins.

Luoma JB, Chwyl C, Bathje GJ, Davis AK, Lancelotta R. 2020. "A Meta-Analysis of Placebo-Controlled Trials of Psychedelic-Assisted Therapy." Journal of Psychoactive Drugs 52 (4): 289–99.

MacLean, K. A., J.-M. S. Leoutsakos, M. W. Johnson, and R. R. Griffiths. 2012. "Revised Mystical Experience Questionnaire (MEQ)." APA PsycTests. Database record.

Macy, Gary. 2012. The Hidden History of Women's Ordination: Female Clergy in the Medieval West. United Kingdom: OUP USA.

Magid, Barry. "'Why I'm NOT a Neuroscientist' Thompson Offers an Incisive Deeply Informed Critique of Buddhist Modernism's Mutual Love Affair with Neuroscience." Facebook, February 14, 2020. https://www.facebook.com/profile/804313867/search/?q=dance%20muscles%20brain.

Malleson, N. 1971. "Acute Adverse Reactions to LSD in Clinical and Experimental Use on the United Kingdom." British Journal of Psychiatry 118: 229–30.

Marek, S., B. Tervo-Clemmens, F.J. Calabro, T.F. Yu, A.V. Holmes, and N.A. Gogtay. 2022. "Reproducible Brain-Wide Association Studies Require Thousands of Individuals." Nature 603: 654–60.

Markel, Howard. "An Alcoholic's Savior: God, Belladonna or Both?" The New York Times, April 19, 2010. https://well.blogs.nytimes.com/19/04/2010/an-alcoholics-savior-god-belladonna-or-both/.

Marks, Mason. "The Disappearing Colorado Psychedelic Advisory Board." Psychedelic Week, March 22, 2023. https://psychedelicweek.com/disappearing-colorado-psychedelic-advisory-board/.

———. "Oregon Psilocybin Emails Show Secret Data Collection Plans." Psychedelic Week, November 20, 2022. https://psychedelicweek.com/oregon-psilocybin-emails-show-secret-data-collection-plans/.

Marseille E, Stauffer CS, Agrawal M, Thambi P, Roddy K, Mithoefer M, Bertozzi SM and Kahn JG. 2023. "Group Psychedelic Therapy: Empirical Estimates of Cost-Savings and Improved Access." Frontiers in Psychiatry 14: 1293243.

Masters, Robert E. L., and Jean Houston. 1966. The Varieties of Psychedelic Experience. United Kingdom: Holt, Rinehart and Winston.

McCoy, A.W. 2007. "Science in Dachau's Shadow: HEBB, Beecher, and the Development of CIA Psychological Torture and Modern Medical Ethics." Journal of the History of the Behavioral Sciences 43 (4): 401–17.

McKenna, Terence. "Opening the Doors of Creativity." https://www.asktmk.com/talks/Opening+the+Doors+of+Creativity. Lecture.

Meriwether, Nicholas. "Documenting The Dead: Joseph Campbell and the Grateful Dead." Dead.net, October 29, 2015. https://www.dead.net/features/blog/documenting-dead-joseph-campbell-and-grateful-dead.

Milhorance, Flavia. "Jump in Child Deaths Reveals Impact of Industrialisation on Amazon's Indigenous Peoples." The Guardian, June 5, 2023. https://www.theguardian.com/global-development/2023/jun/05/jump-in-child-deaths-reveals-impact-of-industrialisation-on-amazons-indigenous-peoples.

Mithoefer, Michael. 2015. A Manual for MDMA-Assisted Psychotherapy in the Treatment of Posttraumatic Stress Disorder. Santa Cruz, CA: MAPS.

Mithoefer, Michael C., Marcela Ot'alora G, Allison Feduccia, Julieann Klaassen, Paula Y. Jerome, Scott Mitchell, Benjamin Malcolm, and Rick Doblin. 2018. "3,4-Methylenedioxymethamphetamine (MDMA)-Assisted Psychotherapy for Post-Traumatic Stress Disorder in Military Veterans, Firefighters, and Police Officers: A Randomised, Double-Blind, Dose-Response, Phase 2 Clinical Trial." The Lancet. Psychiatry 5 (6): 486–97.

Mithoefer, Michael, and Annie Mithoefer. "MAPS training for MDMA assisted psychotherapy for treatment resistant PTSD class." Class lecture, 2021.

Moon, Jane S., Catherine M. Kuza, Manisha S. Desai, and William James. 2018. "Nitrous Oxide, and the Anaesthetic Revelation." Journal of Anesthesia History 4 (1): 1–6.

Moreno, F.A., C.B. Wiegand, E.K. Taitano, and P.L. Delgado. 2006. "Safety, Tolerability, and Efficacy of Psilocybin in 9 Patients with Obsessive-Compulsive Disorder." Journal of Clinical Psychiatry 67 (11): 1735–40.

Muraresku, Brian C. 2020. The Immortality Key: The Secret History of the Religion with No Name. United States: St. Martin's Publishing Group.

Muthukumaraswamy, Suresh D., Anna Forsyth, and Thomas Lumley. 2021. "Blinding and Expectancy Confounds in Psychedelic Randomized Controlled Trials." Expert Review of Clinical Pharmacology 14 (9): 1133–52.

Nietzsche, Friedrich. 1974. Thus Spoke Zarathustra. United Kingdom: Penguin Books Limited.

"Numinus Wellness Gets Health Canada Nod for MDMA Therapy Group Study." patsnap.com, June 7, 2024. https://www.patsnap.com/news/numinus-wellness-gets-health-canada-nod-for-mdma-therapy-group-study.

Ogden, Thomas H. 2004. The Matrix of the Mind: Object Relations and the Psychoanalytic Dialogue. Lanham (Md.): J. Aronson.

Okasha, S. 2024. "The Concept of Agent in Biology: Motivations and Meanings." Biology & Theory 19: 6–10.

Pace BA, Devenot N. 2021. "Right-Wing Psychedelia: Case Studies in Cultural Plasticity and Political Pluripotency." Frontiers in Psychology, December 10.

Passie T. 1997. Psycholytic and Psychedelic Therapy Research 1931 - 1995 a Complete International Bibliography. Laurentius Publ.

Passie T, Guss J, Krähenmann R. 2022. "Lower-Dose Psycholytic Therapy - A Neglected Approach." Frontiers in Psychiatry 13: 1020505.

Paulson, Steve. "Psilocybin, the 'God Molecule,' and the Quest to Revolutionize Mental Health Care." Wisconsin Public Radio, August 6, 2022. Radio broadcast.

Perna, J., J. Trop, R. Palitsky, C. Luckenbaugh, B. Averill, F. Becerra, I. Bhattacharyya, M. C. Mithoefer, and W. D. Walsh. 2025. "Prolonged Adverse Effects from Repeated Psilocybin Use in an Underground Psychedelic Therapy Training Program: A Case Report." BMC Psychiatry 25: 184.

Plato. 2017. Euthyphro; Apology; Crito; Phaedo. Edited by C. J. Emlyn-Jones and William Preddy. Loeb Classical Library. Cambridge, Massachusetts: Harvard University Press.

Reich, Robert B. 2015. Saving Capitalism: For the Many, Not the Few. United States: Knopf Doubleday Publishing Group.

Richards, William A. 2015. Sacred Knowledge: Psychedelics and Religious Experiences. United States: Columbia University Press.

Ruck, Carl P., and Peter Webster. "The Mythology and Chemistry of the Eleusinian Mysteries." Presented at LSD - Problem Child and Wonder Drug International Symposium on the Occasion of the 100th Birthday of Albert Hofmann, Basel, Switzerland, January 13, 2006. Video. https://www.youtube.com/watch?v=uwfkJkvbR-I.

Samuels, Warren J., and William H. Perry. 2014. Erasing the Invisible Hand: Essays on an Elusive and Misused Concept in Economics. Warren J. Samuels. United Kingdom: Cambridge University Press.

Scheurenbrand, Rainer. Private communication. 2015.

————. Private communication.

Schroder, Tom. 2015. Acid Test: LSD, Ecstasy, and the Power to Heal. United States: Penguin Publishing Group.

Schultes, R. E. 1969. "The Plant Kingdom and Hallucinogens: (Parts I-III)." https://www.unodc.org/unodc/en/data-and-analysis/bulletin/bulletin_4_01-01-1969_page004.html.

Schwartz, Richard. "Working With Internalized Racism." Psychotherapy Networker, October 2020. https://www.psychotherapynetworker.org/article/working-internalized-racism/.

"Seeking the Magic Mushroom." Life, May 13, 1959, 100–120.

Silverman, David, dir. 2007. The Simpsons Movie. 20th Century Fox. Film.

Simpson, Sturgill. 2014. "Turtles All the Way Down." Track 2 on Metamodern Sounds in Country Music. High Top Mountain. Music recording.

Smith, Adam. 2000. The Wealth of Nations. United Kingdom: Random House Publishing Group.

Stambaugh, Joan. 1990. Impermanence Is Buddha-Nature: Dōgen's Understanding of Temporality. United States: University of Hawaii Press.

Stauffer CS, Anderson BT, Ortigo KM, Woolley J. 2020. "Psilocybin-Assisted Group Therapy and Attachment: Observed Reduction in Attachment Anxiety and Influences of Attachment Insecurity on the Psilocybin Experience." ACS Pharmacology & Translational Science 4 (2): 526–32.

Stevens, Jose. Personal communication. 2014.

Stone, Will. "Transformation or Trouble? Research into MDMA Plagued with Allegations of Misconduct." National Public Radio, May 13, 2024. https://www.npr.org/1249698428/13/05/2024/mdma-trials-misconduct-allegations-maps.

Strasburg, Sunny. IFS Conference Presentation, Denver, 2023. Conference presentation.

Strassman RJ, Qualls CR. 1994. "Dose-Response Study of N,N-Dimethyltryptamine in Humans: I. Neuroendocrine, Autonomic, and Cardiovascular Effects." Archives of General Psychiatry 51 (2): 85–97.

Strayhan, Robert. Personal communication. 2021.

Juan-Stresserras, J., and J. C. Matamala. 2005. "Estudio de Residuos Microscópicos Y Compuestos Orgánicos En Utillaje De Molido Y De Contenido De Las Vasijas [A Study of the Microscopic Residue and Organic Compounds in Grinding Tools and Jar Contents]." In El Dolmen De Toledo, 235–41. Alcalá de Henares, Spain: Universidad de Alcalá.

Sweezy, Martha, ed. 2013. Internal Family Systems Therapy: New Dimensions. New York: Routledge.

Tarnas, Richard. 1976. "LSD Psychotherapy, Psychoanalysis, and Spiritual Transformation." PhD diss., Saybrook Institute.

———. 2006. Cosmos and Psyche: Intimations of a New World View. New York: Penguin.

———. 2010. The Passion of the Western Mind: Understanding the Ideas That Have Shaped Our World View. United Kingdom: Pimlico.

———. "Psychedelic Initiation in Postmodern Culture & the Contribution of Stanislav Grof." Footnotes2Plato Podcast, December 10, 2021. Podcast.

Tashian, Daniel, Kacey Musgraves, and Ian Fitchuk. 2018. "Oh, What a World." Track 4 on Golden Hour. MCA Nashville. Music recording.

"The Tragedy of Maria Sabina | Singing to the Plants." Singing to the Plants, February 17, 2008. https://singingtotheplants.com/02/2008/tragedy-of-maria-sabina/.

Townshend, Pete. 1969. "I'm Free." Track Music, Inc., July 5, 1969.
Music recording.

———. 1971. "Won't Get Fooled Again." Track Music, Inc., August 1971.
Music recording.

Unknown. "Joseph Campbell and the Grateful
Dead." https://sirbacon.org/joseph_campbell.htm.

Unknown. Through the Gateway of the Heart : Accounts of Experiences
with MDMA and Other Empathogenic Substances. Adamson. Quoted
in Acid Test, by Tom Shroder.

Varoufakis, Yanis. 2023. Technofeudalism: What Killed Capitalism. United
Kingdom: Penguin Random House.

Wasson, Valentina Pavlovna, R. Gordon Wasson, Stephan Francis De
Borhegyi, and D. Jacomet. 1957. Mushrooms, Russia, and History. New
York: Pantheon Books.

Wasson, R. Gordon. "Drugs: The Sacred Mushroom." New York Times,
September 26, 1970.
https://timesmachine.nytimes.com/timesmachi
ne/90615979/26/09/1970.html?pageNumber=21.

———. "Seeking the Magic Mushroom." Life, May 120-100 ,1959 ,13.

Webster, Peter, and Carl Ruck. 2000. "Mixing the Kykeon." ELEUSIS:
Journal of Psychoactive Plants and Compounds. New Series 4.

Weil, Andrew. "IHLP class." Class lecture, 2015.

———. 1998. The Natural Mind: An Investigation of Drugs and the Higher
Consciousness. United States: Houghton Mifflin.

"What Is Integrative Medicine?" AWCIMagazine, April 4,
2024. https://awcim.org/awcimagazine/what-is-integrative-medicine/.

Whitehead, Alfred North, and David Ray Griffin. 1985. Process and Reality:
An Essay in Cosmology. Corr. ed, The Gifford Lectures 1927/28. New
York: Free Press.

Williams, Luke. "Human Psychedelic Research: A Historical and
Sociological Analysis." Undergraduate Thesis, Cambridge
University, 1999.

Winnicott, D. W. 1971. "Transitional Objects and Transitional
Phenomena." In Playing and Reality.

Zagorski, Nick. "Australia Legalizes Psychedelics for Use in Depression,
PTSD Therapy." Psychiatric News, PN, 58, no. 09 (September 2023).

www.ingramcontent.com/pod-product-compliance
Lightning Source LLC
Chambersburg PA
CBHW021607120626
46545CB00001B/105

9 7 9 8 2 1 8 3 0 5 3 7 6